MW01232704

CONTENTS

SECTION I

WORSHIP

SECTION II

ADMINISTRATION

SECTION III

PASTORAL RELATIONS

FOREWORD

No apology is made for the elementary character of this book. It is intended to be not the last but merely *the first word* spoken to young men contemplating a ministerial career, an "*Introduction* to the Work of a Pastor," as its title declares. While it has been written primarily for ministers of the Methodist Episcopal Church, it is hoped that much in the book will be valuable for a wider circle.

Moreover, an introduction should be *comprehensive* as well as elementary, bringing into view *the whole task* rather than emphasizing disproportionately certain special phases. The writer has attempted to present a balanced statement of the entire work of the church and the methods to be employed, not in the exceptional, but in the average community. Necessarily the treatment of each subject is brief.

I have been encouraged in the task of composition by the Commission on Courses of Study, at whose invitation the writing was first begun. Individual members of the Commission have made valuable suggestions which have been incorporated into the volume. I am especially grateful to Bishop Edwin H. Hughes, D.D., LL.D.; Professor Harris Franklin Rall, Ph.D.; and Professor Lindsay B. Longacre, Ph.D., for having read parts of the manuscript, and to the Rev. Charles R. Bair, D.D., for detailed literary criticism of the entire composition. My debt is very large to nearly all the important contributions to the literature of this subject in English. I am grateful to the authors and titles mentioned in footnotes, especially to Washington Gladden's *The Christian Pastor,* which stands as the most impressive description of the work of the Protestant minister in more than a quarter of a century. The patience and kindness, however, of five churches which I have served as pastor, namely, Summerset, and Highland Park (Des Moines), Iowa; Newport, and Saint Paul's (Manchester), New Hampshire; and Englewood, Chicago, have taught me more than many books.

J. A. B.

Boston, April 1, 1923.

SECTION I

WORSHIP

CHAPTER I

THE SIGNIFICANCE OF WORSHIP

MODERN communities will support generously only those institutions which serve them in a large way. Can the church justify its appeal for maintenance on this ground? It conducts "services" indeed, but is this "service"? To feed the poor, find work for the unemployed, provide lunches for underfed school children is service. But most churches do little of this. They merely gather people together for prayer, and praise, and instruction in religious subjects. And not a few arise to inquire if any vital need is met by such exercises. What can be said in reply to the charge that ministers and other religious workers are parasites on society who live off the labor of others without contributing to the common supply of wealth? Clearly, we must be able to assure ourselves concerning the value of public worship.

We may remark, in the first instance, that worship is a necessary expression of man's sense of the Infinite. Given a belief in God, prayer is man's instinctive response to that belief. And this belief is universal. "Go back as far as history extends and man is religious. . . . The pre-historic remains in Europe and elsewhere, as far as they prove anything, show man possessed of certain ideas and performing certain acts which give strong evidence of being religious."[1] Worship then appears inevitable. By the very constitution of their being men relate themselves to the invisible world of spirit and power which lies behind the temporal order. They provide for worship as naturally and instinctively as they provide for supplies of water and food. This was noted long ago by a pagan historian, Plutarch: "You will,

[1]Edmund D. Soper, *The Religions of Mankind*, p. 27.

perchance, light upon cities without gates, without a theater, and without a palace; but you will find no city without a temple." "As the hart panteth after the waterbrooks, so panteth my soul after thee, O God," is ever the cry of man famished for the Infinite. That an exceptional person here and there seldom expresses this hunger for God does not affect the general fact. He only emphasizes the normal by showing how far he varies from it.

Again, reflect upon the value of worship as a method of renewing moral and spiritual forces. Who has not grown weary in well-doing? Who does not know what it means to have his margin of self-control grow perilously narrow? Who does not find his confidence weakening in the worthwhileness of his finest ideals? Who has not lost his appetite for life through the monotony of life? Above all, who does not know the experience of remorse for sin and moral failure? "The internal decay of the incentive of work, the drooping of the sails of ambition, the falling out of humor with one's own humor"—this is a part of the history of every man's inner life. And in searching for means of refreshing the weary spirit we must reckon with worship. It is not the only device by which something of the joy and zest of life may be recovered. A vacation, a favorite book, the companionship of men and women, an evening at the concert, an afternoon on the golf course may give the desired variation in the daily routine which is needful to "restore the soul." There are two defects, however, which make it impossible for these ever to take first rank as means of spiritual renewal. First, they are purely external aids. One who depends upon them exclusively soon loses all power to refresh himself from the springs of his own inner life. Pity that multitude who find it necessary always to go outside themselves for relaxation and excitement, and who, in the absence of accustomed pleasure, are not only cast down but also destroyed! Moreover, these restorative measures have little power to affect the supreme cause of spiritual fatigue—*sin*. They can only anæsthetize the troubled conscience by inducing a temporary forgetfulness. They are unable to remove permanently the sense of guilt, or create a consciousness of strength which will make victorious living possible in the future.

But it is at precisely these points that worship attains to primacy among all other methods of recuperation. Its strength comes from within, and is independent of outward circumstances. One may not always be able to take a vacation from his work, but he may always pray at his work. When changes on the outside cannot be effected by prayer, one may change his attitude on the inside so as to rest himself while he works. And because he does it for himself he never becomes dependent upon outward aids. The great mystics affirm that worship will do all that friendship, amusement, food, medicine, or even sleep can accomplish for the refreshment of the spirit. Furthermore, it relieves the tension of overtaut nerves, not by inducing forgetfulness, but by creating the sense of Another Presence, All-Loving and All-Strong, who has come to help us face the facts of life and energize our weakened wills. In prayer the sin-tortured soul is soothed by the conviction that sin is forgiven and by the assurance that in future conflicts he shall have power to overcome sin. In worship as in nothing else "a self hitherto divided and consciously wrong, inferior, and unhappy becomes unified and consciously right, superior, and happy in consequence of its firmer hold upon religious realities."[2] Thus the greatest American psychologist confirms the findings of an ancient prophet: "They that wait upon the Lord shall renew their strength" (Isa. 40. 31).

Consider a third suggestion as to the value of worship. Men not only grow weary, but they become confused and lose their sense of direction. They require not only means of refreshing themselves but instruments for ascertaining their moral and spiritual bearings. The line be-

---

[2]William James, *The Varieties of Religious Experience*, p. 189. Reprinted by permission of Longmans, Green & Co.

tween virtue and vice is very faint on occasion. A technique is in demand for sharpening such lines. Worship proves competent for this. Everyone who prays knows what it means to have a perplexed mind become quiet and assured in the act of prayer, forming judgments, reaching conclusions, taking new points of view as one worships. The writer of Ephesians had this in mind when he prayed "that the God of our Lord Jesus Christ, the Father of glory, may give unto you a spirit of wisdom and revelation in the knowledge of him" (1. 17). A distinguished American physician understands it who affirms that to pray is to do what the woodsman does, who, uncertain of his whereabouts, climbs the highest tree to take a look around.[3] The mystics uniformly describe an experience which they call "the illumination of the soul" in which the ordinary powers of perception are heightened and insights deepened. Psychologists may refer all this to the "unconscious mind" out of which suggestion is supposed to come when the nervous system is relaxed. This does not satisfy the true mystics, however, who are philosophers in search of reality, and scientists describing their own states of mind, as well as devotees. They are convinced that the cause of these enlightening experiences does not lie wholly within themselves. They have a feeling of "otherness." "Another" instructs, suggests, inspires, and guides. They are overwhelmingly sure that they have established communication with the Infinite Source of all life and being. The "unconscious mind" cannot be more than the organ of the Holy Spirit.

Mr. H. G. Wells is not accustomed to defend traditional views in religion. But on this matter he writes very much like Saint Paul. "Then, suddenly, in a little while, in his own time, God comes. This cardinal experience is an undoubting, immediate sense of God. It is the attainment of an absolute certainty that one is not alone in oneself. It is

---

[3]R. C. Cabot, *What Men Live By*, p. 277.

as if one were touched at every point by a being akin to oneself, sympathetic, beyond measure wiser, steadfast and pure in aim. It is complete and more intimate, but it is like standing side by side with and touching some one that we love dearly and trust completely. It is as if this being bridged a thousand misunderstandings and brought us in touch with a great multitude of other people. . . . The moment may come while we are alone in the darkness, under the stars, or while we walk by ourselves or in a crowd, or while we sit and muse. It may come upon the sinking of a ship or in the tumult of battle. There is no saying when it may not come to us. But after it has come our lives are changed. God is with us and there is no more doubt of God. Thereafter one goes about the world like one who was lonely and has found a lover, *like one who was perplexed and has found a solution*. One is *assured* that there is a Power that fights with us and against the confusion and evil within us and without. There comes into the heart an essential and enduring happiness and courage."[4]

Now, the experience of the mystic does not differ in kind from that of all who genuinely worship. It differs only in degree. Everyone is a mystic to whom God is consciously real as he prays. To worship is to go on a great adventure that brings up at last in the very presence of the Father, and in this adventure we acquire knowledge about God and our relation to him.

Again, consider the contribution which worship may make toward the solution of our social problems. The most impressive fact about modern society is its high degree of "mutualism." Never were men dependent upon each other as now. Professor Ross describes this condition accurately, if imaginatively: "Nowadays the water main is my well, the trolley car my carriage, the bankers' safe my old stocking, the policeman's billy my fist. My own eyes and nose

---

[4]Reprinted by permission of The Macmillan Company from H. G. Wells, *God, the Invisible King*, p. 23f. The italics are the author's.

and judgment defer to the inspector of food, or drugs, or gas, or factories, or tenements, or insurance companies. I rely upon others to look after my drains, invest my savings, nurse my sick, and teach my children. I let the meat trust butcher my pigs, the oil trust mold my candles, the sugar trust boil my sorghum, the coal trust chop my wood, the barb-wire company split my rails."[5] He might have added that we look to others for the opportunity of earning a living as men never have done before. For the first time in human history the tools of industry are too expensive for the workers to own, so that the man who uses the instruments of economic production must ask the privilege of others. On the whole, this interdependence of each upon all and all on each has greatly multiplied our comforts and increased our happiness. It has increased also the number of friction points and thereby the possibilities of misery. Men are in each other's power and at each other's mercy to a degree altogether unprecedented. This is the very essence of "the social problem."

Now, we may safely assume that our social organization will never be less intricate than at present. On the contrary, it may become more complicated. The "solution of the social problem" obviously calls for a higher degree of intelligence to administer this complex social organization. More imagination and more technical knowledge will help us greatly. *But chiefly we shall need more good will.* Our confusion is due less to lack of knowledge than to lack of brotherliness. A little selfishness now may work greater hardship than much selfishness in a simpler social order. A method must be found to generate altruism, to increase the sense of brotherhood and obligation to our human kind. In the search for an agent to accomplish this spiritual transmutation, we find nothing more promising than worship. Humility, reverence, affection, kindliness are all essential

[5]E. A. Ross, *Sin and Society,* p. 3. Used by permission of Houghton Mifflin Company.

to the prayerful frame of mind. The mood of worship cannot tolerate any sentiment of ill will. To worship is to love. To admit any unsocial feeling while one prays is to dispel the worshiping mood. As a generator of altruism worship has the very greatest social significance. No one is doing more to promote the spirit of brotherhood and increase the available supply of social sympathy than he who induces his fellow men to pray.

Yet again, consider the significance of worship for physical health. The early history of the Christian Church is "permeated with a sense of conquest over sickness, disease, and moral ills of every kind." Gibbon mentions "the miraculous powers of the primitive church" as the third cause for the spread of Christianity—though personally he deemed it an unworthy cause. And while our theories of disease have changed radically, the history of the modern church supplies incontrovertible evidence of the therapeutic value of faith and prayer. Doctor McComb declares "that throughout later history the appearance of any great religious personality synchronized with an outburst of healing power. Francis of Assisi, Luther, George Fox, and John Wesley were not only great spiritual thinkers but also, by the strength of their faith, were able in certain cases to set up a powerful physical stimulus which resulted in the restoration of health to the sufferers; and whenever there has been a revival of religious life it has been accompanied by a more abundant sense of well-being both in soul and body."[6]

The explanation which modern psychology gives of the process of psychical healing is entirely acceptable to orthodox believers both in medicine and religion. Mind and body are one. Their relation is so intimate that each reacts upon the other definitely and promptly. Physical conditions affect the mind, and mental states in turn influence the body. Anxiety, worry, grief, fear, anger interfere with

[6]Worcester, McComb, Coriat, *Religion and Medicine*, p. 299. Used by permission of Moffat, Yard and Company.

the proper working of almost every organ in the body. On the other hand, faith, hopefulness, confidence, trust, love, good cheer stimulate helpfully every organ. Whatever will induce and make permanent these latter states makes for health and long life. Worship is such an agent. Practically every psychologist and physician agrees with William James in affirming that under certain circumstances prayer may contribute greatly to recovery from illness and should be encouraged as a curative method. This recognition of the restorative power of prayer in illness carries with it no approval of the extravagant claims of faith-healing cults which have sprung up outside the church, setting themselves against scientific medicine. In sickness one's first duty is to consult a reputable medical man. We are insisting on no more than this—that the sense of peace, and rest, and confident hope that is inspired through worship will greatly assist the physician in his work and facilitate the patient's recovery. The failure of the church to recognize this value in worship has opened the way for certain religious bodies, usually regarded as outside the pale of the Christian Church, to grow powerful through capitalizing the idea. It is the one good thing in a blend of false philosophy, pseudo-science, and bad theology. By it "all these cults heal the sick, dissipate various kinds of miseries, afford moral uplift to the depressed, and create an atmosphere of faith, hope, and courage in which achievements are wrought that recall the early springtime of Christianity." Is it not time that the church should proclaim again her earliest message, since physicians and psychologists of first rank encourage her to do so? That message is contained in the following paragraph of *Religion and Medicine:*

"The prayer of faith uttered or unexpressed has an immense influence over the functions of organic life. It is significant that a great English newspaper in an article on sleep recommended sufferers from insomnia to betake themselves to prayer. The advice was eminently sound, for in true prayer the mind is in a receptive attitude. It is open to the inflow of the divine forces that bless and heal. Now, the great hindrances to sleep are worry, anxiety, remorse, shame, sometimes fear of not sleeping. Prayer calms and soothes the soul, lifts it into a higher region than the earthly, and thus conduces to the state in which sleep becomes possible. Suppose, now, that our whole waking life were to be lived as Christ's was lived, in an atmosphere of prayer; that is, in a sense of oneness with the Infinite Life, the Soul of our souls, so that we should become channels through which the thought and love of God might have unhindered course. Must not the body so closely connected with the soul feel a new uplift and virtue? This is especially true of all nervous disorders, because the mind has especial relations to the brain and nervous system."[7]

In the light of all this, the need for prayer is imperative. It is not quite evident, however, that a community is under obligation to provide facilities for *social* prayer. Is not *individual* prayer adequate for all spiritual needs? Great souls in all ages have nourished their spirits on *private* devotion. Jesus bade us enter into our chambers and pray in secret, and was himself accustomed to go into the mountain and the solitary place apart for prayer.

What legitimate demand is there for *public* worship? We answer, "The demand of the *social nature* which caused Jesus to form the habit of joining his prayers with his fellow men in the synagogue as well as going into a secret place for solitary communion with God." He took upon himself the form and nature of a man—and man was not made for solitude. It is impossible for him to develop normally except in the midst of his kind. Companionship is quite as necessary in his worship as in his work. Private devotion alone cannot satisfy his total need. The lonely soldier on outpost may hold himself heroically to a proper performance of his duty in spite of the terrors that fill his imagination. But his steadiness and clear-sightedness—and, in-

[7]Worcester, McComb, Coriat, *op. cit.*, p. 312. Used by permission of Moffat, Yard and Company.

cidentally, his usefulness—will be greatly increased by the presence of comrades in arms. With insight Doctor Cabot remarks that it means as much for believers as for soldiers to touch elbows. The benefits of private prayer are magnified many times by social worship, which exposes us to the contagion of other men's faith. An atmosphere of belief is created in which our own faith is strengthened through the realization that others share enthusiastically in those beliefs.

Moreover, fellowship in prayer is the only corrective for eccentricities of belief which inevitably characterize those who do not join with others in prayer. On our Western ranges may be found the sheep-herder who lives alone so much that he becomes unlike other men in some essential respects. An air of detachment and aloofness distinguishes him in the centers of population on the occasion of his rare visits. A similar difference is seen among believers. One who lives in religious isolation may be genuinely devout, but he will almost certainly be "queer" in his devotion, varying from the normal in doctrine and belief. For the standard for faith must be set by the worshiping group rather than the worshiping individual.

It must follow, then, that to "conduct services" is to render service of the highest sort. It need not be a serious fault that the church does nothing except gather the people for worship and instruction, provided it does this effectively. It may well be that some churches should close their doors, but never those which create an atmosphere quickeningly religious in the place of public prayer. To such churches men will ever turn as to their best friends for inward comfort and strength.

Books Recommended for Further Study[8]

R. C. Cabot, *What Men Live By.* Part IV.
Worcester and McComb, *Religion and Medicine.*

---

[8]Any desired book in these lists at end of chapters may be secured from your own publisher.

Washington Gladden, *The Christian Pastor,* Chapter VI.
Harry E. Fosdick, *The Meaning of Prayer.*
E. Herman, *Creative Prayer.*
B. H. Streeter, *et al., Concerning Prayer,* Chapter XI.
H. S. Coffin, *What Is There in Religion?*

CHAPTER II

IDEALS OF WORSHIP

It may be that the lack of popular interest in public worship is not due primarily to the religious indifference of the community, but rather to the failure of the churches to conduct worship effectively. Only rarely does one find a service characterized by an atmosphere genuinely devout or quickeningly religious. This applies to large churches as well as small, to those which use "prescribed prayers" as well as those which enjoy "free worship." On the one hand, mechanical orderliness and ritualistic decorum are emphasized at the expense of life. On the other, freedom has admitted slovenliness and irreverence to the sanctuary. Under both circumstances one misses the dynamic quality which is associated with reality in spiritual things. It is inexcusable that a church or minister should do little else than conduct services of worship, and yet do that so unimpressively that the weary spirit finds no rest in collective prayer.

1. Ideals of Worship. This ineffectiveness is due to the control of false ideals of worship. One of these is the *sacerdotal conception* of public worship as "Divine Service," or a way of serving God. Doubtless there is a measure of truth in this view. If God covets the fellowship of men, as the New Testament represents, men render him a service when they give themselves to him in love. But this thought is obscured by undue regard for the exact performance of the ritual which in the end implies that God is primarily interested in the manner in which men offer their worship. With true religious insight Doctor Fosdick has suggested that public worship is not divine service but *preparation for divine service* in daily living. Again, the *æsthetic* ideal is sometimes in the ascendant. Public wor-

ship is not distinguished from public entertainment. The aim is to give pleasure to the congregation rather than to induce the people to pray. The musical numbers are professionally excellent. The prayers are rhetorically perfect. The sermon is oratorically effective. One may depart from such a service in the pleasant frame of mind in which a good concert leaves him. But it is not a worshipful frame of mind. God is not necessarily in his thought, though the sermon, the music, and prayers may have dealt with religious themes. More commonly, however, the *homiletical ideal* controls in evangelical communions. The sermon is exalted to the place of primary importance in the service. Everything else is incidental. Historically the reformers of the sixteenth century who substituted the sermon for the sacrifice of the mass, and, in their reaction against everything Roman, either abolished from the public service that which appealed to the æsthetic sensibilities or assigned it to a distinctly subordinate place, are responsible for this "sermonolatry." The influence of this ideal is still powerful, as the common custom witnesses of announcing services of worship as "preaching services." Under this ideal the pastor permits himself to become absorbed almost exclusively in the preparation of the sermon, giving little or no attention to the music or public prayers. These are regarded as unimportant "preliminaries" to the real means of grace. The congregation too regards them in like manner and is satisfied if it is finally assembled by the time the sermon has begun. Under this ideal the value of the service is determined by the accident as to whether or not the sermon is "good."

Each of these ideals emphasizes something that deserves careful consideration. There should be enough of ritualism in public worship to make the service reverent and orderly. There should be sufficient respect for æsthetic values that the sensibilities of the ordinary person shall not be offended. And the educational value of the sermon should be appreciated to the extent that the minister shall always put into it his best thought and effort. But to emphasize unduly any one of these admirable qualities defeats the end of social prayer by substituting a subordinate for a primary aim. This aim can never be to teach correct ritualistic action, or to affect pleasantly the æsthetic feelings, or to impart knowledge of religious subjects. *It is nothing less than the development of proper attitudes of soul toward God and men—to induce the great worshipful moods and give them stability.*

In his excellent volume on *Worship in the Sunday School*[1] Professor Hartshorne groups the more important Christian attitudes under five heads: Gratitude, Good Will, Reverence, Faith, and Loyalty. Each of these is a composite emotion including many others which in themselves are legitimate ends of worship. For example, gratitude is compounded of joy, tenderness, and the feeling of obligation. Good will embraces joy, pity, sorrow, forgiveness, and kindness. Reverence is a blending of fear, wonder, admiration, tenderness, respect, dependence, love, and penitence. Faith is made up of hope, assurance, joy, freedom, aspiration, confidence, and trust. Loyalty involves the sense of ownership, devotion, and self-surrender. *The problem that is set for the leader of public worship is to conduct himself in such a manner and lead the people in such exercises as will arouse one or more of these emotions.* Whatever other values the service may possess, if it fails to do this, it cannot properly be called "public worship."

2. Psychology and Worship. The leader of worship should be a student of modern psychology. Educators have long understood the value of this science and no one can be regarded as equipped for the work of teaching who is not familiar with its principles. But Professor Gardner's comment on the relation of psychology to preaching applies with equal force to the whole matter of public worship: "The works discussing the preparation and de-

---

[1]Pp. 50-58.

livery of sermons rarely, if ever, approach the subject from the standpoint of modern functional psychology. The psychological conceptions underlying most of these treatises belong to a stage of psychological thought long since past. But there seems to be just as much reason for applying the principles of modern psychology to preaching (or worship) as to teaching."[2] The minister who desires to become skillful in the art of conducting social worship will take into serious account the literature of this subject, especially that part of it which treats of the psychology of the crowd. His first task is to create mental unity, induce the people to think and feel together. This suggestion may be resented by those who believe that the "crowd mind" is hopelessly inferior in every way.[3] But Gustave Le Bon, the great pioneer in this field, insists that while the crowd is intellectually and volitionally inferior to the individual, emotionally it may be worse, or *better,* according to circumstances. If human nature sometimes degrades itself in collective action, it likewise, on occasion, glorifies itself thus. "Doubtless a crowd is often criminal, but it is also often heroic," says Le Bon. "It is crowds, rather than isolated individuals, that may be induced to run the risk of death, to secure the triumph of a creed or an idea, that may be fired with enthusiasm for glory and honor, that are led on almost without bread and without arms, as in the age of the crusades, to deliver the tomb of Christ from the infidel, or, as in '93, to defend the Fatherland. Such heroism is without doubt somewhat unconscious, but it is of such heroism that history is made. Were people only to be credited with the great actions performed in cold blood, the annals of the world would register few of them."[4]

---

[2]Reprinted by permission of The Macmillan Company. Part in parenthesis the author's. Charles S. Gardner, *Psychology and Preaching,* Preface.

[3]See Martin, *The Behavior of Crowds.*

[4]Reprinted by permission of The Macmillan Company. Gustave Le Bon, *The Crowd,* p. 37f.

If it is possible to lift one to higher levels of feeling and acting in the crowd than he is likely to reach as an individual, surely it is entirely legitimate to manipulate the crowd to that end. This is the justification of many revival campaigns which are open to criticism from other points of view. After all the objections are entered, the fact remains that for a little while men thought, felt, and acted on higher levels than they were wont to do in "cold blood."

It may be helpful to summarize the essential characteristics of the crowd mind. A multitude need not be a psychological crowd. It is not, so long as its component individuals think and act for themselves. On the other hand, widely scattered individuals may display the marks of a crowd. You do not have a crowd until mental and emotional fusion has taken place and the individual mind is sunk in the collective mind. This group mind is not a mere summing up of all the individual minds composing it. "What really takes place is a combination followed by the creation of new characteristics, just as in chemistry certain elements when brought into contact combine to form a new body possessing properties quite different from those of the bodies that served to form it."[5]

In quality this collective mind resembles the "primitive" or "barbarian mind." It is impulsive, credulous, unstable, mobile, highly suggestible. It does no critical thinking, and quickly transforms feeling into action. The consciousness of numbers gives it a sense of power, and the disappearance of self-conscious individuality creates a condition in which ideas and feelings are very contagious, running quickly from person to person. In these qualities we find the secret of a crowd's intolerance and also of its generosity, of its distrust and its faith, of its irritability and its patience.

The leader of worship must understand the nature of the crowd mind, utilizing its suggestibility to make higher moods and thoughts contagious. *His first task is to create*

[5]Reprinted by permission of The Macmillan Company. Le Bon, *op. cit.*, p. 30.

mental unity, induce the people to think and feel together. In the beginning of the service there is always a high degree of "self-conscious individuality" in the assemblage. The people are gathered in one place, but they are not of one accord, or one mind. Each is concerned with his own special interests and there is little common feeling. Some are coldly critical, others relaxed and drowsy, while still others permit their attention to wander uncontrolled among their personal affairs.[6] The minister must fuse the people mentally so that he can direct their thoughts and feelings into the desired channels.

It would be too much to assert that there is no common feeling at all at the beginning of the service. That would be true only of an assembly which had gathered accidentally. In the ordinary service the fact that persons have come together impelled by a common purpose gives somewhat of psychical unity to start with.[7] This sense of oneness is intensified if the assembly gathers within four walls, and is thus protected from distracting influences from without. The degree in which physical segregation helps to unify the congregation intellectually and emotionally may be realized by holding an out-door service occasionally. Furthermore, if the architecture, decorations, and symbolism of the room are attractive and suggestive, and the organist is playing softly, the sense of unity is deepened.[8] But at best the state of psychical fusion in the beginning of the service is low, and the problem is to increase it to the point where the congregation will receive uncritically the ideas of the leader.[9]

Let it be said that absolute fusion is neither to be expected nor desired. This is accomplished only when "the crowd" becomes a "mob" in which the individual ceases to exercise his mental or volitional powers and responds in-

---

[6]Gardner, *op. cit.*, p. 240.
[7]Gardner, *op. cit.*, p. 237.
[8]Cutten, *Psychological Phenomena of Christianity*, p. 395.
[9]Gardner, *op. cit.*, p. 210.

stinctively to the influence of crowd-suggestion. To suppress entirely the personality of the individual would be immoral, though it has been done repeatedly in religious revivals and regarded as evidence of the power of God. The leader may attempt nothing more than to secure the interest of every person in the congregation without robbing any of his intellectual independence or paralyzing his will. As a matter of fact this is all that can be accomplished any way except in case of the purely passive. Persons of good mental equipment will resist immediately any unwarranted attack upon their individuality.

Many ministers untutored in the principles of psychology have employed with great skill the methods best suited to promote the process of mental fusion. Great revival preachers have always been masters of applied "crowd psychology." First, the scattered congregation is brought close together. When people are near each other, ideas and feelings are more readily communicated from one to another because the subtle physical changes of body and countenance are more easily recognized. Close crowding restricts freedom of bodily movements than which nothing tends more to depress the individual self. Professor Ross observes that "the strength of multiplied suggestion is at its maximum when the individual is in the midst of a throng, helpless to control his position or movements. . . . Often a furious, naughty child will become meek and obedient after being held a moment as in a vise. On the playground a saucy boy will abruptly surrender and 'take it back' when held firmly on the ground without power to move hand or foot. The cause is not fear, but deflation of the ego. Here is the reason why individuality is so wilted in a dense throng, and why persons of a highly developed but somewhat fragile personality have a horror of getting nipped in a crowd."[10]

After bringing the people close together, the leader will

[10]Reprinted by permission of The Macmillan Company. E. A. Ross, *Social Psychology*, p. 43f.

require them *to act* together. A hymn is announced, and the request is made, "Let all stand and join in the singing." The creed, recited by all, follows the hymn. After the prayer, the congregation unites in repeating the Lord's Prayer, minister and people kneeling. And later in the service other provision is made for concerted action on the part of the worshipers. This has the same tendency to wilt the individual self as close crowding. "If all stand or leap or shout or kneel, . . . or do anything else which may occur to the leader, it develops a consciousness of oneness and breaks up the personal isolation in which the sense of individuality is at a maximum."[11] Furthermore, if the bodily posture is related to the feeling which the leader desires to awaken, it tends to produce that feeling, or to intensify it, if already present. It is hard to be sad for long if one forces himself to smile. To fall into the physical attitude of prayer tends to create the desire to pray.[12]

The emotional unity produced by crowding and concerted action is unstable. The mind instinctively begins searching for some object, or thought, or experience which will justify the emotion that has been induced. If no such object can be found, the sense of individuality begins to rise again in the congregation, and the leader has "lost his crowd." The skillful minister will see to it that there is no delay in presenting to the congregation those religious ideas upon which he desires them to fix their attention and which correspond to the mood that has been induced. This he may do by following the organ voluntary or the opening hymn (chosen for its rhythmical qualities which promote mental fusion) by an invocation in which there is expressed briefly the desire for the sense of God's presence, or by a recital of the creed which directs the attention of the believer to the great affirmations of his faith. The hymns, the prayers, the anthem, and the sermon will be used likewise to direct the thought of the worshipers toward those spiritual subjects

[11] Gardner, *op. cit.*, p. 250.

[12] Cutten, *op. cit.*, p. 395.

that are related to the feelings which have been aroused, and which will deepen them. Only thus can the condition of psychical unity be maintained and filled with religious significance.

3. PRINCIPLES OF WORSHIP. The attention of the congregation must be held once it is won, and such direction must be given their collective thinking as will intensify the higher emotions and increase the will to goodness. In order to do this, the leader must have regard for certain great principles which always control social worship when it is conducted skillfully.

a. The first of these is *unity.* It implies that all the several acts of worship shall be subordinated to the control of a single purpose and filled with a common spirit. This does not mean that the sermon is to be preached repeatedly in the hymns, prayers, and anthems before the time for the sermon itself arrives. It will be enough if the thought and feeling induced by the music and prayers shall accord with the spirit of the sermon, and nothing incongruous shall be admitted to set up a counter movement of feeling.

Great variety of intellectual content may be entirely consistent with this kind of unity. Let us suppose that the aim of the service is to lead the congregation into a deeper love for Christ. Love, we have noted, is a composite emotion in which adoration, respect, tenderness, reverence, joy, trust, and devotion are blended. The service, ideally, should awaken all these feelings, and they are sufficiently varied that hymns, anthems, and prayers may make their respective contributions without duplicating in the least that which is made by the sermon. The music need not deal directly with the subject of Christ so long as it evokes some of the emotions associated with love. Or, again, the subject is so many-sided that every act of worship may deal directly with it in some aspect without making the service monotonous.

b. The second great principle is *variety.* The occasion for it is twofold. The congregation is a heterogeneous group composed of old and young, children and adults, men and women, cultured and uneducated. It is not to be supposed that these diverse elements can be interested in the same thing or, at least, to the same degree. Yet each person in the congregation has a right to get something out of the service. If the sermon does not appeal, then the hymns, the Scripture, or the prayers may. But more important, the psychical nature of every person in the congregation demands variety if his attention is to be held throughout the service. The attention cannot be focused for long upon a single object. It is impossible for me to hold my thought to the desk upon which I write unless I break up the one object of thought into many by considering it from different points of view. By directing the attention now to this aspect and now to that, it is possible to make the desk an object of interest for a long time, but in no other way. Of what material is it made? What is its shape? What are its dimensions? How much drawer space does it contain? Is it preferable to a roll-top desk? Only thus can I keep the desk long in my thought, for it is the nature of attention to wander from one object to another. The skillful leader of worship must present varying objects to the attention that will gratify its appetite for change and at the same time keep it close to the main matter. Only so may the thought of the congregation be controlled. And this is as true for every part of the service as it is for the service as a whole. The preacher will soon lose the attention of the congregation during the sermon unless he passes swiftly from one phase of his theme to another. The hymns will grow uninteresting if all are of the same type. It is better for the choir to sing but one number than two which produce the same emotional effect.

c. In applying the second principle we are limited by the first. This gives us a third, *progress*. In seeking variety we are not permitted to seek merely "something different." It must be that particular different something which will assist the movement of thought and feeling in the desired direction. Conceivably it might be so different as to be incongruous, and divert the service entirely from its proper channels. The demand here is precisely that which we make upon a story for movement and action toward some well-defined end.

d. The foregoing principles combine to suggest a fourth. The service should have *a definite plan*. The leader should know exactly what is to be accomplished by the service as a whole and just what contribution each act of worship will make to the realization of the plan. He will not go to the service without giving the most careful thought to every detail. Hymns, prayers, Scripture, music, and sermon will be woven "into a harmonious whole which shall in its total effect induce the desired change in the minds of the audience."[13]

e. A fifth principle which must control, at least in Protestant worship, is *democracy*. The Roman Catholic theory is that the clergy, especially the bishops, constitute the church. The laity are admitted only to a position of passive obedience. Participation in worship is the exclusive privilege of the clerical orders. The laymen are only onlookers. The Reformation, however, democratized the priesthood by regarding all true believers as priests. The effect of this upon public worship was revolutionary. Worship became immediately the prerogative of the congregation, and congregational singing was substituted in large part for the chanting of priests. Congregational prayers were introduced, and the whole service was conducted in the language of the people. This was a return to the ideal of the early church, in which all with one accord and one mouth glorified God.[14]

The Protestant theory of public worship is that all the action in the service is the collective action of the congregation. In the special musical numbers the choir represents

---

[13]Hugh Hartshorne, *Worship in the Sunday School,* p. 115f.
[14]Romans 15. 6.

the congregation. Likewise the prayers of the leader are, in fact, congregational prayers uttered by him in a purely representative capacity. He is only the mouthpiece of the people expressing for them their praise and petitions.

But the representatives of the congregation should never overshadow the congregation itself. The leader should hold up continually the obligation of the whole assembly to participate heartily in the many parts of the service designed for collective use—creed, hymns, prayers, etc. No congregation should permit the minister and the choir to monopolize the service. Its rights in this regard are very precious and were won at great cost.

We should be warned that democracy is threatened by mediocrity of taste and standards. Under an aristocratic ideal the service is in danger of becoming mechanical and unreal from excess of ritualism. Under a democratic ideal it is menaced by disorder, irreverence, extemporaneousness, unwarranted assertion of individuality by minister and members of the congregation, maudlin sentimentality, general cheapness in tone and ideals. One of the chief problems of the leader of social prayer is to open the door for the many to participate in worship without loss of dignity and impressiveness in the service.

f. Finally, public worship should be *beautiful*. God is the source of all beauty, and in his worship "tasteless and misshapen" forms should have no place. This applies, first of all, to the place of worship. It is difficult for a congregation to worship in an environment that offends the æsthetic sense. Unlovely surroundings will continually obtrude themselves upon the thought of the worshipers, heightening the self-consciousness of the individual and tending to destroy the psychical unity that is essential to social worship. Yet how commonly are things tolerated in the place of prayer which are unfriendly to the spirit of worship—architectural styles that are pagan rather than Christian, bad acoustics, poor ventilation, improper lighting, crude attempts at interior decorating, and often uncleanliness! Such things "impede the spirit's upward aspiration." Our churches need not be unbeautiful because we believe in the simplicity that goes with democracy. In reacting from the Roman type of architecture we need not revert to the Greek temple. In protesting against the Roman use of symbols we need not make our places of worship resemble concert rooms. If we do not introduce anything into the environment that suggests religious thoughts, at all events we can see to it that nothing in the surroundings shall offend the good taste and peace of mind of the worshipers.

Moreover, regard for the principle of beauty has to do with orderliness and reverence. There is something very pleasing in a service which begins promptly at the appointed hour and in which it is at once evident that everything has been anticipated and nothing left to haphazard—ministers, lay assistants, choir, ushers, and sexton cooperating together with perfect understanding. Furthermore, the service should be radiant with the beauty which inheres in reality in worship—worship that is "in spirit and in truth." Whatever else may be true of it, unless the service is electric with the Divine Presence and worshipers are made to realize the nearness of an invisible world of spirit and power, it cannot be "a beautiful service" in the highest sense of the term.

4. Prescribed vs. Free Worship.[15] In applying the proper ideals of collective worship, some communions provide an order of service in which every element is prescribed by ecclesiastical authority, and nothing is left to the individual judgment of the leader of the congregation or to the congregation itself. Others delight in free worship, which permits the leader to determine for himself what shall go into the service. The Methodist Episcopal Church

[15]This section is little more than a digest of the chapter on "Free Worship versus Formularies" in M. P. Talling's excellent book *Extempore Prayer,* p. 20ff. Used by permission of Fleming H. Revell Company.

uses both types of service, and her ministers should understand the values of each.

A ritualistic service is justified for some by their view of authority in religion. They regard the priesthood as the "exclusive channel of regenerative grace." The laity are incompetent to think for themselves or to express themselves in religious matters. Hence the need of fixed formularies in which the exact words of prayer, and praise, and instruction are set down for the leader and congregation to repeat according to specific directions. But "prescribed worship" is found among other communions who disavow this notion of authority. Theology has little to do with forms of worship. "Any church of any faith might adopt without modification of its tenets a fixed order of worship." In the Established Church of England and the Protestant Episcopal Church in the United States may be found great variety in theological points of view. These differences seldom manifest themselves in public worship, however, for every priest, whether conservative or progressive, uses the same order of worship. Perhaps this is the reason why a proposal to alter or amend the *Book of Common Prayer* is regarded as much more momentous than a charge of theological errancy.

a. Talling states the case for a liturgical service as follows:[16]

(1) *It has a certain stateliness of thought and charm of style which satisfy the ear and cling to the memory.*

(2) *It makes the worshipers independent of the officiating clergyman, so that his faults do not hinder their devotions.*

(3) *Affording a common and uniform means of worship, it serves to bind together all the members of the church into one fellowship and loyalty.* This unity embraces the past as well as the present. For persons who possess a strong historical sense, the thought that they are using the very same words of prayer and praise that have been found upon the lips of believers in all generations is profoundly inspiring.

---

[16]*Extempore Prayer,* p. 20f. Used by permission of Fleming H. Revell Company.

(4) *It is especially suitable for old people, because of its unchanging form of words, . . . and for young people, because their interest is sustained and they have some part in the worship.*

(5) *Nonliturgical or free worship possesses no uniformity, and the people take but little part in the service, and are exposed to the doctrinal bias and personal peculiarities of the minister.*

(6) *Free worship is in great danger of suffering from the unchastened promptings of the mind and uncorrected effusions of the heart.*

b. The case for free worship is summarized thus:

(1) *Prescribed worship makes overmuch of method, failing to distinguish between the spirit and the form of prayer.* Free worship in the nature of the case regards the spirit of worship as all-important.

(2) *Free worship trusts the renewed life to express itself in forms that are entirely appropriate.* It believes that where the head and the heart are right the worship will not go far wrong. . . . If man were vacant of God, worship would need to be a prepared article offered by hearts incapable of real emotion, but while God is above and within us, worship will tend to take on a suitable mood and a reverent expression.

(3) *Fixed forms of worship are the work of periods of calm in religious life, and they tend toward formalism.* On the other hand, every great crisis or religious activity called a "revival" or "reformation" has been marked by the casting off of religious ceremonial. . . . For the church, as for the individual, intense religious life takes on its own expression, and it is direct, simple, and spontaneous.

(4) *Prescribed worship is not sufficiently elastic to meet the demand made upon it by special occasions.* When some years ago Edward VII, then Prince of Wales, was ill, and a call for national prayer on his behalf was issued late in the week, the only church which failed to respond on the following Sabbath was the National Church. Because the bishops had not had time to send down prayers for the use of the clergy, there was silence in Anglican Churches that day upon the very theme which most occupied the British heart.[17]

(5) *"Unchastened promptings" are not inherently necessary in free worship.* It is possible for the individual leader to correct the "effusions of the heart" by giving careful attention to every

[17]Talling, *op. cit.*, p. 136f. Used by permission of Fleming H. Revell Company.

detail of worship and combine the grace of the liturgy with the warmth and spontaneity of free worship. If nonliturgical worship is often marred by indecorum, that proves only that we should teach decorum—not that we should take away all freedom of expression.

(6) *True worship is always creative effort—"an exercise in thinking."* To this end free prayer must be more helpful than liturgical formularies. To express one's own mood compels an attempt at original thought that is not demanded in reciting a fixed form.

Books Recommended for Further Study

Hugh Hartshorne, *Worship in the Sunday School.*
Charles S. Gardner, *Psychology and Preaching,* Chapter XI.
E. A. Ross, *Social Psychology.*
M. P. Talling, *Extempore Prayer.*
Washington Gladden, *The Christian Pastor,* Chapter VI.
L. C. Clark, *The Worshiping Congregation.*
B. H. Streeter, *et al., Concerning Prayer,* Chapter VIII.
T. Harwood Pattison, *Public Worship.*
N. J. Burton, *In Pulpit and Parish,* pp. 187-204.

CHAPTER III

MATERIALS OF WORSHIP—MUSIC

UNDER ordinary circumstances social worship is expressed in Music, Prayer, Reading of the Scriptures, the Announcements, the Offering, the Sermon, and the Benediction. The leader should understand the contribution which each of these exercises may make to the service and should constantly endeavor to make himself increasingly skillful in their use.

The relation of music to worship is so intimate that in both its vocal and instrumental forms it is a powerful agency for expressing and developing religious sentiment.

1. THE ORGAN. Its unique adaptability for accompanying choral song makes the organ the sacred instrument *par excellence*. The pastor cannot be expected to be an expert performer, but he should know the religious value of organ music and what is to be accomplished by preludes, interludes, offertories, and postludes. Otherwise he may find himself at the mercy of an organist who takes only professional interest in his work, or, more likely, at the mercy of a congregation whose inattention defeats the noblest efforts of the organist. More regrettable still, in the absence of proper ideals he may himself create the impression that the organ is only "a piece of sumptuary elegance" by his lack of respect for its contribution.

We have already called attention to the organ as a useful agent in fusing the congregation into an emotional unity at the beginning of the service. By the beauty and strength of its tones it commands immediate attention and creates a hospitable state of mind. Lorenz says, "If there were no other justification of the organ prelude, . . . its influence as mere music in organizing the crowd of individuals into a psychical unity were enough. The mere fact that they are listening to the same music, are having a common experience, creates a composite personality that becomes an induction coil intensifying the current of feeling that is to flow to the individual listener. . . . The opening music is not the negligible matter it is usually considered to be."[1]

Just as the organ prelude promotes unity of spirit in the beginning, so the interludes, responses, and offertory are useful in stabilizing emotion when there is danger of it being broken up by interruptions or sudden changes of direction in the service. For example, most congregations are disturbed by the belated arrival of many persons after the general prayer. Again, the offering tends to retard the movement of the service. And during the holy communion, the movement of the congregation threatens the social self that has been created by the prayers of the service. An organ interlude at such times may intensify the prevailing mood, and retain the attention of the congregation in spite of the distraction. In like manner the postlude should stabilize the feeling in which the congregation finds itself at the close of the service. As a matter of fact, however, many organists manage to dispel that feeling immediately by the crashing, militant kind of number selected for this part of the service.

We have been thinking of the pipe organ. But the congregation which cannot afford such an instrument need not despair of having its service enriched by instrumental music, for these effects may be approximated upon a reed organ or piano by a good musician. Indeed, some leaders of church music are not at all sure that a pipe organ is an unmixed good. "Given a small congregation that is not hearty in its participation in the service of song, given an organist who thinks that he is the whole thing and that the more stops he pulls out the more evident is his musical capacity, and the organ becomes a thing of evil, smothering

[1]E. S. Lorenz, *Practical Church Music*, p. 40f. Used by permission of Fleming H. Revell Company.

and submerging the choir and congregation, and absolutely domineering over the whole service and neutralizing all its possibilities for good. . . . The very bigness of the pipe organ magnifies the mistakes and inefficiency of an incompetent organist."[2]

The personality of the organist is more important than the instrument. His function is ministerial and his music should be a genuine expression of his personal faith, hope, trust, and love. Only to the extent to which his playing is self-revelation will he contribute largely to worship. It must follow that lack of respect on the part of the congregation for the work of the organist is exceedingly reprehensible. Yet how commonly members of the congregation feel at liberty to visit with each other during the musical parts of the service! And how frequently one sees even the minister conversing with a guest in the pulpit at these times! It is always a solemn thing for a human being to unveil the deepest feelings of his heart to public gaze. This the minister does in his public prayers and sermon, as the organist should do when he plays, or the soloist when he sings. If irreverence and inattention are unseemly in the presence of the one at such a time, it is equally so in the presence of the others.

2. The Choir. The mediæval church regarded membership in the choir as a clerical office. This view gradually developed under the control of the ascetic ideal which required that the choir should be composed only of men and boys, and, later, only of priests. Under this theory the choir came to monopolize the musical part of the service and the congregation was reduced to silence. This theory still exists in the Roman Church, but is modified greatly in its practical working.[3] The Protestant conception of the priesthood restored to the congregation its right to participate in worship. Nevertheless in some modern Prot-

[2]Lorenz, *op. cit.*, p. 373. Used by permission of Fleming H. Revell Company.

[3]J. J. Van Oosterzee, *Practical Theology*, p. 386.

estant churches the choir has again absorbed largely the musical part of the service and the congregation participates most sparingly in song. This has come about through a false notion of the function of the choir—that it is a device for adding variety to the service, or a means of elevating the musical tastes of the congregation, or of ministering to its artistic pride. *The democratic ideal of worship requires that the choir shall be thought of as a "specialized segment of the congregation."* As such it must assist the congregation in congregational song and express, as the representative of the congregation, the worship of the people in musical forms that are beyond the ability of the untrained multitude. I have not found a more satisfactory statement of this principle than the one made by Pratt in his *Musical Ministries in the Church*:[4] "The first purpose of the choir is to support and foster congregational singing. . . . Here I mean much more than a vague moral sympathy. I mean, of course, that a first reason for a choir's existence is that it may furnish a vocal nucleus to which the voices of the people can attach themselves, a positive mass of harmony in which every singer in the congregation can find his place with confidence and comfort. . . . The second function of the choir grows directly out of the first. . . . Congregational hymn-singing has obvious limitations on the musical side. It can hardly be expected, save in exceptional cases, to pass beyond the use of simple forms like the chant and the hymn tune. Yet the tonal embodiment of prayer and praise and of declarative utterances of all kinds tends constantly to stretch far beyond these smaller musical forms. The uses of music for these expressive purposes are surely not to be confined wholly to what an accidental, heterogeneous and untrained assembly can accomplish. . . . Here the choir comes in to extend and supplement congregational action as a vicarious agency. Choir music, then, is partly designed to supply forms of congregational expression that

[4]Waldo Selden Pratt, *Musical Ministries in the Church*, p. 86ff. Used by permission of Fleming H. Revell Company.

the people in general are technically unable to offer in person."

But there is a large measure of truth in the mediæval conception of the choir. It is the teacher and inspirer of the congregation as well as the instrument through which the congregation expresses its adoration and praise. In the latter respect its service parallels that of the minister in prayer; in the former, that of the minister in preaching. At one moment it faces toward God in worshipful address and at another it faces the congregation with instruction and exhortation.[5]

If these constitute the true function of the choir, it is obvious that the purely artistic and professional interests of the singers must always be subordinated to the religious in selecting and rendering choir music. *They do not sing primarily to entertain the congregation, but to lead the people into a spirit of prayer and worship.* However great may be the musical skill of the choir, its work is a failure if it is not done in a manner which increases the devotion of the congregation.

As to form, choirs vary greatly in America. Some churches prefer the choir composed of men and boys. Others have especial regard for the mixed quartet. Generally, however, the choir is a chorus of male and female voices. Each of these types has advantages and disadvantages. The fresh voices of a boys' choir are delightful, but the problems of discipline and irregularity of attendance make it difficult to maintain. The quartet is easily managed, but is likely to be controlled by purely professional, artistic, or even commercial considerations. The volunteer chorus is democratic, and is capable of producing under proper direction effects far beyond the power of the quartet. But while democracy solves some problems it creates others. The irregularity of attendance of a volunteer chorus, its quarrels and misunderstandings, the musical shortcomings of many of its members, and the wide diversity of musical

[5]Pratt, *op. cit.*, p. 100f.

tastes are sources of constant anxiety. The ideal choir is a volunteer chorus built around a quartet so that there will be at least one trained voice for each part. In the interest of variety it may be wise to substitute occasionally an "adjunct choir" composed of boys, or girls, or young people of both sexes, for the regular chorus.

In the selection of music,[6] the leader should have regard for *the capacity of the choir.* A quartet should not select music which can be rendered effectively only by a chorus, and a chorus should not choose a grade of music beyond its ability to sing well. *The capacity of the congregation must be considered, also.* A kind of music that will serve admirably the needs of some congregations will distress others. *And the temporary mood of the congregation must be taken into account.* If the choir is to express for the congregation its worshipful feelings, its musical forms must accord with the spirit of the special occasion. *Finally, the preference of the minister who has charge of the service must be respected.* In the interest of unity the prevailing consideration in selecting the music cannot be the preference of some member of the choir who "likes" a certain anthem, but what will make the largest contribution to the service as the leader has planned it. This implies, of course, that there must be the closest cooperation between minister and choir leader.

The subject of dress may become engrossing in a choir. Tastes in millinery and clothing vary so greatly and strangely that the array of colors and styles in the choir may interfere with the spirit of worship. This problem may be solved in one of two ways: require all to wear vestments of black or white, or insist upon modest, inconspicuous clothing of a certain general type. In most cases the latter course will be more advisable.

If the choir is the mouthpiece of the congregation expressing vicariously the praise and petitions of the whole assembly, it should be composed ideally of none but those

---

[6]Lorenz, *op. cit.*, pp. 293-298.

who love God and desire to worship him. How can they worship for others who do not worship for themselves? It does not follow, however, that a pastor or Music Committee should be in haste to expel from the choir all so-called unconverted people. And, certainly, there is no warrant for making church membership a condition of membership in the choir. Religious experience is always relative, and there are many whose hearts reach Godward but whose spiritual attainments have not seemed to justify a public confession of faith. Let the pastor speak often to the choir of the ideals that should control them in their work, exalting the ministerial character of their service, and this will create an atmosphere in which one will not tarry long who does not find it congenial.

Repeated reference has been made to the relation of the pastor to the choir. The importance of this relation cannot be overemphasized. The finest results are never secured where the choir has a large sense of independence, presuming to select not only the anthems but the hymns without regard for the plans which the minister may have for the service. This lack of cooperation, however, is chargeable against the pastor quite as often as against the choir. The wise pastor will take the choir into his confidence, revealing his ideals for their common work, meeting with them frequently at rehearsals, not to direct them but to show appreciation of them, and he may well meet them as they prepare to enter the service for a moment of earnest prayer that the spirit of worship may be upon him and them as together they attempt to lead others in worship. This will result in a fellowship which will be mutually delightful. The pastor should be final authority in the selection of hymns and anthems, but he will be careful to exercise this authority in tactful ways. He will come with requests rather than commands, and will covet and act upon, as far as possible, suggestions from the choir. The initiative, of course, in all these matters, must come from him.

3. Congregational Song. *Important as the organ and*

choir may be, "the true center of Protestant music must always be the music of the congregation." The reason appears in the fundamental theory of Protestant worship—that worship is the common right of the whole body of believers. The principal means through which the congregation may express itself collectively is congregational song. This is one of the indispensable agencies for creating and developing religious sentiment—an important means of impression as well as expression. On these accounts every pastor should be eager to make the singing of the congregation as effective as possible. To do this he must know something of the history and religious value of hymns.

Congregational singing in the language of the people antedates the Reformation.[7] As early as 1505 A. D. the followers of John Hus had a well-developed body of hymns and tunes for congregational use. Both Luther and Calvin exalted this element of worship, but the influence of the German reformer was very different from that of the Frenchman. Luther cherished a great affection for the German folk-songs and the old Latin hymns which were a part of the Daily Office of the Roman Church. The fact that the hymn was a free composition, and not merely a paraphrase of Scripture, did not make it objectionable to him. On the contrary, he found it to be a most effective instrument for spreading the new gospel. At once he began to write German hymns based without prejudice upon the Scripture, the old Latin and Bohemian hymns, and his own religious experience. These were set to suitable music and placed in the hands of the people. The result is that the history of German hymnody continues without interruption from the beginning of the Reformation until the present, and is much richer in the number and quality of its hymns than is English hymnody.

Unlike Luther, Calvin had no taste either for the popu-

[7]The reader is referred to the excellent work on *The English Hymn,* by Louis F. Benson, for the history and development of English hymnody, to which work I am greatly indebted.

lar songs of the people or for the hymns of the Latin Church. He approved of no congregational songs except those based upon Scripture, and practically limited himself to metrical versions of the Psalms. Thus it came about that wherever Calvin's influence predominated in the spread of the Reformation, *psalm-singing,* as distinguished from *hymn-singing,* characterized Protestant worship. Because of this, English-speaking peoples became psalm-singers and remained so for almost two centuries after the Reformation.

Unfortunately, the men who made the earliest metrical translation of the Psalms into English—Sternhold and Hopkins—were neither good poets nor accurate translators. Moreover, the Psalms belonged to the earlier stages of revelation, and, however satisfying they may have been for the time that produced them, they could never meet the larger demands of Christian worship, for in them the worshiper could not name the name of Jesus. Again, some of them breathed a spirit that was un-Christian. During the seventeenth century a group, including such Anglicans as Bishop Ken and John Mason, a Catholic like John Austin, and a Nonconformist like Richard Baxter, attempted to "Christianize the Psalms," making them say what modern believers would say, and to find in other parts of the Bible and in the more evangelical Latin hymns the materials for congregational songs. Their work was only preparatory, however, to the more important work of Isaac Watts, whose relation to the Christian hymn is at least comparable with that of David to the Hebrew Psalm.

Watts' work now seems unduly restricted. His hymn-forms were practically limited to the three simplest meters—long, common, and short. For the materials of his hymns he refused to go outside the Bible on the ground that this contained the record of Christian experience in all its ranges, and therefore no occasion was found for going beyond the bounds of Scripture for hymn themes. More strangely still, he declared that hymns could not be poetry since they must be adapted to the capacity of the common mind. He claimed no more for his own hymns than that they were rimed verse. In all of these respects his ideals contrasted sharply with those of the Wesleys.

In the early part of the eighteenth century the conditions of congregational song were more sorry, if possible, in the Church of England than among Nonconformists. The singing of psalms "lined" by a precentor was the universal practice. John Wesley described the custom in the town churches of his day with picturesque adjectives: "the miserable, scandalous doggerel of Sternhold and Hopkins"; at first droned out two staves at a time "by a poor humdrum wretch," and then "bawled out" by a handful of "wild, unwakened striplings," "who neither feel nor understand" what they "scream," while the congregation is "lolling at ease, or in the indecent posture of sitting, drawling out one word after another."[8] His desire to improve the psalmody of the English Church is responsible for his contribution to English hymnody. For, according to Benson, "the leader who played the part in Methodist hymnody which Calvin had taken in Huguenot psalmody was, contrary perhaps to the general impression, John Wesley, and not his brother Charles. He planned it, prepared the ground, introduced and fostered it, molded and administered it, and also restrained its excesses."[9]

The Wesleys were trained to sing both psalms and hymns in Epworth Rectory. They were admirers of the work of Watts and used his *Hymns and Songs* in the Holy Club. But it remained for the Moravians to reveal to them the superiority of a fervid type of hymn-singing over the uninspiring psalmody of the Anglicans and the Nonconformists. This Moravian influence upon Methodist hymnody is marked by the number of hymns translated from the Ger-

---

[8]Reprinted and condensed from *The English Hymn*, p. 222, by Louis F. Benson by permission of the publishers, George H. Doran Company.

[9]Benson, *op. cit.*, p. 220.

man and by the spiritual fervor of Methodist singing, though John Wesley repudiated the "whimsical Allegories" and "perverted spiritualizations" which characterized Moravian hymnody about the middle of the eighteenth century.

The work of the Wesleys in developing the English hymn is admittedly second only to Watts. But for the "reproach of Methodism" which caused Anglicans and Nonconformists alike to hold the followers of Wesley in contempt, their influence might have been even greater. Charles wrote some six thousand five hundred hymns, though it is only fair to say that many of these were so mediocre that never more than seven hundred and twenty-four were admitted to any *Methodist Hymnal,* and in the official *Methodist Hymnal,* adopted in 1905, the number is reduced to one hundred and twenty. The best of these are found in the hymn books of practically all Christian bodies. John Wesley enriched the store of English hymns not so much by original compositions as by translating from the German, by "tinkering" the hymns of others, and by editing a number of hymn books. "His equipment for this undertaking," says Benson, "was his sound musical feeling, a very limited technical knowledge, and an unusual practical sense."[10]

More important than the number, however, was the new type of hymn which they produced, *the evangelistic hymn* based upon individual Christian experience. Charles Wesley "felt an impulse to translate every new spiritual experience into song. . . . His hymns are frankly autobiographical. They portray without any effort to tone down his own heightened emotions to the average level, his personal spiritual history: his unrest and even agony under bondage to the law, his instantaneous conversion and assurance of faith, the period of ecstatic joy, the ups and downs of the pilgrim progress to the 'second rest,' his delight in the anticipation of death."[11] Naturally, this type of hymn sung

[10]Benson, *op. cit.,* p. 239.

[11]Reprinted from *The English Hymn,* p. 249, by Louis F. Benson, by permission of the publishers, George H. Doran Company.

by the multitudes with fervor created the kind of experience which gave it birth, and Methodist singing became the most powerful single agent in the Methodist revival.

Furthermore, the Wesleys improved the literary quality of the hymn. In contrast with Watts, whose measured verse was "written down to the level of the meanest capacity," they insisted that "the hymn should be a religious lyric" and that the capacity of the people should be leveled up to an appreciation of the beauties of true poetry. There is reason to think that some modern Methodists are following Watts rather than Wesley in the use of "rimed verse" instead of poetry in congregational singing.

The history of the English hymn, after Watts and Wesley, breaks up into many diverging streams under denominational, literary, and revivalistic influences. A brief study of the authors' index of the latest *Methodist Hymnal* will suggest the extent to which hymnody was enriched during the nineteenth century by contributions from every one of the more important religious bodies, and of the catholic spirit of their work. The same book, too, shows the influence of broader literary standards which admit a type of religious lyric not regarded heretofore as adapted to public worship, for example, Holland's "There's a Star in the Sky," and Lanier's "Into the Woods My Master Went." The revival movements of the last century created a new body of spiritual songs designed to make an immediate appeal to the popular mind. The inferior quality of most of these songs will prevent their admission into church hymnody, though this may not apply to some of the nobler "Gospel Songs" of Moody and Sankey when the copyrights expire.

Change in religious thought and feeling is bound to be reflected in time in a new type of church song. The influences at work at the present time to modify the English hymn are mainly theological and social. The modern point of view respecting these matters appears conspicuously in the new Congregational Hymn Book, *The Pilgrim Hymnal,* published in 1904. Doubtless we shall see further evidences of these influences in other denominational hymnals in the near future.

The value of a hymn is determined, of course, by the degree in which it serves the purpose of congregational song. We have noticed already that it is useful in unifying the many individualities into a single group-self. This may justify at times the use of an inferior or even a nonreligious song at the beginning of the service. Such songs as "The Church in the Wildwood," "Beautiful Isle of Somewhere," and "Brighten the Corner Where You Are," possess in themselves little or no religious value, for they do not express any definite religious faith. They are sentimental rather than religious. It is the music rather than the stanzas which accomplish the effect produced by such songs. The rhythm of the music tends to bring all together into a common state of emotion that is indispensable to a successful service. "I Love to Tell the Story," "He Leadeth Me," and "O Sometimes the Shadows are Deep," set to the tunes commonly associated with them, possess the same unifying power and, in addition, have a definite religious content, for they are genuine expressions of personal faith in God. The former type of song could never be used appropriately in any except an informal service, and even then only at a point in the service where the rhythm of the music was more important than the thought expressed in the words.

Again, congregational singing is the most effective method of expressing collective prayer and praise. For this purpose the ephemeral "gospel song," whose effect is physical rather than spiritual, and due to the music rather than the words, is unworthy. As an expression of faith it is too often inane. John Wesley instructed his preachers to interrupt the "noisy hymn" and ask the congregation a few questions like the following: "Now, do you know what you said last? Did it suit your case? Did you sing it as to God, with the spirit and understanding also?" Such an interruption is not only a test of the soberness of the congregation but also a very severe test of the quality of the hymn. To raise such questions about some of the songs used commonly in public services would be deadly. For no one really means what the songs say, and the realization of this would cause the congregation to turn away from them in disgust. There is a place in social worship for the rhythmical, mediocre song—*but it is not a large place.* "God has a right to be worshiped with the best we have." And when the aim of the song is to express a living and rational faith, none but the songs that are lofty in thought and dignified in expression are worthy either of God or the congregation. It may be that for a time a minister must accommodate himself to the limitations of a congregation that is lacking in appreciation of the better hymns and is incapable of singing them, but he should be ashamed to leave them long in that condition. He can do nothing that will have a more favorable effect upon their spiritual lives than teach them to express their praise in worthy musical forms.

A third function of congregational singing, which constitutes a third test of the value of a song, appears in its effect upon the individuals that compose the congregation. It is a means of impressing as well as expressing religious truth. Doctor Pratt says, "The value of any particular hymn is partly to be judged by the state of opinion and sentiment in which it actually leaves you. Is it true in its thought of God and Christ, in its reference to all the manifold aspects of sin and salvation, in its representation of the spiritual life? And is it healthy in general tone, affecting in its imagery and masterful in its progress, and sufficiently noble to awaken enthusiasm for what it treats? These are severe tests, but are they not fair ones?"[12] In this respect the modern gospel song again appears unworthy. Its thought of God and Christ is often very far from true, its ethical tone is generally individualistic, and its imagery and

---

[12]*Musical Ministries in the Church,* p. 67. Used by permission of the publishers, Fleming H. Revell Company.

forms of expression often are so lacking in nobility that one is repelled rather than attracted to the subject.

If these constitute the true function of congregational singing, it must be that the hymn stands in its own right in the service, co-ordinate with, and not subordinate to the sermon. Both, however, must contribute cooperatively to the movement of the service in a given direction. The hymn need not deal directly with the subjects treated in the sermon, but it should create a congenial atmosphere and express a spirit that is kindred to that of the sermon. This is especially true of the first and second hymns of the Methodist Order of Worship. Many ministers prefer that the closing hymn should reinforce directly the thought of the sermon, intensifying the emotional response of the congregation. Finally, it is evident that the leader of public worship is the only person who is in position to select the congregational songs intelligently.

Let us attempt to select some hymns by way of illustrating the principles just stated. Assume that the aim of the service is to lead the congregation into an appreciation of the value of prayer. The sermon, of course, should deal with the subject in a way to clear up intellectual confusion and arouse the will to pray. What hymns should be chosen from *The Methodist Hymnal* for this service? Inasmuch as prayer is communion with God, the opening hymn may properly express the joy which the devout heart experiences in divine fellowship and should be set to a rhythmical tune whose spirit accords with that of the hymn. We might well use hymn No. 330, beginning,

"My hope is built on nothing less
Than Jesus' blood and righteousness";

or better, perhaps, hymn No. 364, beginning,

"My Saviour, on the word of truth
In earnest hope I live";

or hymn No. 540, which begins, "O could I speak the matchless worth." If the Creed, Prayer, Anthem, and

Scripture Lesson shall have been used advantageously, the atmosphere will be sufficiently worshipful, that the second hymn may be much more stately than the first. Cowper's hymn, No. 454, is now appropriate:

> "Sometimes a light surprises
> The Christian while he sings."

For the closing hymn, one should be selected with the wistful note, dealing directly with the subject of prayer and strengthening newly formed resolutions to pray. Hymn No. 495 is good: "From every stormy wind that blows"; or hymn No. 355, "Love divine, all loves excelling."

In announcing hymns the leader is bound to give them the consideration to which they are entitled as the most important means for the expression of collective worship. They should not be announced indifferently, as though the aim were simply to do a conventional thing or to fill up the time, but earnestly as though there were nothing more important at that moment than to sing that particular hymn in the right manner. Whether or not the hymn shall be read, wholly or in part, depends upon the purpose of the leader in reading. If he desires to call attention to its significance for life and religious experience let him read by all means. But if the reading is done mechanically and for no serious purpose, the door is opened immediately to unreality. Better no reading at all than this kind.

It follows that the minister should be a diligent and lifelong student of hymns and tunes. He should see to it that his own acquaintance with congregational song is constantly growing and should manage to introduce such variety of singing into the worship of the church and Sunday school that the people will come to love the best in church music. Let him magnify the official hymnal of the church and master its music and poetry. He should teach a new hymn to the congregation frequently, and sing it often until it is familiar. He may give pleasing variety to regular services by telling historical incidents connected with many of the great hymns. To guard against a narrow range of choice, he should keep a record of hymns used on the successive Sundays of the year, avoiding frequent repetition of the more familiar numbers.

Books Recommended for Further Study

Waldo Selden Pratt, *Musical Ministries in the Church.*

E. S. Lorenz, *Practical Church Music.*

Louis F. Benson, *The English Hymn; Studies of Familiar Hymns.*

Edward S. Ninde, *The Story of the American Hymn.*

Edward Dickinson, *Music in the History of the Western Church.*

Peter C. Lutkin, *Music in the Church.*

Nutter and Tillett, *The Hymns and Hymn Writers of the Church Hymnal.*

Carl F. Price, *The Music and Hymnody of the Methodist Hymnal.*

John M. Walker, *Better Music in Our Churches.*

CHAPTER IV

MATERIALS OF WORSHIP—PRAYERS

Worship is prayer, and in social worship the prayers normally should be the strongest parts of the service. As a matter of fact, they are generally the weakest, overshadowed by both the sermon and the music. A thoughtful liturgist inquires, "Is it not true that you have heard from the same lips a sermon orderly, clear, virile, and a prayer rambling, indefinite, and vapid; the former being a presentation of well-considered, well arranged and important truth, felicitously expressed; the latter ill-considered, poorly arranged thought, born of struggle so apparent or following a rut so wearily worn as to destroy all sense of spirituality?"[1] To learn to pray is the most important part of a minister's task. Beecher used to declare that "he who knows how to pray for his people need not trouble to preach for them or to them."[2]

1. Defects in Public Prayers.—*a.* Among the more common defects which mar public worship, *unreality* must be named first. This may appear in mock humility and exaggerated self-depreciation on the part of the liturgist, in affected fervor and highly rhetorical address to Deity, or in the mechanical manner in which the prayer is made. Whatever else should be true of it, a worthy prayer must be a sincere and unaffected expression of feeling.

b. Carelessness, amounting to flippancy and irreverence, destroys the value of many prayers. This may appear in the formlessness of the prayer—wandering, incoherent, empty of intelligible ideas, as if no preparation had been made for this act of worship. Or it may appear in the

[1]Talling, *op. cit.,* p. 16f.

[2]Yale Lectures, II, p. 47.

manner of him who leads—matter-of-fact, familiar, lacking awe and humility.

c. Other prayers are spoiled by *flattery and complimentary references* to men in their presence. Who has not been sickened by something as reprehensible as the following: "Bless, we pray thee, our beloved brother. We thank thee for the wonderful work he is doing and the powerful sermon to which we have just listened"? The author of a valuable treatise on worship well says, "Appreciation of God's servants at home or abroad has a rightful place in prayer, but is no warrant for fulsome praise in their presence."

d. Charles H. Spurgeon was particularly provoked with prayers *overloaded with endearing words.* "When 'Dear Lord,' and 'Blessed Lord,' and 'Sweet Jesus' come over and over again as vain repetitions, they are among the worst of blots," he believed.

e. Prayers are denatured when, under the guise of addressing Deity, they become *sermons to the congregation* on doctrinal, political, historical, or personal matters. Such "preaching prayers" are not prayers at all.

f. Frequent repetition of the divine name is to be avoided. A good rule in this matter would be to use the name of God only when it will add emphasis. Likewise all other repetitious words and phrases detract from the impressiveness of devotion. This is always due to disconnected thought. One who has a perfectly clear notion of what he wants to say will express it freely.

g. Other common faults, without attempting an exhaustive catalogue, are shouting, wild gestures, rapid speech, drawling, monotone, crudities of all kinds. In addressing the infinite God we should be at least as circumspect as when speaking to "the leading citizen" in our town.

2. The Principles of Effective Prayer. In correcting the faults of public prayer one should keep before him the great principles which make for effectiveness in this act of worship, and seek constantly to apply them to himself.

a. It must be evident that the very first of these is *reality in religious experience.* To pray well in public one must pray much in private. And he must carry the atmosphere of one who knows God at first hand, who is sure of the unseen world of spirit, and power, and goodness, and who speaks with the quiet assurance of perfect knowledge and sincerity.

b. The second principle derives from the Protestant theory that worship is the function of the entire congregation, and that all public prayer is "common prayer," even when expressed by a single person. *One who "leads in prayer" speaks not for himself alone, but in a representative capacity.* He is merely the mouthpiece through which the congregation pours its collective confession, repentance, adoration, and praise. He must, then, not only identify himself with God through the transparent genuineness of his religious faith, but also with the congregation in those experiences and feelings which all share together. It is the *common* sorrow, the *common* sin, the *common* need, and the *common* aspiration that should find expression in his public prayers—not the experiences that are purely personal to himself. To this he pledges himself when he suggests, "Let *us* pray," rather than, "*I* shall pray." He must not allow himself under these circumstances to be mastered by private considerations of health, weariness, depressing moods, or individual sorrow. One of the greatest things the late Theodore Roosevelt ever did was to make an address before a political convention the day after his son Quentin was reported lost, without referring in any way to his individual grief, though the whole country knew about it. In similar fashion the minister must repress in his public prayers all personal matters, giving right of way only to that which is general. Only so can he make himself a perfect mouthpiece for collective prayer. Henry Ward Beecher expresses this sense of oneness with the congregation admirably:

"Hundreds and hundreds of times as I rose to pray and

glanced at the congregation I could not keep back the tears. There came to my mind such a sense of their wants, there were so many hidden sorrows, there were so many weights and burdens, there were so many doubts, there were so many states of weakness, there were so many dangers, so many perils, there were so many histories—not world histories, but eternal-world histories—I had such a sense of compassion for them, my soul so longed for them, that it seemed to me as if I could scarcely open my mouth to speak for them. And when I take my people and carry them before God to plead for them, I never plead for myself as I do for them—I never could."[3]

c. The third principle is preparation. If speaking *to* the people is a solemn privilege for which one should make the most careful preparation, speaking *for* them in prayer is no less solemn, demanding equal diligence beforehand. But, strangely enough, comparatively few ministers prepare their prayers as painstakingly as they do their sermons. With some this is sheer negligence. With others it is the result of a fanatical notion that such preparation would interfere with the movement of the Holy Spirit—as if the Holy Spirit despised our normal faculties and declined to operate except through the impulsive, the unpremeditated, and undisciplined moods of the heart and mind. Let us "no more venture into the pulpit with an impromptu prayer than with an impromptu sermon."

This preparation should be double—(1) a preparation of the heart of the liturgist by private prayer and meditation to induce the mood and spirit of worship, and (2) a preparation of the mind by carefully selecting the ideas that are to be incorporated into the prayer and arranging them in the most effective manner so that the prayer will be something more than a disorderly "medley of phrases devoid of intelligible order." This latter preparation may well go as far as the actual writing of the prayer. It is not incompatible with extemporaneousness, which implies merely the

[3]Yale Lectures, II, p. 46.

free utterance of that which has been well considered previously.

In organizing the materials of the prayer we must have regard for the principles of composition which control in the creation of all literary forms.

(1) First, the prayer must have a definite plan. Its character will depend upon the nature and the occasion of the service. If there is nothing exceptional in the setting, the prayer may be general in its scope, comprehensive, rather than particular, in its emphases. If the occasion is "special," the plan will be shaped accordingly, larger place being made for the matter rendered conspicuous by the time and place. The one who prays should know exactly the direction his prayer will take and the particular steps by which he is to proceed.

(2) A plan implies a *sense of completeness and unity* when the prayer is finished. Every part must be related to the central idea which unifies all into a single whole. Respect for this principle of unity, moreover, will keep out everything that is foreign to the main matter. Again, it will not overlook any important item that should be included. "How often in extemporaneous prayer one hears many subjects introduced, none of them completed, nor the whole rounded out in such proportions as to have a distinct effect—a bundle of scraps, no more like an organism than a parcel of legs, arms, fingers, and ears resemble the human body."

(3) The plan can be unfolded only gradually. This requires *movement and action* in the development of the prayer, precisely as is required in the development of a story. In the absence of this "travel of thought" from point to point, producing a sense of change, the attention soon wearies, and interest fails through monotonous repetition. Movement, then, should be rapid enough to hold the attention. And under the control of the unifying idea it should be orderly enough to be followed easily.

(4) This movement should rise steadily from point to

point until the highest of all—*the climax*—has been reached. Then the prayer should be concluded. This upward movement is not merely one of thought, but of feeling as well. For a prayer is less a "train of thought" than a "train of emotions."

(5) The introduction of the prayer usually consists of such ascriptions to Deity as are appropriate to the dominant note in the prayer. If it is a prayer of thanksgiving, then God may be thought of as the gracious Father and Benefactor of men. If a prayer for help, as the Almighty and Omnipotent. For a typical example, take the familiar collect for purity which is a prayer for cleansing:

Introduction: "Almighty God, unto whom all hearts are open, all desires known, and from whom no secrets are hid:"

Petition: "Cleanse the thoughts of our hearts by the inspiration of thy Holy Spirit, that we may perfectly love thee, and worthily magnify thy holy name; through Jesus Christ our Lord. Amen."

(6) The conclusion of the prayer should be appropriate to what has preceded, and should be brief. Most of the prayers in that excellent volume, *The Temple,* by W. E. Orchard, close almost abruptly with a simple *"Amen."* More commonly the conclusion cites the authority by which the requests are made or consists of an adoring phrase addressed to some Person of the Trinity:

"Through Jesus Christ, our Lord. *Amen."*

"For Jesus' sake. *Amen."*

"That we may glorify thy holy name. *Amen."*

"Through the merits of thy Son, Jesus Christ. *Amen."*

"Through him who liveth and reigneth with thee and the Holy Ghost, now and forever. *Amen."*

"To the honor and glory of thy name. *Amen."*

(7) The ideal public prayer will be simple and chaste as to language. There will be no long or involved sentences. The words, for the most part, will be of one or two syllables. Vulgarisms and slang will have no place in them

Terms that are low and coarse and also high and inflated should be avoided.

d. The materials of public prayer consist of Confession, Petition, Thanksgiving, and Intercession. It is possible to avoid monotony of subject and method by tabulating, for one's private use, under these general headings, items that properly may be incorporated into one's prayers. The following catalogue, which is only suggestive, is an abbreviation of the "Summaries" made by James Burns, M.A., in *A Pulpit Manual,* pages 67-77,[4] though I have presumed to add certain themes suggested by our new social ideals.

Confession

(1) *Sins of Daily Life*

Love of self; of ease; of money; of display. Indifference to spiritual things; neglect of duty; blindness to the unseen.

(2) *Sins Against Our Fellowmen*

Unkindness in judgment; lack of courtesy and forbearance; selfishness and hardness of heart toward the needs of others; lack of sympathy with their sorrows and losses; neglect of the poor, the weak, and the erring.

(3) *Sins Against God*

Ingratitude for daily mercies; unfaithfulness in duty, and constant forgetfulness; neglect of prayer; indifference in worship; want of love and zeal for spiritual things; betraying Christ through the worldliness of our lives.

(4) *Sins of Mind and Heart*

Vanity, pride, boastfulness, impatience, intolerance, lack of consideration for the opinions of others. Want of love and compassion toward others; selfish absorption in ourselves which makes us callous; insincerity; indulging in vain, frivolous, and empty conversation; using the language of devotion without the spirit; uttering hot, passionate, and unkind words when we ought to have remained silent; remaining silent when we ought to have spoken. Our indolence and evil temper; our worldly discontent at the success of others; our acts of dishonesty and deceitfulness in our relations to our fellowmen. Our forgotten vows and neglected

[4]Used by permission of The Pilgrim Press.

opportunities; the sorrows which have brought no repentance, and the heavenly pleadings which we have disregarded; the things left undone, and those which we ought not to have done; the sins and weakness which mar our best moments, so that even when we would do good, evil is present with us.

(5) Sins of the Congregation

The poverty, languidness, and frequent irreverence of our worship; the worldly thoughts and business cares which we allow to distract our minds; the coldness of our praises and the feebleness of our prayers; our unwillingness to part with our possessions for the extension of Christ's kingdom; our indifference toward the sinful without and the lost and erring around our doors.

(6) Sins of the Nation

Our love of wealth, and greedy pursuit of material prosperity; the pride and haughtiness which we show toward other peoples; our increasing love of luxury and display in our public life; the decline of worship, the public neglect of the Day of Rest; our indifference toward social wrong and injustice, and our neglect of the poor, the suffering, and the weak.

(7) Sins of Social and Industrial Groups

Our failure to apply Christian principles of conduct to industrial relationships; our disregard of human values; the subordination of human welfare to profit and power; and inability to do the work of the world in the spirit of brotherhood; our exploitation of childhood and womanhood; our indifference to the effect of industry upon the home; our industrial wars.

Petition

(1) For Forgiveness

For all sins; for omissions of duty; for every unkind word, evil thought or imagination; for every sinful deed, for everything in past conduct which has merited judgment.

(2) For Cleansing

From the stains and impurities wrought in us by sin and the world; cleansing of the conscience, of the mind, of the heart, of the will; cleansing of the eyes, the hands, the lips.

(3) For Renewal

In faith and love; brought back to sense of divine favor;

strengthened with might to withstand temptation; reassured of Christ's presence, protection, love.

(4) *For Protection*

In time of temptation, trial of faith, spiritual weakness; in time of sorrow, sickness, affliction; in time of worldly loss, discouragement, disappointment; in time of doubt, difficulty, and perplexity.

(5) *For Grace*

To forgive; to possess the soul in patience; to maintain peace of conscience, joy in the Holy Ghost, assurance unto the end; to witness a good confession; to persevere unto the end.

(6) *For Courage*

To follow in the footsteps of Christ; to bear His Cross and do His will; to testify our allegiance to Him before the world with boldness; to willingly sacrifice for His sake; to endure hardness as a good soldier of Jesus Christ.

(7) *For Deliverance*

From vain imaginings; foolish repinings; needless care; vain regrets; embittered speech; love of coarse enjoyments; the scornful spirit; compromising with sin; ingratitude, and distrust of the divine love.

Thanksgiving

(1) *For Daily Mercies*

Food; raiment; comforts and protection of home; health of body and mind; strength to labor; life's daily tasks and opportunities; love which shields and supports us.

(2) *For Our Education*

Friends, teachers, and instructors of youth; example of those around us; education and inspiration which come from past history, literature, art, and daily activities; life's disciplines and experiences; trials which train us in patience, humility, and in fortitude; sacred ties which bind us to the Unseen.

(3) *For Our Country*

Its history and traditions; its civil and religious freedom; its justice and good government; the growth of charity, consideration for the wants of the weak and poor, and national responsibility.

(4) *For Spiritual Mercies*

Day of rest—its opportunities, associations, and obligations.

House of God—its ministry and sacraments; sacred ties and holy worship.

Gift of Christ—His Incarnation, Ministry, Atonement, Death, Resurrection, Ascension, and Intercession.

Holy Spirit—guidance of His Church and people; revelation of truth; inspiration for holy conduct.

Holy Word—its revelation of divine purposes; its inspiration and promises.

Saints and teachers; prophets and evangelists; all who serve in faithfulness.

Intercession

(1) *For Native Land*

The President and his family; his Cabinet and Counselors; both Houses of Congress; Army and Navy, and all engaged in service of the Commonwealth; Judges and Magistrates; all who occupy places of trust and responsibility.

(2) *For Other Nations*

All kings and rulers, together with peoples under their sway; the growth in the world of freedom, justice, and good government; the overthrow of tyranny and oppression; the spread of the spirit of love and brotherhood; the hastening of the reign of the Prince of Peace.

(3) *For City*

City, town, parish, or district; magistrates and public men; its public institutions and benefactions; its efforts to improve the health, happiness, and comfort of inhabitants.

(4) *For Social Classes*

(a) The poor—those working under hard, depressing, monotonous, dangerous, or unremunerative conditions; those suffering through unjust social or economic laws; those who are physically or mentally unfitted for engaging in life's battle; those who are depressed, or worn out, or dispirited.

(b) The rich—that they may be good stewards of God's bounty; defended from pride, selfishness, vain display, love of luxury, hardening which comes from success; that they may maintain a lowly and obedient heart.

(c) Those engaged in commerce—that prosperity may be granted to all engaged in business and various industries; that divisions between class and class may be healed; that all engaged in business may be men of integrity, rectitude, and known for their fair dealing.

(d) The unfortunate—those losing heart; those crushed down by debt, by loss, by failure of their hopes; those embittered by adversity; those becoming hard and defiant because of prosperity of others; those who have found life a disappointment, and the multitude of the miserable around our doors.

(e) The afflicted—those who are suffering in mind or body; the inmates of our workhouses, hospitals, or kindred institutions; those who tend them, doctors, nurses, and all engaged in alleviating human distress; those who mourn; those drawing near to death, and those in bondage to its fear. Those grievously tempted; those who have gone astray—the prodigal, criminal, abandoned; those in doubt and spiritual perplexity; those hindered through circumstances, weakness of faith, or lack of courage; those who have not the courage of their best convictions; those who are growing blinded to spiritual realities.

(f) Employees—women, children, men who work under depressing, dangerous, and unremunerative conditions. Labor organizations, that they may be wisely led and saved from bitterness and malice.

(g) Employers—that they may be wise and patient, exercising their great power over the workers in the spirit of brotherhood; that they concern themselves with working men as well as dividends —that they be saved from the sin of using other men as tools to further their own self-interest.

(h) For business men—that they be saved from the deceitfulness and materialism of trade—that they may realize that they are engaged in useful social service—that all engaged in business may be full of integrity and honor.

(5) *For the Church*

Ministers, teachers, missionaries, evangelists, all engaged in her service; for spread of Gospel in heathen lands; for missions and native Christians; for church with which we are connected; for congregation, its minister, office-bearers, members; for all its societies, its work, and interests. For the coming of Christ in great power.

(6) *For Home*

Parents, and children; those in distant lands; those who have gone out into the world; those at school; the lambs of the flock; any in sickness, trouble, anxiety.

e. The enrichment of prayer is a matter of never-ending concern to the leader of worship, who should constantly strive for worthier expression of religious feelings. He will need, first, a high *standard.* This will be found in the best liturgical prayers of the church, of which he should be a lifelong student. These prayers will assist him in his private devotions by suggesting themes for meditation, and will be a productive source of new words and synonyms. By reading them aloud and memorizing the shortest and noblest of them, one will enlarge his vocabulary and accustom himself to dignified, varied, and forceful utterance in prayer. Moreover, through these prayers one may become acquainted with the collective mind of the church in all generations and so understand the *common* need, the *common* sin, the *common* aspiration which he must interpret.

f. How long should one pray? Long enough, but not too long. Abruptness must be avoided on the one hand, and weariness on the other. "He prayed one into a good frame of mind and out again by keeping on," is a complaint that might be made against many ministers. The longest prayers recorded in the Bible could not have required more than ten minutes to deliver. As a rule, the general or pastoral prayer should not consume more than five or six minutes. Invocations, and prayers after the offering and the sermon should be condensed into from one to three sentences.

g. If prayer is the office of the congregation, and the leader is only speaking for the people in a representative capacity, they have responsibility for the successful ministry of prayer. That responsibility requires that the congregation shall assemble in a devotional mood, each person deliberately quieting his heart in silent prayer on entering his pew. (How seldom this is done in Methodist churches!) In liturgical services, where certain printed prayers are arranged for the congregation, all should participate heartily in reading. When the leader prays, there should be a thoughtful following of his speech and such an appropriation of his sentiments as will make them one's own.

h. Since the days of the apostles Christian congregations have expressed their approval of public prayers by audible responses, sometimes in the form of a congregational prayer, but more often by a simple "Amen" (1 Cor. 14. 16). This custom probably was borrowed from Hebrew worship (Deut. 27. 15f.). In a liturgical service these responses may be indicated formally. Sometimes the choir chants the prayer, or merely "Amen." Otherwise the individual members of the congregation respond or not as they are moved by an inward impulse. When the Lord's Prayer is used it is necessary to give the congregation a sign that the leader's prayer is concluded by closing with a customary formula "through Jesus Christ our Lord," or "in the name of Jesus Christ."

Early Methodists individually responded with great freedom to sentiments which pleased them in prayers, sermons, and exhortations by hearty *Amens*. This custom is largely falling into disuse, to the regret of some and the delight of others. It does not follow, however, that we have ceased to respond inwardly. The deepest and most intelligent feeling has never been associated necessarily with the loudest expression of emotion. If one is constituted temperamentally so that it is natural for him to respond in this way, he should feel at liberty to do so. But neither he nor the congregation should feel that his piety is superior to that of the quieter brother who responds by a flash of the eye or flush of the cheek. And let the speaker never lower himself to ask for *Amens* that are not given without solicitation!

i. In free worship it is best not to insist upon a certain posture as obligatory, either for the congregation or the minister. Custom, circumstances, conditions of health, and personal preferences are determinative in this matter. For the shorter prayers, it is probably well to stand. For the longer, tradition and custom favor kneeling among Methodists, though increasingly congregations sit while the minister stands. If the leader chooses to kneel when he enters the pulpit and during the public prayers, let him do so in a manner that is both graceful and devout. There is no spectacle less inspiring than to see a leader of worship kneeling upon one knee, the other foot and knee extended as far as possible, and hanging by one hand to a corner of the pulpit.

Examples of Public Prayers

MORNING INVOCATION

Almighty God, Who hast planted the daystar in the heavens, and, scattering the night, dost restore morning to the world, restore unto us, we beseech Thee, Thy heavenly light; grant us to pass this day in gladness and peace, without stumbling and without stain; that, reaching the eventide victorious over all temptations, we may praise Thee, the eternal God, Who art ever blessed, and dost govern all things, world without end. Amen.[5]

EVENING INVOCATION

Almighty God, Whose light shines undimmed across the restless sea of our lives, look favorably, we beseech Thee, upon Thy Church, upon Thy people worshiping Thee in this place, and upon all our brethren the world over; let Thy light rest upon us to calm and bless; dispel the dark night of our sins and errors; help us now with peaceful and pure hearts to worship Thy Name, and ever in our lives dutifully to serve, and faithfully to follow Thee, Through Jesus Christ, our Lord. Amen.[6]

PASTORAL PRAYER

Almighty God, Whose ear is ever open to the cry of Thy children, hear us, as at Thy mercy seat we plead for all our brethren of the people; for the high and low, the rich and poor, the learned and the ignorant; and especially for the sick and the afflicted and such as are drawing nigh unto death; for all whose sorrows lie heavy upon our hearts.

We remember before Thee those who bear in the secret of their hearts the burden of anxious care or secret sin; those who are passing through times of danger, temptation, or doubt; those who are losing heart in the struggle of life; and those who, neglecting Thee, are falling into sloth, indifference, or despair.

We remember before Thee all in any spiritual doubt or perplexity,

---

[5]From *A Pulpit Manual*, James Burns, p. 19. Used by permission of The Pilgrim Press.

[6]*Ibid.*

and we pray for those who are withheld from following Thee by pride of heart; by love of pleasure, ease, or display; by worldly desires or ambitions; by the fear of man; or by false views of Thee and of Thy truth.

O God, Who dost give the oil of joy for mourning, and the garment of praise for the spirit of heaviness; relieve, succor, and enlighten these our brethren for whose necessities we intercede, and grant them a happy and speedy issue out of all their sorrows and afflictions.

Most loving Father, who hast given Thy Church to be a perpetual witness to Thy Truth, and hast set her as a light to lighten the dark places of the earth, and to draw all men unto Thyself; bless, we beseech Thee, this day, the Church Catholic spread abroad throughout the world. Sanctify and cleanse her by Thy Word; remove all needless divisions, and unite all those who love the Lord Jesus Christ in the bonds of love and charity.

Bless, we pray Thee, the Church with which we are connected; enlighten and direct her professors and ministers, her missionaries and students, her office-bearers and all her faithful people; granting us grace to do Thy will, and to accomplish in this land the task with which Thou hast intrusted us.

Hear us as we intercede on behalf of this congregation, that Thou wouldst bless our fellow members present and absent, the old and the young, the rich and the poor. Prosper our work amongst the children, bless each society and organization in our midst, and as often as we assemble ourselves together in Thy courts help us to render unto Thee acceptable and adoring worship.

Eternal God, Whose kingdom is from everlasting to everlasting, from Whom alone all power cometh, bless, we pray Thee, our native land, our King and Queen, and all the members of the Royal House; give wisdom to His Majesty's counselors; direct the affairs of this empire; bless every part of the public service, and may all who in any way serve the commonwealth do justly, love mercy, and walk humbly with Thee, our God.

Now unto the King eternal, immortal, invisible, the only wise God, be honor and glory for ever and ever. Amen.[7]

FOR THE CHURCH[8]

O God, we pray for Thy Church, which is set to-day amid the

[7]From *A Pulpit Manual,* James Burns, p. 48. Used by permission of The Pilgrim Press.

[8]From *Prayers of the Social Awakening,* by Walter Rauschenbusch, published by The Pilgrim Press. Used by permission.

perplexities of a changing order, and face to face with a great new task. We remember with love the nurture she gave to our spiritual life in its infancy, the tasks she set for our growing strength, the influence of the devoted hearts she gathers, the steadfast power for good she has exerted. When we compare her with all other human institutions, we rejoice, for there is none like her. But when we judge her by the mind of her Master, we bow in pity and contrition. Oh, baptize her afresh in the life-giving spirit of Jesus. Grant her a new birth, though it be with the travail of repentance and humiliation. Bestow upon her a more imperious responsiveness to duty, a swifter compassion with suffering, and an utter loyalty to the will of God. Put upon her lips the ancient gospel of her Lord. Help her to proclaim boldly the coming of the kingdom of God and the doom of all that resist it. Fill her with the prophets' scorn of tyranny, and with a Christlike tenderness for the heavy-laden and down-trodden. Give her faith to espouse the cause of the people, and in their hands that grope after freedom and light to recognize the bleeding hands of the Christ. . . . Make her valiant to give up her life to humanity, that like her crucified Lord she may mount by the path of the cross to a higher glory.—Walter Rauschenbusch.

Books Recommended for Further Study

M. P. Talling, *Extempore Prayer,* pp. 13-219.

Arthur S. Hoyt, *Public Worship in Non-Liturgical Churches,* pp. 49-104.

MANUALS OF WORSHIP

Walter Rauschenbusch, *For God and the People.*
W. E. Orchard, D.D., *The Temple.*
D. R. Porter, *The Enrichment of Prayer.*
Karl R. Stolz, *The Psychology of Prayer.*
M. P. Talling, *Extempore Prayer,* pp. 220-293.
James Burns, M.A., *A Pulpit Manual.*
George W. Coleman, *The People's Prayers.*
Samuel McComb, *A Book of Prayers.*
W. A. Quayle, *The Climb to God.*
W. P. Thirkield, *Service and Prayers.*
Prayers—Ancient and Modern.
The Book of Common Prayer.

CHAPTER V

Materials of Worship—Lessons, Announcements, Offering

1. Reading the Law, and later the Prophets as commentaries upon the Law, was an important part of public worship among the Jews from the time of Moses and Joshua (Judg. 8. 34; Deut. 29). This custom was adopted by the early Christian Church, which soon added the Gospels and Letters to the Hebrew Scriptures. It has been approved by all important branches of the modern church, except the early Puritans of New England, who countenanced no liturgical use of the Scriptures down to a comparatively late period. Gladden quotes from the diary of the Rev. Stephen Williams, a Congregational minister of Longmeadow, Massachusetts, under date of March 30, 1755: "This day I began to read the Scriptures publicly in the congregation." His biographer notes that this was a bold innovation which was sustained in that parish with great difficulty.[1] The approved method of using the Scriptures publicly was to read a portion, expounding it section by section, leaving nothing to private interpretation. Increase Mather declared: "It cannot be proved that Dumb Reading, or Public Reading of the Scriptures without any explication or exhortation is part of the Pastoral Office." This smacked too much of the popishness from which New England Puritans had fled.[2]

At the present time Scripture reading occupies a prominent place in the worship of all Protestant bodies. The Methodist order provides for two lessons—one from the

[1] Washington Gladden, *The Christian Pastor*, p. 150. Used by permission of Charles Scribner's Sons.

[2] T. Harwood Pattison, *Public Worship*, p. 147.

Old Testament, generally from the Psalms, read responsively, and the other from the New Testament, read by the leader to the congregation. The first lesson affords an opportunity for the congregation to express its collective praise directly. Only the poetical parts of the Scriptures are adapted to this manner of reading—the portions in which thought answers to thought and the words are arranged in balanced phrases. The congregation is limited practically to the Psalms, parts of Job, the Prophets, and occasional lyrical passages in the New Testament for such lessons. In *The Methodist Hymnal* the Psalter is arranged with readings for morning and evening worship of each Sunday in the year, and also for certain special days like Christmas, Easter, and Thanksgiving. The imprecatory psalms have been omitted, and David speaks, for the most part, "like a Christian." The leader is not obliged to use this Psalter. He may use any lesson from the old Testament. But the Psalter will be used regularly by the pastor who appreciates the value of democracy in public worship. Any lesson may be used on any Sunday, but to avoid the monotonous repetition of a few favorite selections and to enlarge the acquaintance of the congregation with the devotional literature of the Scriptures, the lessons should be taken in order, beginning preferably with the first Sunday of the calendar year. If the Psalter is used regularly in only the morning services, the evening lessons may be used appropriately for morning worship on alternate years.

No direction is given in the order concerning the posture of the congregation in using the Psalter, and practice varies on this point. The psychological result is better if the congregation shall stand. The signal for rising should be as inconspicuous as possible. Certainly no bald request need be made by the leader, nor awkward upward gesture with the arms. It may be generally understood that the rising of the choir is the sign for the congregation to stand. Or, having allowed sufficient time for each person to find the selection after the announcement has been made, let the announcement be repeated, at which time the congregation will stand. For example, "The lesson in the Psalter for the morning of the twelfth Sunday." Time. "The lesson for the twelfth Sunday." Congregation stands. Or, after announcing the selection, let the minister be seated. When sufficient time has elapsed for all to find the proper page, let him stand to read, and his rising will be the signal for the congregation to rise. An organ interlude might serve the same purpose.

The manner in which the Psalter is used varies greatly. Some communions favor chanting by the congregation in unison, or by the congregation or the choir and the minister antiphonally. Generally, however, the reading is responsive—the leader reciting the verses with odd numbers and the congregation those with even numbers. The reading on the part of the congregation should be characterized by unity and strength of volume, in which, nevertheless, the spirit of thoughtfulness and devotion appears. On the part of the minister there should be intelligent expression—no intoning or mechanical chanting of the words—which will call forth a proper response from the congregation, but nothing in voice or manner that will attract especial attention to himself. He is acting as a part of the congregation in this exercise and should perform his duty in the light of that fact.

The second lesson is read aloud by the leader alone. The aim is didactic—to impress some truth or duty upon the congregation rather than to express worshipful feelings, though, of course, both these ends may be served. It is the custom of many pastors to select a lesson connected with the text of the sermon. This is done when the sermon is regarded as the primary event in the service, to which everything else is subordinate. But we have seen that the controlling ideal should be worship, not preaching, and under this ideal the lesson is coordinate with the sermon and may be independent of it. It need not teach the same truth expressed in the sermon. Indeed, in the interest of variety it is better if it shall express some other truth. And in the course of a year's ministry all the important Christian truths should be presented through this medium. The Anglican and Episcopalian communions accomplish a comprehensive presentation of biblical teaching by arranging the lessons in such a way that the Old Testament may be read through once and the New Testament twice each year in public worship, provided worship is conducted daily. John Wesley provided for the same complete instruction in the "Sunday Service" which he arranged for American Methodists. This service has never been popular, however, and each pastor selects his own lessons. As a result there is no such symmetrical teaching of biblical doctrine through the reading of the Bible as is true of those churches which use a liturgy. To accomplish this without a liturgy the minister must give much more careful attention to the selection of his lessons than many do.

To guard against a narrow range of choice, let a record be kept of all the lessons used during the year, and plan deliberately to read from the less familiar portions of the Bible as well as from the Psalms and the New Testament. Many in the congregation hear little, if any, Scripture outside the church service.

How shall the lesson be read? Certainly not in the mechanical fashion that too frequently mars Protestant worship, whether liturgical or nonliturgical, nor dramatically after the manner of elocutionists. It is obvious that the reading should interest and instruct the congregation. Yet how rarely does it compel the attention of the worshipers! It is essential, first of all, that the reader should re-create for himself in imagination the very thoughts and feelings which the author tried to express. This cannot be done except by much study of the lesson beforehand, study that will familiarize one with the circumstances under which the selection was written and reveal the purpose of the writer, awakening one's sympathetic interest in that purpose. Suppose, for example, the minister should brood over Paul's defense before Agrippa until he sees before him the prisoner in chains, pleading in dignified and earnest fashion more for his cause than for himself, choosing carefully each word and arranging his argument with a view of making the best impression upon his judge, could he then recite that address in the lifeless or careless manner characteristic of many who read the Scriptures in public? When the reader enters sympathetically into the thought and feeling of the writer, that fact will show itself in the inflections and modulations of the voice. The preacher who uses his imagination thus will unconsciously make the reading of the second lesson an event in every service, for he will interpret the Scripture in a way to be remembered, and that without interrupting the reading by comments of his own, "as the manner of some is."

At the beginning of the lesson, let the leader announce where it may be found. At the conclusion, let him announce simply, "Here ends the reading of the lesson." To exclaim, as some do, "May God add his blessing to the reading of his word," is a pious affectation that grates upon the sensibilities of those who would avoid the appearance of unreality in worship. If the lesson shall have been read properly, be sure God will have already blessed it. If not, the reader has made it impossible for his prayer to be answered.

On entering the pulpit, the "pulpit Bible" should be opened, even though one intends to read from his own personal copy. This is the most important part of the furnishings of the church. It contains the truth which is to be read and interpreted by the minister. From it radiates the light which is to illuminate the minds and warm the hearts of all who worship. In recognition of that fact, let it be opened at least symbolically, and remain open until the conclusion of the service.

2. Announcements. Nothing more seriously deflects the movement of thought and feeling in worship than a large number of announcements, especially if they are con-

cerned mainly with the social affairs of the church. An ideal time to make them would be before the opening hymn. The late arrival of many who should hear them, however, makes it necessary to give them at a later time. The next best place is just before the offering.

When it can be afforded, the church should publish all announcements in a weekly bulletin. *This bulletin should never contain business advertisements.* When they are thus printed, there is no need of doing more than to call the attention of the congregation to them in the briefest manner. Where a bulletin is not used, the leader should have the announcements sufficiently well in hand that he can state the essential facts about each one in the fewest possible sentences. It is always his privilege to edit notices in the interest of economy of time and the best good of the service. Circumstances should be very extraordinary to warrant taking more than four or five minutes for this part of the service. It is better to use only two or three.

3. OFFERING. The offering need not retard the service, though some hypersensitive persons complain of it and seek a device which will do away with the necessity of mentioning money in public worship. On the contrary, if it be truly an act of worship, performed in a religious atmosphere as an expression of genuine devotion to God and his church, it may enrich the service. *Giving is the very essence of all worship, and as long as it shall be necessary to maintain Christian institutions, it will be a part of true worship to offer material as well as spiritual gifts in the place of prayer.*

It is customary for the leader to make the offering the concluding announcement. If it is to be devoted to some special cause, that fact may be stated briefly. Then let the collectors come in a quiet and orderly manner to the communion rail to receive the plates either from the leader or some one of their own number. The minister may recite one or two appropriate verses of Scripture on delivering the plates to the collectors. On their return, let the leader make a brief prayer of thanksgiving and consecration, placing the offering in some inconspicuous place within the chancel. If the plates are not to be returned, then the prayer should be made as they are distributed, the ushers waiting reverently until it is finished. The spirit of worship will be greatly stabilized if the organist shall play softly or a good soloist shall sing during this part of the service. Conducted in some such reverent manner, the offering can be made a genuine "means of grace."

The following are excellent models for the offertory prayer:[3]

ACCEPT these our offerings, O God, we beseech Thee, which now we seek to dedicate to the service of Thy Holy Church, and grant us ever to have grateful hearts, through Jesus Christ, our Lord.

HEAVENLY FATHER, Who hast given us all things richly to enjoy, graciously deign to receive these our gifts which now we lay upon Thine altar, and bless us both in the use and the giving of Thy mercies, for Jesus' sake.

O GOD, who dost teach us by this act of worship that it is more blessed to give than to receive, graciously accept these our offerings and give us the right spirit both in giving and receiving, through Jesus Christ, our Lord.

In many churches the congregation consecrates the offering by rising and chanting Number 740, *The Methodist Hymnal:*

"All things come of thee, O Lord,
And of thine own have we given thee."

BOOKS RECOMMENDED FOR FURTHER STUDY

Arthur S. Hoyt, *Public Worship in Non-Liturgical Churches.*
F. H. J. Newton, *The Conduct of Public Worship,* Chapters I-V.
S. S. Curry, *Vocal and Literary Interpretation of the Bible.*
R. W. Rogers, *Book of Old Testament Lessons for Public Reading in Churches.*

---

[3]From *A Pulpit Manual,* by James Burns. Used by permission of The Pilgrim Press.

CHAPTER VI

Materials of Worship—Sermon and Benediction

THE SERMON

1. The History of Preaching. The sermon enjoyed no such unique distinction in the New Testament church as is accorded it in our time. In the beginning it was merely a footnote to the lesson or to a letter from some apostle which was read in the presence of the congregation—a short comment to clear up an obscure passage or an exhortation suggested by something in the reading. It does not appear to have been confined to an official class, but was a privilege open to any who cared to volunteer. After the apostolic age, however, the sermon took on new importance. It became a formal discourse, or oration, pronounced by presbyters and bishops, and in the fourth century preaching even became popular as a kind of indoor sport. "Fashionable people in Constantinople, Alexandria, and Antioch, and hundreds of smaller towns, began to speak (so Chrysostom intimates) almost as enthusiastically about the favorite preacher of the hour as they spoke of the favorite horse in the races or the reigning actor in the theater."[1] After this century the sermon declined in importance until the period of the crusades, which marks another high point in the history of preaching. Again there was a decline, until the Reformation lifted the sermon once more to a place of overshadowing importance in public worship. This place it has succeeded in holding until now among those peoples most profoundly affected by the Reformation.

In a general way the curve of popularity in the history of preaching follows the line of keen theological interest.

[1]John A. Broadus, quoted by E. C. Dargan, *History of Preaching*, vol. ii, p. 64.

The sermon became popular in periods of doctrinal discussion because it was practically the only instrument available for exposition and propaganda. At times other influences affected it, such as imperial patronage, social favor, and the importance of rhetorical studies in education. But these are distinctly secondary to the doctrinal influence.

Moreover, this curve follows the line of prophetic rather than priestly influence. In periods of calm, when doctrines and beliefs are fixed, the priest makes permanent ritualistic and ceremonial forms to contain them. Such instruction as he gives in worship is imparted chiefly through the symbolism of the service with which the congregation is familiar. But when the prophet appears with his demand for a restatement of faith and a revitalizing of religious interest, the old symbols and ceremonials are inadequate. They do not say what he wants said. He has no choice but to use a new symbolism of words and speech to express his new thought, and resorts to the sermon. Where the priestly restraints are too strong to be broken the prophet is silenced and the sermon all but disappears from worship, as in the Greek Church, in which preaching has had almost no history since the days of Chrysostom. To a somewhat lesser extent this is true of the Roman Church and the "High Church" wing of the Anglican and Protestant Episcopal Churches. Not that these have produced no great preachers, but that the importance of the sermon is minimized in public worship. Where the prophet has his way, as in the evangelical communions, the sermon is exalted to a place of primacy in public worship, even to the point of "sermonolatry."

2. Power in Preaching. As an instrument for expressing faith and imparting truth, the sermon, ideally, will never be superseded. Evangelicals are right in feeling that a service is not quite finished in which there is no place for instruction or inspirational address. For a truth or a belief has little power to command others until it takes possession of a human life in such fashion that all instruments—word,

gesture, intonation, eye, posture—cooperate to express originally and creatively what is felt in the deep places of the spirit to be true. The printed Word is potent. But only the spoken word—"truth through personality"—ever becomes omnipotent.

Believing all this—(1) that the sermon is indispensable to the intellectual life of religion; (2) that it has achieved and safeguarded religious freedom and liberty; (3) and that, potentially, it is our finest agent for expressing and propagating faith—it must be recognized, nevertheless, that much which passes for preaching in our modern life fails to accomplish any of this, and the sermon is in disrepute to-day. *As an act of worship the sermon must be religious.* One of our great teachers of homiletics insists that much American preaching is not religious:

"Power is absent from a large part of American preaching because that preaching is not religious. It is not essentially and vitally and experimentally religious. While we recognize much strong, noble preaching, for which we thank God and take courage, is there not also a large amount of preaching that could be put into the following categories, which are not mutually exclusive?—(1) an unconvincing evangelicalism—mere platitudes about redemptive doctrines without clear relation to human life; (2) a solemn pietism—conventional appeals for consecration and separation from the world; (3) a weak sentimentalism—pathetic stories, farfetched religious experiences, general unreality to the healthy-minded; (4) a dry intellectualism—mere discussion of subjects, the sort of thing that can be done better in a magazine; (5) a belated controversialism—fighting over old battles, tilting at windmills; (6) a shallow sensationalism—catching the crowd by the methods of the vaudeville and the yellow press, anything for notoriety; (7) a bumptious egotism—the minister carried away by the self-importance of his leadership, thrusting his views, his hobbies, his methods, himself, and even his family, upon public attention; (8) a shallow socialism—the use of the pulpit for the presentation of particular economic theories and partisan views with no great human appeal. Some of these preachings gain large audiences, even fill up the membership of churches, even secure conversions and reformations of life, but their influence taken as a whole is petty, cheapening to religion, and is not bringing God to men and lifting men to God. If all preaching were of such character, the days of the pulpit would be numbered."[2]

Power in preaching has been defined as "such a presentation of an intense religious conviction as shall tend to produce in the congregation an emotional experience of that conviction." The final test of a sermon as an act of worship is just this power to evoke a sympathetic response from those who hear it. Can the preacher make the congregation feel and think about the theme as he himself does?

The problem here is much the same as in public prayer. This kind of power is conditioned chiefly by two things—(1) the degree to which the preacher has identified himself, in imagination at least, with the joys and sorrows, the victories and defeats of his hearers, and (2) the sincerity with which he speaks the convictions of his own soul. A Sunday-school lad remarked after hearing a simple, straightforward account of the attempt of a Kentucky mountain college to teach mountain boys that the heroism of Jesus is nobler than revenge, "It does make a difference when you hear a man who really believes what he says." Professor Soares asks, "Can it be that congregations are sometimes dismissed asking themselves, Does he mean it, or was he only preaching?"[3]

3. THE TECHNIQUE OF PREACHING. Yet it is not wholly a matter of deep feeling and spirit. Many ministers who do not lack convictions, and who are intelligent and sincere, nevertheless are unable to preach effectively. They have not mastered the *technique* of preaching. This has to do

---

[2]Reprinted by permission of The University of Chicago Press. *University of Chicago Sermons,* edited by T. G. Soares, p. 3f.

[3]*Id.,* p. 6.

with the *materials,* the *form,* and the *manner* of the sermon. Admittedly they are secondary to conviction and sincerity. Probably more preachers fail, however, in the former than the latter. A whole volume would be required to treat these matters adequately. We venture to emphasize here very briefly only those things which are related to the liturgical values of the sermon.

a. The Material of the Sermon. As an act of Christian worship, the sermon must express and interpret the Christian experience of the race. The principal record of this experience is found in the Bible. To explain this book helpfully is the minister's chief business. He is expected to understand it as perfectly as the lawyer should understand the law and the physician his medical science. Yet how rarely do ministers create the impression that their judgment on a biblical matter will be confirmed in the court of scholarly criticism! Many reveal the fact that they know the English and American poets, that no popular books of fiction ever escape them, and that the Saturday Evening Post and, possibly, the Atlantic Monthly come regularly to their reading tables, but neither Hosea, nor Jeremiah, nor Amos, nor Isaiah, nor any other prophet becomes a living personality from anything they say. No one has ever preached commandingly who did not regard the Bible—its prayers, its biographies, its parables, its miracles, its poetry, its philosophy, its history, its letters—as his primary source of sermon material. In the profound religious experience in which Ezekiel received his call to the prophetic office he was commanded *to eat a book* (*roll*) in which was written the message he was to deliver—eat until he had *filled* himself with it! Could there be a more impressive dramatization of this idea that a preacher's Bible is to be thoroughly masticated, digested, and assimilated?

After the Bible, the next great record of Christian experience is found in the doctrinal statements of the church. Unlike the biblical text, these are constantly changing in their outward form. To interpret them helpfully the minister must know them in their history, and in their relations to the changing ideals of thought and life which modify them from age to age. To make sure that he covers the whole field of Christian teaching in the course of a year's preaching, one should plan for himself some such calendar of themes as certain communions arbitrarily impose upon their clergymen—for example, the Protestant Episcopal Church. Otherwise he will overemphasize some truths and underemphasize, or neglect entirely, others equally important.

But it is a part of our Christian faith that God is still active in his world and in the hearts of men. We may know him at first hand for ourselves, and personally verify the findings of others, and add to them. Only as the minister thus lives again in his own experience the truths which others have affirmed can his preaching be self-revelation; and unless it is that, the sermon cannot be called worship. He will be interested, too, in the attempt of his contemporaries to know God, and in their fresh descriptions of religious experience. What latter-day poets, philosophers, essayists, and teachers of social ethics have to say about life and duty is legitimate sermonic material. One will gather the materials of preaching to little purpose, however, unless he is able to interpret them imaginatively. Masters of the art of ritualistic worship know well how to stir the imagination by the use of symbols which appeal to the eye or the ear. As an act of worship the sermon must likewise stimulate the imagination of the hearers, else it will have little power to affect their feelings and induce a worshipful mood. Who does not hold in memory a Scripture or a doctrine which once had no meaning but was made forever beautiful by a preacher who interpreted it with the simplicity and understanding that comes only from imagination?

In emphasizing imagination as a primary source of power in preaching, we should distinguish imagination from fancy. The latter breaks with reality and is a source of danger. By it, the puerilities of the allegorical interpreter are perpetrated, who always is able to make the Scriptures say what he wishes them to say. On the contrary, the constructive imagination, while it transcends facts, never loses its contact with them. The imaginative interpreter proceeds by the historical method. He is anxious to discover, not his own mind, but that of the writer.

As illustrating the difference between the two methods, contrast the fanciful with the imaginative way of interpreting the parable of the good Samaritan. The former assumes that every feature of the parable is a symbol filled with religious meaning. For example, the man who fell among thieves stands for Adam; the thieves were the devil and his angels; the priest and the Levite were the Mosaic dispensation; the good Samaritan was Christ; the beast on which the Samaritan rode was Christ's human nature; the inn was the church; the two pennies paid to the innkeeper represented the life that now is and that which is to come. A truly imaginative interpreter proceeds, however, by inquiring what were the circumstances under which the parable was spoken. He finds that a young man had asked for a definition of the word "neighbor." "Who is my neighbor?" he inquired, and Jesus replied with this story of a neighbor in action in which it appears that neighborliness is not a matter of geography, nor race, nor patriotism, nor religion, but of mere human interest on the basis of human need. This is what Jesus put into the parable and this is what the imaginative preacher takes out. The allegorist misses it entirely.

b. The Form of the Sermon. Imagination is important, too, in expressing one's insights, as well as in discovering them. It frequently happens that of two sermons equally above criticism as to materials, one will have power to command the interest of the congregation that the other lacks. Quite generally the explanation will be found in the literary form of the respective sermons. One preacher is a master in the art of organizing his material; the other is not. The first expresses his thought clearly from the opening sentence, and before six sentences have been spoken the congregation knows exactly what theme is to be discussed. In thirty minutes he has said (1) this, and (2) that, and (3) a third specific thing about the theme. Everything is easily grasped. It requires no effort to listen. Indeed, one cannot help listening. There are no digressions of thought. Nothing is put into the sermon which does not contribute directly to the main stream of interest. No stories are told for their own sake. No poetry is quoted to display the preacher's acquaintance with the poets. If poetry is used, it is because some singer has said what the preacher needed to say at a certain point better than he can possibly do. All is compactly arranged and expressed simply and clearly. The sermon is a single organism, a perfect unity, and easily remembered.

The other sermon is a multiplicity, a heterogeneous collection of statements, sentiments, poetry, and historical references gathered from everywhere with no inner coherence holding them together. If there is a main line of thought, it is difficult to find it; or finding it, to hold it, for irrelevant matter is constantly introduced which diverts attention from the principal subject. Only by a conscious effort of will is the attention fastened upon the sermon at all. To carry away more than a fragment of such a sermon would require superhuman power. Yet these very same materials, organized more perfectly, would make a worthwhile utterance. And the only difference would be in the literary form. Some one has remarked that while an arrow and an ordinary stick of wood may be made of exactly the same material, one may be hurled from a bow very much farther than the other. This difference in carrying power is due entirely to the difference in their respective shapes. One was formed to go far, cleaving the air with a minimum of resistance, and the other was not. And that explains the difference in the carrying power of sermons.

Everything which has to do with literary style should receive the most conscientious consideration of the preacher throughout his ministerial life. *Synonyms* should be studied with a view of enlarging the vocabulary and using words more accurately. A sermon should be written completely each week, not with a view of reading from the manuscript, but for the drill of composing *sentences* which will express clearly and forcibly the exact thought that is in mind. The dictionary should always be at hand as one reads, and no unfamiliar word should ever be permitted to escape until its meaning is known. In planning the sermon as a whole one must keep in mind the great principles of literary composition which control all forms of effective discourse, whether spoken or written; namely, (1) *unity,* (2) *coherence,* and (3) *orderly development* toward a climax of thought and feeling.

One would do well to read each year a good treatise on English composition to keep his ideas of style constantly fresh. Such a volume would be much more helpful than most of the textbooks on homiletics.

c. The Manner of the Sermon. Though subordinate to material and form, *the manner* of the sermon is nevertheless highly important. Everyone can recall a public address which was ruined by awkwardness and self-consciousness on the part of the speaker; by action that was unrestrained or too much restrained; by a voice too big or too small; by pitch too high or too low, or that did not vary. These technical matters cannot be treated here at length. We may emphasize only their importance. This is illustrated in George Whitefield, who is said to have been able to make a congregation weep by the way in which he pronounced the single word, "Mesopotamia." If that story be legendary, it is beyond all doubt true that a popular living American preacher produces the most astounding effects on the nervous systems of his hearers by the modulations and flexibility of his voice. Another distinguished clergyman puts himself under the tutelage of a teacher of public speaking for a short period every year to correct bad habits of speech and action which he may have fallen into unconsciously. Every minister could wisely take himself in hand at this point. Ideally he should take a course of training under a competent instructor. If that is impossible, he may do much for himself by following the suggestions of such a text as C. Edmund Neil's *Sources of Effectiveness in Public Speaking*.

d. The Length of the Sermon. Since the sermon is only one of many elements in public worship, all of which must cooperate to produce a designed effect, the question of its proportionate length is important. Certainly it should never take more than half the time available for the whole service. Generally it should take less. More time must be spent in careful preparation if one is to preach only twenty minutes than if forty are at his disposal. But the appreciation of the congregation will be correspondingly greater.

4. THE BENEDICTION. The manner in which the service of worship is concluded will determine largely whether or not the impression made during worship is to be permanent to any degree. It is possible to dismiss the people in such a fashion that the results of the service shall be dissipated before they leave the church. The Methodist Order of Worship provides that the sermon shall be followed by prayer, the people kneeling, and this by a congregational hymn, the people standing. In a footnote it is suggested that this order of prayer and song may be reversed. If an invitation is to be given at the close of the service to unite with the church or confess discipleship, it is better to have the prayer precede the hymn, giving the invitation when the hymn is announced. In that event the Doxology may be sung and the benediction given, the people standing after the candidates have been received. If the invitation is omitted, or given during the hymn before the sermon, then the sermon may well be followed immediately by a hymn, the people standing, and this by a prayer, the people kneeling or sitting in a prayerful attitude. The value of this prayer will be increased if the congregation shall pray silently for a moment before the leader shall voice their collective prayer. If this

order be observed, the benediction should be given while minister and people are in the position of prayer.

It should be remembered always that the benediction is a part of worship, and not merely a signal that worship is finished. The apostolic benediction[5] prescribed in our order is a wonderful prayer that minister and people together may continually experience the redeeming power of Jesus Christ, and be constantly aware of God's love for men, and walk in never-ending fellowship with the Holy Spirit. To recite this prayer mechanically is to make only a motion for the congregation to depart. Rendered in this way, it has no religious value whatever. But pronounced thoughtfully and reverently, it becomes the great prayer of the service, gathering up all lesser petitions into one final request for the highest blessing, fixing in the last moment the thought of the people upon the Great God in whom they live and move and have their being, and to know whom is eternal life.

5. The Ushers. A most important post in the service of worship is that filled by the ushers, who are in charge of all matters which pertain to the physical comfort of the congregation. They should greet the people cordially, though quietly, as they enter the church, not with the professional air of a butler or theater attendant, but in the spirit of a man welcoming a guest to his own home. If a stranger enters, and time permits, the usher will ask a few courteous questions. If there is a choice of seats, he will ask the worshiper what his preference may be. At the communion service, the ushers may helpfully direct the movement of communicants to and from the chancel so that there may be no crowding or confusion. They will see to it that no belated worshipers take their seats during any act of worship, whether prayer, or anthem, or lesson, but only between these. They are the "aides" of the pastor for special errands. If the ventilation needs attention, the pastor should signal an usher to attend to it—not leave

[5] 2 Cor. 13. 14.

the pulpit himself. If a visiting minister is seen unexpectedly in the congregation and the pastor desires his presence in the pulpit, whenever possible let him send his message by an usher. Once he enters the pulpit, the pastor should stay there until the service is over. The ushers should be elected by the official board, and where there are several, one should be "chief usher," directing the work of all the rest. That none may be overburdened, one set of ushers may serve at the morning service and another at the evening. In some churches the ushers are regularly organized and have delightful social occasions together.

Books Recommended for Further Study

A. E. Garvie, *The Christian Preacher.*

Charles S. Gardner, *Psychology and Preaching.*

D. J. Burrell, *The Sermon.*

L. O. Brastow, *The Modern Pulpit.*

H. W. Beecher, *Yale Lectures on Preaching.*

Phillips Brooks, *Yale Lectures on Preaching.*

W. F. McDowell, *Yale Lectures on Preaching.*

S. Parkes Cadman, *Ambassadors of God.*

F. J. McConnell, *The Preacher and the People.*

C. Edmund Neil, *Sources of Effectiveness in Public Speaking.*

P. T. Forsyth, *Positive Preaching and the Modern Mind,* Lecture III.

Charles R. Brown, *The Art of Preaching.*

CHAPTER VII

THE SUNDAY EVENING SERVICE

TWENTY-FIVE years ago Washington Gladden wrote: "In America, at least, the problem of the evening service is one of considerable difficulty. . . . In most of our churches the service is thinly attended, and the question of its maintenance weighs heavily on the minds of the pastors. Where it has not been abandoned, various devices have been resorted to for increasing the congregation—praise services, musical services, spectacular services with lanterns, and such like."[1]

The problem has become much more difficult in the time that has elapsed since this distinguished pastor complained thus. Then the automobile was still a curiosity which thousands had never yet seen, not the familiar possession of every third family even in rural communities. Nor had the moving-picture industry yet made the theater the chief social and recreational center in every hamlet. When Gladden wrote, only pastors in cities were worried about the Sunday-night service. Now every country pastor, as well, anxiously considers what can be done to offset the enticements of the "auto" and "movie." And the same two conclusions are still reached. An increasing number decide to abandon the service, while another growing multitude feverishly attempt to enhance its attractiveness by spectacular features, some legitimate and some highly questionable. He is rash indeed who presumes to dogmatize about that which is confusing to many. Nevertheless, there is always need to keep before us certain ideals whose validity is undisputed with reference to this service.

1. *The success of a service of worship is not to be meas-*

[1] *Op. cit.*, p. 121. Used by permission of Charles Scribner's Sons.

ured chiefly by the number of persons present. Great multitudes are seldom very important in religion. Let us be reminded often that Jesus was content to do his work with a small group and that he deliberately sought to keep his congregations from becoming "great." Like Gideon, he seemed to regard a crowd as an embarrassment. Their unwieldiness, their instability, their fickleness, their irresponsibility, their quick response to an appeal to prejudice, their inability to think deeply or with discrimination make it impossible for mere numbers ever to give worth or distinction to a congregation. Catholics and Protestant Episcopalians, for whom the size of the congregation makes little difference in the success of the mass or the communion service, have much to teach non-liturgical churches in this matter. Of course, one must guard against complacency and contentment with inferior achievement. The normal pastor will covet as large a congregation as possible. His motive, however, will not be to get a crowd for its own sake, but to render spiritual service to all for whom he has responsibility. When this motive is in the ascendant one will not be unduly elated, or depressed, by the size of the congregation, if only the service itself shall possess inspirational value for those who are present. Let us not ask, "How many came?" but, "What was done for those who came?"

2. *The function of the church is very different from that of the theater.* Comparisons between the size of theater audiences and church congregations are not very impressive. For it is impossible to contrast things that have no common resemblance. The chief justification for the theater is that it provides for relaxation through amusement. But amusement is distinctly not the primary business of the church. Services should be beautiful and interesting indeed, but they are not conducted to entertain the congregation. One goes to the theater to "let down." He goes to the church for instruction and worship, and this requires creative effort of the highest sort—the very opposite from letting down. The "movie" makes no demand upon one's

intellectual or volitional powers. The church taxes these faculties to the utmost. In the nature of the case the church can never be popular with that large element in the community which has little power to refresh itself from within and is drawn as by a magnet to that in its environment which promises the most excitement and the greatest number of thrills. Whenever the church resorts to the methods of the theater to "get a crowd," a distinct loss of respect usually follows; first, because the community feels that the church either does not understand its own peculiar mission or has lost confidence in it; and, second, because the theatrical manager is very much more expert in the show business than is the average pastor. It would seem to be better policy every way for the church to spend its strength on its legitimate task than to attempt to brighten its services by features that are purely diverting or amusing. Gladden's findings twenty-five years ago have been confirmed, on the whole, by the experiments of thousands of perplexed pastors and official boards since: "It is not to the æsthetic nature that the services of the church make their appeal; and the moment it becomes evident that pleasure, no matter of how refined a sort, has been exalted in those services above serious thought, the power and the glory of the church are gone."[2] It may be that on week days some church will conclude that a part of its task is to provide amusement, but "the use of its Sunday night services for this purpose is nothing less than the prostitution of a high office."

3. The feeling prevails that it is generally unwise to conduct two services of exactly the same type on the same day. This suggests that *the Sunday-evening service should vary in its aim and method from the morning service.* The latter should be more dignified and worshipful. The former may well be less stately, brighter in color, more rapid in action, and, while maintaining an atmosphere of worship,

---

[2] *Op cit.*, p. 122.

featuring certain matters as a rule unprovided for in the morning service.

In every church there are persons thinking seriously upon the subject of personal religion, but who have never made public confession of their discipleship. These should have frequent opportunity to declare themselves before the congregation, and a service should be provided with an atmosphere warm with expectation in which they are frankly encouraged to make their decisions at once. To serve such the Sunday-evening service should often be made evangelistic. It may be the part of wisdom to do this without elaborate announcement beforehand, but let it be done as frequently as the leader feels there is any strong probability that anyone present would be glad for such an opportunity.

There is an important educational service expected of the ministry at this time when the area of ethical obligation is widening to include the field of social as well as private relationships; and the Sunday-evening service, better than any other, can be devoted frequently to this purpose. No subjects are more fascinating to the present generation. And all come well within the scope of the minister's business, for all sustain a vital relation to the spiritual life. Needless to say, "preaching of this kind makes unusual demands upon the intelligence of a minister." He has no right to speak until he has prepared himself thoroughly. But the preacher who intelligently applies the great Christian ideals to the problems of industry, poverty, vice, delinquency, education, government, etc., keeping clearly in view all the while their religious bearings, will show himself a workman who has no need to be ashamed, and at the same time will find a way to make the service attractive without making it merely amusing.

It does not follow that the Sunday-evening service should be converted into a "forum" for the presentation of these subjects from every point of view. The forum, as popularly known, while ethical, is not necessarily religious. Its atmosphere is one of debate rather than worship. There should be a place where every community may assemble to do what is done in the forum. But wherever possible it is wiser to meet in a public hall than a church. If the church is the only available meeting place, the forum should be held at some other than an hour set apart for worship.

Interpreting in modern terms the great doctrines of Christianity is also a part of the educational task of the minister. Neglect of this matter has resulted in filling our churches with a generation of Christians who neither know what to believe, nor why. Any babbler, with a positive air, can disturb them. The blame must fall upon a ministry which forgot to expound in untechnical language the fundamentals of Christian belief—the doctrines of God, sin, redemption, immortality, biblical inspiration, revelation, and infallibility, and the like. Nothing will give stability to faith except clear thinking on these high themes, and for leadership in this the church has a right to look to the minister. Within recent months a "summer preacher" filled one of the most famous Methodist churches on warm Sunday evenings by preaching a series of sermons on these substantial and presumably unpopular subjects. A few years ago another preacher in another city maintained a strong Sunday-evening service throughout a whole summer by interpreting the message of one of the Old Testament prophets. Still another found that an unsuspected number were interested in Christian biography, as he spoke helpfully concerning the great personalities in modern church history. The experience of these preachers opens the way for believing that when the minister addresses himself earnestly and intelligently to the educational phase of his task, so far as it concerns his pulpit utterances, that fact will be appreciated by many.

4. *Clearly, the maintenance of the Sunday-evening service calls for the most conscientious labor.* It has failed often because it has had only fragments of time for preparation that remained after the minister had exhausted himself on the morning service. It is not well attended in many in-

stances because it is not worth attending. The pastor must find a way to keep himself *physically* fresh for this service. A tired man is incapable of inspiring leadership. And he must keep fresh *mentally*. Study, *study*, STUDY must be the dominant passion of his life! How to do it all in view of the manifold demands upon his time may be a very great problem. But he must find a way or suffer the consequence —that is, a devitalized evening service. And the way may be found by the minister who puts his mind into his work.

Books Recommended for Further Study

Washington Gladden, *The Christian Pastor,* Chapter VI.
L. H. Bugbee, *Living Leaders Judged by Christian Standards.*
H. S. Coffin, *Some Christian Convictions.*
C. E. Jefferson, *Things Fundamental.*

CHAPTER VIII

MID-WEEK SERVICES

MANY Catholic and Protestant Episcopalian churches are open every day that individual worshipers may enter for rest and prayer. Some provide, in addition, one or more services of worship daily. The so-called evangelical churches, however, usually maintain but one service between Sundays, designated variously as the "midweek service," or the "prayer meeting," or the "social meeting." The service, as a rule, is not largely attended. Because of this, it is considered quite as much a problem as the Sunday-evening service. As with the evening service, the first long step toward the solution of the problem is to understand clearly the proper function of the service.

1. Two great reasons appear to justify a midweek meeting for the church. *The first is the need of individual Christians for frequent conference concerning the spiritual life.* Among Methodists this need has dominated the service so completely that only the name "prayer meeting" accurately describes its nature. Very properly it differs greatly from the more formal services of the Sabbath. The leader usually is the pastor, or one whom he has selected, who gives direction to the meeting without too much insistence upon a prescribed order. The customary features of the service are songs, prayers, a Scripture lesson, a brief address, and testimonies. The notable fact about the meeting is its democracy. The songs, while "congregational," are frequently chosen by persons in the audience; the prayers are generally extemporaneous prayers by the laity, both men and women; and the testimonies, having to do with the inner aspirations and longings, or failures and defeats, are made by devout men and women.

Non-Methodists are sharply aware of the weakness of this service. Of the "testimony meeting" Gladden writes, "Such a recital, if modestly and honestly made, by persons who are living serious lives, might often have great value; but it is greatly to be feared that those whose lives are most serious are least inclined to give absolutely truthful reports of their own spiritual states; and of that which is most intimate and vital it is hardly possible to tell the story. The danger is that 'experience meetings' will degenerate into a recital of well-worn phrases which represent no real facts of the inner life. The mischief of such insincerity must be very great. When one who has scarcely thought of spiritual things during the week—his mind having been wholly absorbed in the pleasures and strifes of the world—goes into the weekly meeting and fluently expresses his deep interest in the great things of the Kingdom, and testifies that he is making steady progress in the religious life, the injury to his own character must be deep, and the effect upon the minds of those who know him well, most unhappy. To this insincerity the cut-and-dried experience-meeting affords a strong temptation. Everyone is expected to give some account of his own spiritual condition, and no one likes to give a discouraging report. It is too easy to assume a virtue which one does not possess, and to avow an interest which is optative rather than actual."[1] It is only fair to say that this does not represent Gladden's whole thought of this type of service. In other connections he is very appreciative. Many Methodists will thank him, however, for his criticism, for he expresses precisely what they feel, yet hardly dare to say. If the prayer meeting could be rescued from the control of "ignorant, effusive, opinionated persons, who have no wisdom to impart and no inspiration to convey, . . . who only succeed in gratifying their own vanity or in confirming their own delusions, while they irritate and disgust the sensible people who listen to them," doubtless thoughtful and substantial people would attend in larger numbers.

[1]*Op. cit.*, p. 241f. Used by permission of Charles Scribner's Sons.

This constitutes the great problem of the prayer meeting—to save it from the "prayer-meeting killer," and make it a source of spiritual power for the whole church, without destroying its democratic character or changing it into a pale imitation of a Sunday service.

That the prayer meeting has survived the strain put upon it by its weak, ignorant, insincere, and sometimes pharisaical friends, suggests strongly that it is well designed to serve a fundamental need of the religious life. That need is found in the demand for verbal expression which is made by a genuine religious experience. The redeemed of the Lord ever have felt impelled to say so. Whenever God becomes very real, and the soul is filled with a sense of power, joy, and safety, from conscious fellowship with the Infinite, the lips will not be restrained. An attempt to suppress the feeling only turns it into a "fire in the bones" which threatens to consume one. If any fear that immodesty attaches to the expression of such intimate emotions, let Horace Bushnell, who cannot be accused of Methodist fervor, reassure them: "No one ever thinks it a matter of delicacy, or genuine modesty, to entirely suppress any reasonable joy; least of all, any fit testimony of gratitude toward a deliverer for deliverance. . . . In the same simple way, all ambition apart, all conceit of self forgot, all artificial and mock modesty excluded, it will be the instinct of everyone who loves God to acknowledge him."[2] And not only is testimony essential to him who knows the "joy of salvation," but it is exceedingly helpful and interesting to those who hear, *provided only that the note of reality appears all the way through.* So long as the recital is simple, clear, and unaffected, having to do only with that which the speaker himself has verified or is trying to verify in Christian experience, it has power to encourage the hesitant and faltering as almost nothing else does.

It should be said that there is no special virtue in num-

[2]In *Sermons for the New Life,* quoted by Gladden, *op. cit.,* p. 247.

bers of testimonies as such. One testimony of the right sort is worth many of the mechanical, rapid-fire, sentence-testimonies so much in vogue in young people's meetings. And this applies to prayers as well as testimonies. They are too fragmentary and too lacking in reflection to be very valuable. On the other hand, there is little profit in the words of one or two individuals, blessed with "the gift of continuance," who take all the time available for this part of the service.

After sincerity and reality, the average prayer meeting is in sore need of improvement at the point of its music. The songs, of course, should be simple, but they may be that without being silly and inane. It is not too much to say that a thoughtful Christian cannot join in the singing in many prayer meetings and keep his self-respect. There is an abundance of music in the Methodist Hymnal beautifully adapted to prayer-meeting purposes. One will lose nothing in passing by entirely all compilations which were prepared with an eye more open to the commercial profits of the publisher than the spiritual edification of the worshipers. "The vulgarization of the tastes and the depravation of the sentiments of worshipers through the use of sensational and sentimental prayer-meeting hymns and tunes has been a grave injury to religion in America."

And after the music, the next great need of many a prayer meeting is more conscientious consideration on the part of the pastor. If he does not regard it as deserving of his time and thought in planning and preparation, he cannot reasonably expect it to be attractive. In any case, scolding the people because they do not attend is not likely to draw them. Make the service as helpful and attractive in itself as possible, invite the congregation pleasantly and cordially, and then believe that where even two or three are gathered together *in Christ's name,* Christ himself will be in the midst. And those who do attend will always be glad to go again.

2. The second fact to justify a midweek service arises in connection with the work of the church as a corporate body. Larger use of the prayer meeting to serve this need has redeemed several midweek services in a notable manner. The work of the church requires trained lay leadership. The membership generally is uninformed concerning the great community problems—philanthropy, public health, education, industry, etc.—and the proper relation of the church toward them. The missionary task, at home and abroad, is unfamiliar. The Christian Bible is unknown, except in the most superficial way, to most Christians. These facts, and others, make imperative demands for consideration. When and how may the church intelligently address itself to them? There is no better occasion than the midweek service. So "Prayer-Meeting Night" has become "Church-Training Night" in many churches. The congregation assembles for supper at half-past six, coming directly from their daily labor. An hour is devoted to the meal and social fellowship. This is followed by three quarters of an hour of praise, prayer, and testimony. The company then breaks up into several study groups, the Sunday-school workers to consider their problems, the Epworth Leaguers theirs, others for Bible study, still others for mission study, and yet others for the consideration of community matters, each for another three quarters of an hour. The whole program is completed in two hours and a half. It is easy to see how prayer-meeting night might thus become a real event in the life of the church.

This kind of program, of course, requires careful planning. The most important matter is the leadership of the several classes. No groups should be organized which cannot be provided with competent guides. Where the whole number is small, the pastor himself may take charge of them during the study hour as a single group, considering now one and now another subject. *Some such combination of worship with instruction can be effected in any church, large or small.* A few who do not like innovations may complain at first, but even they will be won at last by the success of the plan.

3. The class meeting, as a formal organization, has all but disappeared from American Methodism. This fact is an occasion for dismay to some, while others, of equal piety, regard it as natural and inevitable. It came into existence to serve a specific need, but in these days of complex organization, when other agencies do its work, it is no longer vital to the life of the church. In the beginning Methodism was only a "movement" within the Anglican Church. All Methodists were Anglicans, though not all Anglicans were Methodists—only that portion of them who were stirred by Wesley's interpretation of the doctrines of Christian experience, such as justification, regeneration, assurance, and sanctification. These came together in their respective communities for mutual counsel and fellowship after Wesley or his preachers had gone. One of the number was appointed to receive the contributions of the group for the support of the movement. Gradually this leader became a kind of subpastor charged with responsibility for the spiritual care of the society between the rare visits of a "traveling preacher." Throughout Wesley's lifetime "the class" was the unit of his movement, and the class leader was as important as the modern pastor.

Likewise for many years in America "the class" and "the class leader" were indispensable elements in the life of the church. There were no "settled" pastors, such as Congregationalists and Presbyterians knew—only "itinerant preachers" each of whom was in reality a bishop or superintendent who supervised a large number of classes grouped together into a "circuit," called his "pastoral charge." Though he traveled constantly, the preacher could visit each "point" on his circuit only a few times each year. Meantime he must depend upon the local class leader for that intimate pastoral oversight which settled ministers gave in other communions. And between visits of the preacher, this leader, chosen for his piety and good judgment, would meet the class weekly for prayer, interchange of experience, exhortation, and advice. Out of this simple form grew the complex organization known as the Methodist Episcopal Church.

To-day the "circuit system" is being rapidly abandoned. At best it was only a makeshift, justified by the poverty of the settlers and the inability of the church to serve otherwise a rapidly advancing and widely scattered population. The ideal of the present is to appoint a trained pastor for each church just as rapidly as the individual churches become able to support them. Thus the pastor takes the place once held by the class leader, and under him a rather extensive corps of lay officials in charge of the several organizations within the church. The weekly prayer meeting affords the opportunity for spiritual culture once provided by the class meeting. The Finance Committee and the collectors receive the gifts of the people. So that, all in all, it would appear that the spiritual nurture of the membership of the church is adequately provided for, even though the class meeting has ceased to function in its old-time way.

Recently the class-meeting idea was revived in the so-called "unit system," which requires that every member of the church be assigned to a group of ten or twelve. One in the group is appointed "unit leader," and he, in turn, assigns responsibility to other members for particular tasks. For example, one will distribute missionary literature, another will be stewardship secretary, and yet another will propagate the life-service idea. This was the class meeting galvanized into new life for a special emergency. The unwieldiness of the organization, however, prevents it being popular in a church already elaborately organized, now that the emergency has passed. The real "class" in Methodism to-day is the Sunday-school class, and the "class leader," the Sunday-school teacher, who has all the responsibility of the former leader and more.

In a few churches what is called "the class" in the older sense meets weekly, generally on Sunday before morning worship. This has great value for those who attend in preparing the mind and heart for the service which follows.

It is likewise helpful to the pastor, who knows that this group of devout persons support him sympathetically as they pray.

4. The Epworth League came into being a third of a century ago to render a manifold service to the young life of the church. Within that period, the organized Bible class has made its appearance and now undertakes in many churches much of the work formerly done by the League. Nothing, however, has superseded the League as an instrument for devotional culture among young people. If it does no more in the local church, at least it conducts a young people's prayer meeting, sometimes midweek, but more generally on Sunday evenings. Here immature believers receive most valuable training in expressing religious experience and in leading religious meetings. Besides this, the general organization conducts several score of Summer Institutes in every part of the country each year where delegates from almost every church are trained in the art of lay leadership. No society in the church is doing more to make an effective church in the future than the Epworth League. The wise pastor will bend every effort to secure a large attendance from his church at these summer conferences.

Books Recommended for Further Study

Committee on Conservation and Advance (pamphlet), *Church Training Night.*

Dan B. Brummitt, *The Efficient Epworthian.*

Luccock and Cook, *The Mid-Week Service.*

CHAPTER IX

LITURGICAL SERVICES

THERE are occasional services of such nature and importance that the church has prescribed in great detail the lessons, prayers, and addresses which shall be used. Of course these are not commanded in the sense that a minister would be brought to trial for disregarding them, but it is expected that he shall use them in conducting the services for which they are designed, and any unauthorized departure therefrom is more likely to offend than commend itself to good taste. The originality of the minister may better show itself in filling these forms with life and power than by changing them.

The ritual is for the most part adapted from the *Book of Common Prayer* of the Anglican Church. Its history carries back directly to the *First Prayer Book of Edward VI,* which was generally used for the first time on June 8, 1549. This book was the work of the English National Church under Archbishop Cranmer when the leadership of the bishop of Rome was repudiated. The aim was to compile a Service Book from materials long in possession of the church, which would be free from the false doctrines and superstitious practices which characterized the several Roman liturgies in common use in England, and which would be in the language of the people rather than Latin. The book has been revised a number of times, but the present *Book of Common Prayer* is substantially the same as the *First Book* of Edward. John Wesley admired this liturgy greatly. The "Sunday Service" which he prepared for American Methodists is but an abbreviation of the *Prayer Book.* In the preface to that service he wrote: "I believe there is no liturgy in all the world, either in ancient or modern language, which breathes more of a solid, scriptural, rational piety than the Common Prayer of the Church of England. And though the main part of it was compiled more than two hundred years ago,[1] yet is the language of it not only pure, but strong and elegant in the highest degree. Little alteration is made in the following edition of it." In the use of these forms, crudities and carelessness of administration destroy their value, and every minister should learn to conduct them with such grace that the congregation will be impressed with a proper sense of their beauty and worth.

1. Baptism. Baptism is recognized as a sacrament by all evangelical Protestant bodies except the Friends. Christianity adapted the rite from the Hebrews, who in common with other Semitic peoples used water freely in symbolic washings in worship. The act of baptism represents the Spirit of God as cleansing and renewing the spirit of man. At the same time it marks those who are included in the Christian fellowship, the church, and has done so from New Testament times. We do not believe in baptismal regeneration. The rite merely recognizes the inward action of the Spirit which takes place independently of the outward washing.

Three modes of baptism are recognized by Methodists as equally valid—immersion, sprinkling, and pouring. Since one is admitted into the church once for all, this rite is to be performed but once in the lifetime of a Christian, though we have no patience with the extreme teaching that "the act can never be repeated without sacrilege."[2] Since it is a sign of admission into the church, the proper place for the service is in the church, though, of course, it may be performed elsewhere whenever the circumstances seem to warrant. The real church is found where two or more believers are met together in Christ's name. Methodists make no attempt to justify baptism by unordained laymen because

[1]Wesley wrote this in 1784.

[2]E. L. Temple, *The Church in the Prayer Book*, p. 247.

they do not regard the performance of the rite as essential to redemption. They find it impossible to believe that the guilt or innocence of the soul is determined by this outward washing.

Two forms of the service are provided—one for infants and small children, and the other for persons of "riper years," those who are capable of taking upon themselves vows. In the order for infants three great assumptions give character to the whole service. The first appears in the opening address to the congregation—that little children are already within the kingdom of God and the church, and that God's spirit is already given to them. The second is that the parents or legally appointed guardians are the natural sponsors of the child, and the major responsibility for his spiritual training cannot be transferred to godfathers and godmothers. Any number of persons may stand and take the vows with the parents, but no one can act as a substitute for them in this matter. In this respect our service contrasts notably with the *Prayer Book.* The third assumption is that the church publicly acknowledges its obligation to provide for the spiritual nurture of the child which belongs to it. Apart from these assumptions, the service is only a superstitious practice. He is a wise pastor who visits in advance the parents of children to be presented for baptism and makes sure that they understand the obligations which they are to assume.

Except when administered privately, the service is usually a part of the public worship of the congregation. The parents and other sponsors are invited to present the child (or children) near the baptismal font, generally during one of the regular hymns. The minister, standing before them, addresses the congregation, inviting their prayers on behalf of the child to be baptized, and leads in that prayer. The address to the parents follows, in which a promise is exacted that the child shall be instructed in the meaning of the rite and given such other religious discipline as shall bring it to spiritual consciousness in due time. After the pledge is given, the congregation rises while a short lesson is read, and should remain standing during the act of baptism unless the number of candidates is very large. Immediately after the lesson the minister *takes the child in his own arms* and, asking, "What name shall be given to this child?" dips up a little water in his right hand and pours or sprinkles it upon the head of the child as he repeats the Christian name only (for example, *Charles Edward*—not *Charles Edward Jones*) together with the baptismal formula. Returning the child to the parents, he leads the kneeling congregation again in prayer, concluding with the Lord's Prayer, in which all participate audibly. Dignity and impressiveness may be given to the service if the congregation shall join heartily in those parts of the service printed in heavy type.

It is the habit of some ministers to kiss the baptized child before returning it to the parents. This affectation should be avoided since it adds nothing to the impressiveness of the service and is an unnecessary and sentimental assertion of the minister's individuality. The minister should give the parents a certificate of baptism for the child and enroll its name in his own record of baptized children, whose status is that of probationers in the church.

The order for persons of "riper years" differs from that for infants only in such respects as the difference in maturity and spiritual condition requires. The promises are exacted of the candidates themselves and have to do with matters of belief, ethical practice, and religious purpose. The baptismal formula is the same in both orders. Following the act of baptism the congregation kneels and repeats audibly the Lord's Prayer, which may be followed by extemporaneous prayer. The answers to the questions are prescribed in the ritual, a copy of which should be in the hands of each candidate. If the candidate does not have the printed service, it is much better to let him frame his own answers than to tell him aloud what he is expected to repeat parrot-fashion. This inevitably produces a sense of unreality that jars upon the spirit of true devotion. It applies as well to the answers made to the questions asked of persons being received into the church. When performed privately, the service, in either of its forms, may be abbreviated according to circumstances, provided, of course, that the essential parts—the interrogations and the formula—shall never be omitted.

2. THE HOLY COMMUNION. The value of this sacrament depends largely upon the way in which it is administered. The administrant may put so little of his individuality into it as to make it purely mechanical. Or, he may show in word and action such understanding of the significance of the rite, such appreciation of its beauty, such a sense of joy tempered by humility and reverence at the privilege of participating in it as to make it the chief means of grace to believers.

To administer in this way involves, of course, much more than the mastery of the technique of the service. On the other hand, it cannot be administered effectively without this knowledge, and the mastery of these details becomes an important part of the duty of anyone who undertakes to use a ritual. The more important instructions are printed in the order. Certain minor matters, however, are overlooked which have much to do with the impressiveness of the service. In the absence of specific direction, we are to be guided, in part, it is assumed, by the practice and ideals of the Anglicans from whom we received the service, and in other part, by the preference of those among us who possess the most discriminating taste in such matters.

a. Ordinarily the service is made a part of the regular worship of the congregation once every two or three months, the communion being preceded by the usual hymns, prayers, a short sermon, and reception of members. Before the hour appointed for worship it is customary to cover the table which stands behind the rail and in front of the pulpit with a "fair linen cloth," upon which are set plates of bread conveniently cut into strips or broken into small pieces, and a pitcher of unfermented grape juice, together with an empty cup or a number of small individual cups. These in turn are all covered with another white cloth awaiting the moment when they shall be used.

b. Inasmuch as the service is a memorial of the sacrifice of Christ, it is fitting that it should begin with a special offering on the part of the congregation, which is received by the collectors while the minister reads a number of hortatory verses selected from the Scripture. This offering is generally used for the relief of the poor in the church and the community. If time permits, it is well to use the Ten Commandments as a Litany (see *Hymnal,* Number 738) before the offering or as a substitute for the offering in the event that, for a good cause, it is omitted.

c. After the offering the minister removes and folds carefully the cover which is spread over the bread and wine, laying it conveniently near for use again. He should then take his place *at the right side of the table* as he faces the congregation,[3] which is the station from which he is to administer the whole service, and read the Invitation to the *standing* congregation. Those who are to assist him should come within the chancel at this time. Then follows the General Confession, in which ministers and people participate audibly as they kneel, the ministers about the table *facing toward the elements.*

d. It is customary for the administrant to ask his assistants to read the prayers which precede the Prayer of Consecration. Lack of familiarity with congregational prayers may make it necessary to urge the people at the beginning of the service to join heartily in the General Confession, the Collect for Purity, and the Ter Sanctus. The Prayer of Consecration is made by the administrant himself, who should take the plate and cup in his hand at the appointed places.

e. After the Prayer of Consecration, the minister him-

---

[3]So the Anglicans and Protestant Episcopalians. See Samuel Hart, *The Book of Common Prayer,* p. 167.

self receives the communion in both kinds before administering the same to his assistants. A mistaken sense of courtesy has caused some protest against this practice as being inhospitable. It becomes singularly appropriate, however, once it is understood that this is a symbolic act which suggests that he who would minister grace to others must first receive that grace himself. After serving his assistants, he resumes his place at the right side of the table, leading in the prayer and the Ter Sanctus, which is to be said or sung by the people.

f. After the Ter Sanctus, the minister proceeds to serve the people "in order." Presumably this means in an orderly manner. This must imply that only as many are to be allowed to kneel at the rail at one time as can be accommodated comfortably. Confusion and disorder result if the people kneel two or three rows deep. It is likewise in the interest of order that as the first retire, a second group shall come from *the opposite side* of the house. Ushers, properly instructed, may direct the movement of the congregation. The singing of devotional hymns and the playing of proper selections on the organ will do much to create an atmosphere of worship during this part of the service and stabilize the emotion of the congregation. The time may be most profitably employed in intervals of the service in meditation and introspection, for only as there is a conscientious endeavor to realize the spiritual aspects of the sacrament can one eat and drink worthily so that he "may live and grow thereby."

In view of the ministerial character of their service, the choir probably should precede the congregation in communicating, though usually they are the last. On coming to the rail, each communicant should go to the farthest unoccupied space and kneel in an upright manner, the women with veils raised and hands ungloved. Persons may receive the communion, however, sitting or standing if there is good reason for not kneeling. It is the practice of Anglicans to break a small piece of bread from strips which are held in the left hand, and drop this into the open palm of the right hand of the communicant. The prejudice which exists, however, in the minds of most people against handling food unnecessarily makes it more advisable to have the bread cut into small bits upon the plate and permit the communicant to help himself. For sanitary reasons individual cups too are to be preferred to the common cup. The empty cups may be collected in a tray provided for that purpose after all have been served.

It is the common custom to repeat the administrative formula for each element a number of times as it is passed. This is not always edifying, and since we do not hold, as does the English Church, that each communicant has an inherent right to an individual repetition, it is probably better to repeat the formula clearly and distinctly once each time the elements are served, and then pass them to the communicants in silence.

There is no ritualistic authority for the time-honored practice of dismissing communicants with an exhortation. But some signal is needed for all to retire at once, and this may well justify the practice. Better than the impromptu exhortation, however, is a single verse of Scripture or a hymn, concluding with the formal dismissal: "Arise, go in peace. Amen." Or, better yet, the dismissal itself is sufficient after a moment has been allowed for silent prayer and thanksgiving.

g. As soon as all have been served and *before the concluding prayers,* the unused portion of the consecrated elements should be covered again with the cloth that was removed at the very beginning of the service. Then the minister and people kneel, joining together in the Lord's Prayer and a Prayer of Thanksgiving, at the conclusion of which all stand to repeat or chant "Gloria in Excelsis." The service concludes with the Benediction.

3. The Marriage Service. Unlike Catholics, Protestants do not regard marriage as a sacrament. It is a most sacred service, nevertheless, and no minister should ever

perform the rite without revealing in the manner of its performance his own sense of its deep sanctity. The form provided in the Methodist Episcopal ritual can hardly be improved, and the directions are too clear to need any supplementary statement.

At a time when public opinion generally subscribes to a view of marriage contradictory to the teaching of the New Testament, the Christian minister should exercise scrupulous care lest he contribute to the destruction of the family by performing marriages where one or both parties have been divorced. At the most, Jesus allowed but one cause as sufficient warrant for breaking the marriage relation. And the Methodist Episcopal Church does not permit its ministers to remarry any divorced persons except the innocent party in a divorce on the ground of adultery. It may be embarrassing to refuse one's services at times. This is a small matter, however, as compared with the stultification of oneself to avoid embarrassment or to earn a fee. Nothing is more significant of the power of the church in a materialistic age than the eagerness with which nearly all persons covet the blessing of the church in the hour of marriage and the hour of death. Marriages *may* be performed by civil magistrates. Most of them, however, are performed by ministers. And the church will keep the respect of the community by declining to adjust its views on matrimony to those of a gainsaying generation. He is no true minister of Jesus Christ who performs the marriage ceremony "for anyone who can secure a license." In a courteous manner one may inquire whether either party has been divorced, should the license indicate a previous marriage, and why. If a divorce has been granted for any other than the cause allowed by Jesus, the minister may simply say that the law of his church forbids him to perform the ceremony. Moreover, if for any reason whatsoever he may feel that the proposed marriage is ill-advised—the youth of the parties, or a frivolous view of matrimony, or unsound conditions of health or mind—he should decline to perform the service, though a license from the State be presented authorizing it. To consent on the ground that "some other minister will marry them if I do not" is utterly contemptible. "If I ever dare to marry, I should want Dr. B. to marry me," said a woman professor in a large women's college. "It was a solemn thing getting married by Dr. B. Groom and bride had to have separate interviews with him. They used to say the brides came out of his study tearful and the grooms sober-faced; but his marriages always turned out happy ones."[4] All marriages should be recorded carefully in the official records of the church as well as certified to the State in the blank usually provided for that purpose. Needless to say, all marriages should be properly witnessed.

4. The Funeral. In time of death, as in marriage, most families covet the help that religion affords. However critical men may be of the church, they do not care to have those whom they love lowered into the earth without the prayers and blessing of the church. In such an hour the pastor has a supreme opportunity to render a spiritual service.

If the deceased be a member of the church, the pastor will call on the family as soon as he is informed of the death, offering to be helpful in any way possible. In other cases he will call as soon as he knows that his services will be needed. On these occasions usually he may make preliminary plans for the funeral service, gathering such data concerning the deceased as he may care to use in the address. And within a few days after the service he should call again. In making these calls it is very much more important that he be a warm-hearted, sensible friend than an ecclesiastic doing and saying the professional things which he believes are expected of him. If the family is notably devout, it may be perfectly natural to offer the consolations of prayer. If they are not, or if there is confusion and distraction which would make the suggestion of prayer an embarrassment, he will render his largest service through being just humanly sympathetic.

[4]From an article in "The Christian Advocate," July 6, 1922, p. 834.

As for the service itself, the Methodist Episcopal Church provides a ritual that is solemn and beautiful, adapted from that of the Anglican Church. Frequently the service will consist only of the lessons and prayers of this service—*and nothing can be in better taste!* More commonly, however, one or two numbers of special music and an address in addition are expected. A "funeral sermon" is almost never in order, even in the rural districts to-day. The address should not take more than eight or ten minutes, and the whole service should be concluded in a half hour, as a rule. Any biographical sketch of the deceased that may be desirable should be incorporated into the address, and while proper appreciation is ever in order, overstatement and eulogy are distinctly bad form. If the departed was a saint, that fact will be already widely known. If not, only embarrassment can follow from an attempt to "whiten a sepulcher." Any effort to stir up the emotions of the company, particularly of the family, is reprehensible. Rather the service should soothe the harrowed feelings of those who mourn by its quiet tenderness. The proper material for an address at a funeral consists of the fundamental doctrine that God is love, and all other doctrines that are implied in it. Many things may happen that we cannot explain, but nothing can carry us beyond the reach of his love. Thus those who stay are safe, and those who go. "If we have such a Father in heaven as our Lord sought to reveal to us, then there are no sorrows that cannot be healed."

It is a commendable custom of many ministers to insert blank leaves in their rituals on which they may write, from time to time, verses, sentiments, and poems, gathered in their reading which may be appropriately used on funeral occasions. Selections from this compilation may be read as a part of the address, or a substitute for it.

Methodist ministers are forbidden to charge a fee for burying the dead. Where one is put to considerable expense to render this service, it is assumed that the family will reimburse him. But if they should not do so, he could hardly present a bill for it. On the other hand, he is not forbidden to accept an honorarium if one is offered without solicitation. When the offer comes from a family not connected with the church, there is no good reason for declining it, if they can afford to make it. It is probably the only way in which they ever contribute to the support of the ministry. But if it comes from one of the families in the church, the minister will do well to return it with a brotherly statement that a good shepherd will not profit from the distress of one of his sheep. Undue readiness to accept gifts has ruined the usefulness of many ministers.

5. "THE LITURGICAL PERSONALITY." It may appear that rather unusual emphasis has been laid upon the mechanics of public worship. But it has never been forgotten that "the best precepts with regard to liturgical matters run the risk of failing of their object unless powerfully supported by the liturgical personality."[5] Behind the pulpit decorum of the minister, the congregation must feel the throbbing of a heart that loves God devotedly and a spirit that is sensitive to the most appropriate means of expressing that affection. *In free worship we speedily reach the point where no rule of action can be prescribed. The only safe guide is a sound liturgical instinct.* In the development of such an instinct instruction in principles and methods of worship, the study of liturgical writings, conversation with skilled liturgists, all have an important place, but a place that is subordinate to the cultivation of the minister's own spiritual life by private prayer and meditation. To give his life a "spiritual bent" must be the liturgist's first concern. There should be "no day without special secret prayer, without definite reading and reflection on Holy Scripture, without, in a word, an inner laving in the refreshing and invigorating well-springs of a higher life."[6] In the interest of developing a "liturgical personality" we

---

[5]Van Oosterzee, *op cit.*, p. 443.

[6]*Id.*, p. 445.

do well to heed Spurgeon's exhortation: "We cannot be always on the knees of the body, but the soul should never leave the posture of devotion. The habit of prayer is good, but the spirit of prayer is better. As a rule, we ministers ought never to be many minutes without actually lifting up our hearts in prayer."

Books Recommended for Further Study

R. J. Cooke, *History of the Ritual of the Methodist Episcopal Church.*

C. C. Hall *et al.*, *Christian Worship.*

W. P. Thirkield, *Service and Prayers.*

Discipline Methodist Episcopal Church, 1920, The Ritual.

SECTION II

ADMINISTRATION

CHAPTER X

IMPORTANCE OF ORGANIZATION

THE essential fact in Christianity from the beginning has been an experience of fellowship between the individual believer and Jesus Christ. It was most natural that those who enjoyed this experience should have been drawn together into a brotherhood of believers. The mutual love which characterized the earliest Christians in their relations each to the other was a new thing in the world—so unselfish and beautiful that they themselves explained it as a divine creation, the work of the Holy Spirit who filled the body of believers with his presence, binding the many together into a single organism. This fellowship dates from Pentecost, which was not the time, as some suppose, when the Holy Spirit first came into the world (God's Spirit has been here since he brooded over primeval chaos), but the day when the Spirit created "the Beloved Community."

The atmosphere of good will which prevailed in the early church was very attractive to outsiders and very helpful to new converts, whose faith was fortified not only by the teaching of the apostles but by companionship with fellow believers. "They devoted themselves to the instruction given by the apostles *and to fellowship,* breaking bread and praying together" (Acts 2. 42, Moffatt's translation). The quality and strength of this corporate unity are suggested by the figures of speech employed in the New Testament to describe it—"the temple of God" (1 Cor. 3. 16), "the body of Christ" (1 Cor. 12. 27), "a kingdom" (1 Thess. 2. 12), "a household" (Gal. 6. 10). The essential idea in each instance is that the many, mutually related and dependent, were arranged into a systematic whole under the influence of a common spirit so that they lived and wor-

shiped together with the greatest harmony. The church has kept this ideal of fellowship before it continually by thinking of itself throughout its history as "the communion of saints."

As time passed, problems arose within the brotherhood which called for solution. Moreover, it appeared that the Christian propaganda could be carried on more effectively by collective than by individual action. So the fellowship became formally organized with officers whose respective duties were clearly defined. The type of organization seems to have varied, in different localities, though generally the Jewish synagogue was the model. And from that day to this the organization has been increasing in complexity.

It is quite the fashion to complain that organized Christianity has lost Christ's vision of saving the world and is chiefly concerned these latter days with saving itself. The critics render a valuable service in so far as they merely warn us against the danger of permitting the organization to become an end in itself. When they suggest, however, that organization is inherently bad, they do violence to the truth. There is no important achievement in the history of the church that would have been possible to an unorganized Christianity. The critics should reflect upon the futility of certain attempts to bring in the Kingdom which discounted the importance of organization. The contrast between the work of George Whitefield and John Wesley is familiar. The former was the greater preacher, judged by popular standards, and probably the more winsome personality. But his influence upon the English-speaking world was insignificant as compared with that of the latter, who organized his followers into "societies." Less frequently is attention called to the difference between the Old Testament prophets and the New Testament apostles. They matched each other in zeal and religious passion. But the former had very little influence upon their own generation, failing to avert the calamities which they saw impending; while the latter turned the Roman world upside down.

Humanly speaking, this difference seems to be due largely to the fact that the prophets were isolated voices, while the apostles, in addition to preaching, left organizations behind them in all the great cities of their day.

One can imagine how little headway individual Christians would have made in the task of Christianizing the world, each attacking the evils of paganism in his own way without reference to what any other was doing. Just as little as a patriotic young man would make in fighting his country's enemy with impetuous zeal, but refusing to join an organized body of soldiers! He would contribute more to the cause he loved by merging his identity with a group in which the many act as one. This principle holds to-day. We are still fighting against great evils. There is need of assistance from every high-minded man and woman in this war. But we shall make our blows more effective if all strike together rather than separately. We read that while one shall chase a thousand, two shall put ten thousand to flight. How? Obviously by careful cooperation in plan and effort. The difference between ten and two more or less fairly represents the difference in effectiveness between organized and unorganized effort. And the task of a pastor is the twofold one of (1) keeping in the church a spirit of divine fellowship, and (2) molding that fellowship into an instrument by which Christ can do his work in the world. The New Testament figure of the church as the body of Christ expresses both ideas—a form which is filled with his spirit, and which puts eyes, ears, hands, feet, and voice at his disposal that he may coordinate their several activities and so increase the effectiveness of each.

The Methodist Episcopal Church believes in organization to an unusual degree for a Protestant body. It has a highly centralized form of church government which invests its general officers with almost despotic power. Churches accept pastors, whose names they may not know, merely on the appointment of a bishop. Ministers sometimes find their pastoral relations broken in one place and new ones established in another without their permission being asked. Great benevolent boards are trusted with vast sums of money and their executive officers clothed with extraordinary authority. In a way, it appears to be anachronistic—"a church of the people, yet so autocratic!" But one does not create an autocracy by centralizing authority *so long as those who possess power are held to a high degree of responsibility!* The autocrat is accountable to no one. The agent of a democratic society, say the President of the United States, may for the time being have all the power of a Czar, but he is responsible to the people who conferred the power, and must make an accounting every four years. Similarly with the general officials of the Methodist Episcopal Church. They possess extraordinary power, but their work is subject to frequent review. Ministers and laymen trust them very far for the time being. But the day of accounting is always ahead. This keeps the church democratic—its power, in fact, widely distributed—but a democracy which believes in collective effort and is not afraid to delegate great authority temporarily to a few individuals. In this manner the church attains to something like the "efficiency" of an autocratic organization without sacrificing real freedom.

Organization is as significant for the local church as it is for the general body. The pastor deals in the small with precisely the same problems that bishops and general secretaries face in the large. Therefore he must learn to approach them intelligently. He may not like them, but they are unavoidable. He may not withdraw from his prophetic office, but, in addition, he must acquire "the gift of administration."

CHAPTER XI

PRINCIPLES OF ADMINISTRATION

THE principles of administration are the same for the church as for any organized group, whether commercial, industrial, social, economic, political, or religious. They are not arbitrary ideals laid down by general officials, but great laws of life which control human beings in group relations.

1. *The first is to conceive intelligently the proper function of the organization.* The pastor must ask himself continually, "What is the whole business of the church in the community?" The answer which he makes will determine the form of the church organization. An organization whose function it is to make shoes will not be identical in every respect with one whose business is to wage war. One whose aim is to relieve distress will differ greatly from one whose purpose is education. This principle is often disregarded by those who insist that the church should be "run on business principles." If that means only that the church should be administered intelligently in the light of the great ends to be served, it is good advice. But if it means that the church is to be run like a bank, it is bad counsel for the simple reason that banking is not the business of the church. The church will have its own methods because it has its own work.

Broadly speaking, the ends toward which the church should move are worship, evangelism, education, and service. Necessarily the organization designed to serve these ends will be complex. To direct this work properly the pastor, ideally, should have expert assistance in the form of paid workers who are specialists in their respective fields. Practically, however, most pastors must do their work with volunteer helpers.

2. *It is important that the members of an organization shall be imbued with loyalty to a common ideal.* Every high class organization is careful to receive and retain in its membership only such persons as are in sympathy with its aims and methods. Some organizations necessarily require certain physical and mental qualifications in their members. The church demands only moral and spiritual fitness. Do candidates for membership hate sin and love righteousness? Is God a reality to them and his will their highest law? Do their daily lives give evidence of these desires? Are their religious beliefs and ideals such as to make it possible for them to live and work harmoniously with other members of the church? The church should make its standards as broad and few as possible, but there can be no doubt as to its right and obligation to guard its membership against divisive and disintegrating elements.

The "morale" of the church can seldom be built up or maintained by harsh disciplinary measures. Only in the rarest instances is it profitable to proceed against a member with formal charges and church trials (though one should not flinch if duty points clearly in that direction). Only the spirit of generous, patient, intelligent love radiated by the pastor in his life and words will fuse together the many with diverse minds and tastes into a unified "communion of saints." After three years of fellowship with Jesus the Twelve sat down the last night in an irritable mood, their unity spoiled by distrust and jealous ambition. To unite different types into a brotherhood for unselfish service is still "the most stupendous and heart-breaking labor to which a minister of the gospel can set himself."[1]

3. *No good administrator ever dreams of doing himself all the work of his organization.* The pastor who would become a competent manager of the church organization must depend upon the help of assistants. He should not do anything in the way of a minor task that can be delegated to others. Yet at this point many pastors fail hopelessly.

[1]Charles E. Jefferson, *Building the Church*, p. 76.

Tasks are so numerous, competent lay workers are so few, and time is so short, that the impulse is strong to undertake everything oneself, or fill the important posts in the church with members of one's own family. Times without number when the pastor removes to another charge, the church is stripped of practically all its leadership, for he takes with him in the parsonage household the Sunday school superintendent, several Sunday-school teachers, and the presidents of the Epworth League and most of the women's organizations. The helplessness of Methodist churches without pastors is almost proverbial. This is not creditable to the type of pastoral oversight that has failed to develop lay leadership prepared to carry on the work in the absence of the pastor.

Not only does the pastor do the church an injustice by assuming posts of subordinate leadership, but he renders himself incompetent to do effectively the work which only he can do. The life of bustling activity incapacitates him for the quiet study and brooding that is indispensable to effective preaching. Constant immersion in minor details lessens his power to see his task as a whole and to discriminate between the primary and the secondary. The church may foolishly applaud for the time being the young minister who acts as janitor, leader of the men's class, Sunday-school superintendent, scoutmaster, choir leader, as well as shepherd and prophet. But in ten years that restless activity will smother the spirit of prophecy within him, and prophets are too rare to waste in this fashion. By middle life it will be clear that it would have been wiser to have secured and trained laymen to fill these lesser posts so that he might have had time to keep his intellectual strength from abating and his spiritual vision from growing dim. Many a pastor, who at thirty was an energetic youngster in great demand, has become a problem for district superintendents and bishops by the time he has reached fifty. In the beginning he did his work by a vast expenditure of physical energy. He was always "on the go" and was regarded as a "hustler." But in every man the tides of physical life begin to run low at forty-five and it is necessary then to do by mental and spiritual power what was formerly done by physical. So it comes to pass that the pastor in middle life who has always been "too busy to study" is in some such position as a squirrel might be in midwinter who was too busy in the autumn to lay in a store of nuts. He has no resources to draw upon that will get him by the hard place.

The problem of securing competent lay helpers is very much more difficult for him than for the manager of a business organization. He seeks volunteer and unsalaried service. The worker must find his reward in the doing of the work itself. It is easy, however, to exaggerate the advantage which economic power gives the entrepreneur in business. The successful manager is not always cracking the whip of authority over the heads of his subordinates. Rather he makes the same appeal which the pastor must make—helps men to see that the work in itself is important, holds before them constantly the ideal which he cherishes for the enterprise, creates a sense of responsibility by delegating authority to them, and gives all consideration possible to their opinions. Even in business the pocketbook is not always the paramount consideration, and the best managers know this full well. But be this as it may, the pastor must prevail upon men and women to assume posts of leadership in the church without hope of financial reward. If he cannot get the persons he wants, he must take the persons he can get. And he must see to it that they become as efficient as possible under the limitations which are imposed. He will encourage them by words of commendation when it is possible to do so. He will offer helpful suggestions as to the way in which their work may be made more effective. He will meet them frequently for private and group conference. He will put into their hands the best literature on their respective tasks. And gradually he will build around himself a corps of teachers and assistant executives thoroughly imbued with his spirit and sharing his ideals.

Having once delegated authority to some one for a particular task, the pastor should advise with that person with reference to all matters in his department. For example, he should not go over the head of the choirmaster in musical matters. If some special arrangement seems desirable, the leader should be requested to make it. If the pastor should make it himself without consulting the leader, that official would have a right to suspect that he was not trusted, and would be irritated. If the subordinate will not give cooperation, he should be removed, but as long as he is in charge, he should be consulted.

4. *It is a weakness in much so-called "scientific management" that the administrator takes an impersonal view of the human elements in the organization.* Men are regarded as so many mechanical parts of a gigantic machine which have no will of their own and act only at the command of the master. It is this treatment of men as if they were inanimate things that is the chief cause of unrest in industry. Workers care less about more wealth just now than they do about more freedom. And the most successful business executives are devising means whereby employees may make their voices heard in the management of affairs.

If the despotic boss is undesirable in business, he is impossible in the church. Democracy in religion requires that every member of the church shall have an opportunity to express his view on any vital matter connected with the life of the church. It is not enough that the pastor should have a policy or a program. He is bound to win the enthusiastic consent of the church to it so that it shall be the collective program of the whole organization. There is no place in Methodism for the pastor who feels that the church must obey when he speaks simply because he has spoken. If the people adopt his judgment, it must be because it is worth adopting. He should never be satisfied with carrying a vote on any vital matter by a narrow majority. Any notable changes in policy should be made only when the judgment of the church as a whole is practically unanimous as to its wisdom. "Conference," "discussion," "education," "respect for the people's judgment," are words with which the wise pastor will conjure. By them he will move the spirit of the congregation toward himself and command the cooperation of their wills. And if it be that they do not vote as he desires, it is supreme folly for him to complain childishly that the people will not follow his leadership. If his was a good cause, it can afford to wait for the hearty support of the church. If it was not, it should have been lost.

In the development of opinion favorable to any project, it is important to win the approval of the men of sober wisdom in the organization whose views carry great weight with their fellow members. Every church has one such person, and some have several. If a majority of these will not indorse the plan, action should be deferred until such a time as their consent can be won. To force the issue prematurely may result not only in the defeat of the plan but also in arraigning the strong man against the pastor. Of course we are not suggesting unmanly servility, much less insincere flattery, in the effort to win others to one's way of thinking, but only that Christian respect for the opinion of others which is always becoming in a brotherhood like the church, and which is essential in dealing with a group committed to democratic ideals.

5. *Another principle for which the wise administrator must have great regard is that of properly coordinating the work of the several departments of his organization.* It is not enough that an army commander shall be courageous on the field of battle. He must correlate the work of his staff so that all departments shall work together toward a common end. His army must be fed, clothed, and equipped, and all at the same time. If the quartermaster's department gets up the clothing and the commissary department brings up the provisions, but the ordnance officers do not bring up the guns and ammunition, the army will suffer defeat in spite of the personal heroism of the general and

his men. The responsibility for the disaster must be charged to poor staff work, which in turn is traceable to poor generalship.

Similarly the wise pastor must correlate the work of the several departments of the church so that all will cooperate intelligently in working out a common purpose. He should endeavor to eliminate all waste and needless duplication of effort, and see that no department fails to function in the proper manner. In this connection attention is called again to the large number of organizations in many churches doing some form of educational work regardless of whether or not the same work could be done more effectively by another group. For the missionary societies, the Epworth League, and the Sunday school all to offer mission study courses, for example, is much as if the ordnance, commissary, and quartermaster's departments should all provide the army with shoes. There is an oversupply of one article and an undersupply of others.

6. *Every authority on business administration regards "system" as "the basic structure of organization."* It consists of a well defined routine for controlling the methods and processes of production. The wise manager, nevertheless, understands that while system is a good servant, it is a poor master. Impatience with "red tape" is thoroughly justified when system has become so elaborate or is so venerated that it retards the dispatch of business. Wherever it is possible, however, to turn work over to routine it will be wise to do so. The nervous system does exactly this when any form of conduct has become habitual, for habit is only another word for system. Proper system in church work is as desirable as right habits in religion. But it must be remembered that no hard-and-fast system can be brought in from the business world and applied directly to the work of the church. A workable system must emerge naturally from within the organization on the basis of experience. The work of the church should be done in orderly fashion, but the particular order will be its own.

Every pastor can introduce system to advantage—

a. In his study. Where the pulpit is lacking in intellectual vigor, desultory reading and bad habits of study on the part of the minister are generally the cause. Too many pastors have *no fixed hours for intellectual work and no permanent intellectual interests* which control in the selection of books and periodicals. Regular study hours have been jealously observed by all great pastors.

b. In pastoral work. The control of impulse is responsible for inefficiency in pastoral work quite as certainly as in the intellectual work of the study. Too many pastors call only as the mood for calling is on them. This may seem to be justified by the fact that to be helpful to people in our calling we must be at our best emotionally as well as intellectually. On the other hand, it is fatal to pastoral work that it should be wholly at the mercy of our moods.

c. In evangelism. Inadequate results in the work of evangelism are more often than not due to the fact that the minister does not go about this work systematically. In another place particular programs of evangelism will be mentioned. For the present it is enough to say that at the beginning of each year every pastor should plan his evangelistic work very definitely for the whole year. He will understand that the people who are to be won are not people in general but particular men and women and boys and girls whose names and addresses he should have on a constituency roll or card index. He will know too that these people must be won by the people who are already interested in the things of the Kingdom, and he will likewise make a list of those persons who may reasonably be expected to do personal work. He will plan his special meetings both for the church and the Sunday school, and as the time arrives for particular services in his calendar he will give careful attention to every duty, seeing to it in so far as possible that nothing is left to chance. If this seems like reducing the work of soul-winning to mechanics, let us remember that God works through the ordinary and the natural powers of man quite as certainly as he works through the extraordinary and the unusual.

d. In religious education and community service. The work of religious education and community service suffers, as does the work of evangelism, because it is not organized in a systematic fashion. Moods or impulses may render us impotent here as well as any other where. It ought to be obvious that the educational work of the church calls for the closest planning and the most consistent application of time and energy through a long period. And the church can render only inadequate service in solving community problems if its interest in those problems is occasional and spasmodic rather than permanent and intelligent.

e. In preaching. As suggested above, no pastor is likely to present a comprehensive teaching of Christian truth from the pulpit unless he plans far in advance his themes and subjects.

f. In church finance. Many a church, brought to the verge of bankruptcy by lack of system in financial methods, has adopted a more intelligent plan with results that were little less than miraculous. In place of letting unpaid bills accumulate until the credit of the church was almost ruined and meeting these bills by a frenzied appeal to men when there happened to be a good congregation assembled for worship, the plan of intelligently making a budget of expense for the twelve months in advance, and informing the congregation as to the legitimacy of the several items in this budget, and finally canvassing every member of the church for subscription to this budget, has raised many a church from the dead.

7. *Modern administrators, within and without the church, have much to say about "efficiency."* This is the result of an effort on the part of "scientific management" in industry to handle huge volumes of business by standardizing, wherever possible, the processes of mass production and turning them over to "routine." Necessarily it is highly mechanical, reducing the demand for creative

thought on the part of the workers and requiring special skill in making a few motions which soon become almost instinctive and involuntary.

It should be understood that efficiency in this mechanical sense for church work is neither desirable nor possible. Efficiency in industry converts the worker as certainly into a machine as the clanging thing of iron and steel which he handles. And, surely, we do not expect men to be treated by the church in the impersonal way that they are treated in a mill. Moreover, it is impossible to standardize very extensively methods and processes in an organization whose aim is to develop certain *moods* and *tempers,* to induce an attitude of *faith* and *good will* toward God and men. The "efficient church" is the one which finds a way to produce "the believing soul." This is more largely a matter of "atmosphere" than of technique or organization. It never can be said that a specific number of prescribed actions will always and everywhere produce this state of belief.

It does not follow, however, that there is no need for more intelligence and better practical judgment in doing the work of the church, which is what we really mean when we demand "greater church efficiency." The pastor who enters his study well past the middle of the morning with no definite schedule in mind for the next four or five hours, spending a half hour on the morning papers, an hour on letters, followed by a visit to the post office, returning to weed the garden or tinker the automobile, failing to get in sixty minutes of conscientious mental labor on a worthwhile book or problem of thought, is wasteful and lazy—and that is inefficient. The Sunday-school teacher who permits a pupil to be absent two Sundays in succession without getting in touch with him is careless and indifferent—and that is inefficient. For two or more organizations to plan social affairs for the same or successive evenings which appeal to the same constituency for financial support is stupid—and that is inefficient. For several societies, the Sunday school, the Epworth League, the Men's Club, for example, to attempt to do separately something that could be done together better shows lack of coordination—which is inefficient. To organize a group of women, girls, and children first as a Woman's Foreign Missionary Society, King's Daughters, and Little Light Bearers; and then as a Woman's Home Missionary Society, Queen Esther's Circle, and Home Guards is bad management—and that is inefficient. An official, whose duty requires that plain and accurate records be kept of business transacted or moneys handled, but whose minutes or accounts are in disorder and confusion is surely inefficient. A church badly located and poorly equipped for its work when a better site and adequate facilities are really available, is inefficient. More precision, care, painstaking conscientiousness, imagination, earnestness, intelligence—these can all be introduced with advantage into the work of the church—which is all that is meant in suggesting more efficiency.

8. A final principle which should control a pastor of a Methodist Episcopal church is derived from the federal character of the church. There is probably no ecclesiastical organization in the world, except the Roman Catholic, in which the cohesion of its several parts is so great. Its bishops are all "general" superintendents. In practice the authority of each may be limited to a group of Conferences, but in theory this authority is church-wide. Its ministers are "transferred" with the greatest ease from one Annual Conference to another, and the lay membership, while localized and counted in some particular church, as a matter of fact rests in the general denomination. This produces a strong "connectional" consciousness, which affects each pastor to a notable degree. It obligates him to exalt before his own congregation the best in the denominational tradition, without boastfulness or unbrotherliness toward other communions. *Moreover, it requires from him loyalty toward the general officers and heads of the church and willingness to cooperate in executing properly authorized programs.* This loyalty does not require that he be servile.

He is to think his own thoughts and express his own mind when the time for discussion has arrived. But when discussion has ceased and the will of the denomination is expressed in legislation, he has no choice but to conform to this general will. If one cannot give this loyalty, he may honorably withdraw from the ministry of the church, but cannot honorably continue in it.

Books Recommended for Further Study

Charles E. Jefferson, *Building the Church.*

Albert F. McGarrah, *Modern Church Management; A Modern Church Program.*

Albert J. Lyman, *The Christian Pastor in the New Age.*

Frederick Lynch, *The New Opportunities of the Ministry.*

Shailer Mathews, *Scientific Management in the Churches.*

F. A. Agar, *Manual of Church Methods.*

William H. Leach, *How to Make the Church Go.*

R. W. Babson, *The Future of the Churches.*

CHAPTER XII

PLANS OF ORGANIZATION

THE General Conference of the Methodist Episcopal Church has prescribed a plan of organization for the local church. The governing body is called the "Quarterly Conference"[1] and is composed of all ministers, local preachers, exhorters, stewards, trustees, class leaders, and deaconesses on the charge, together with the chief executive officers of the several major organizations within the church (superintendent of the Sunday school, president of the Epworth League, presidents of the several women's organizations, and the directors of religious education and social activities, etc.). This Conference usually meets from two to four times a year under the presidency of the district superintendent. It operates through numerous committees, and to it the several officers, organizations, and committees report at least once a year.

The long interval between meetings of the Quarterly Conference makes it an impractical instrument for handling business which must receive regular and frequent attention. To meet this defect, the Board of Stewards and the Board of Trustees were separately organized. This gave rise to a species of dual control in the church, for the division of labor agreed upon was that the stewards should have charge of "spiritual matters," while the trustees should give themselves to "temporal affairs." The lack of coordination between the two bodies proved embarrassing, and eventually, in many churches, one of them came to feel itself superior to the other. To make possible a return to a more democratic and unified control the Quarterly Conference now

[1]An amendment is now pending proposing to change this name to "Local Conference."

may authorize the organization of an "official board," whose personnel is that of the Quarterly Conference, and which largely does the work both of the stewards and trustees. Some states require that the trustees must be separately organized to hold and transfer property. But for this fact, in most churches neither stewards nor trustees would be independently organized. The official board meets regularly once each month, and special meetings are held on call of the pastor. The pastor is presiding officer, ex officio. Additional officials are usually a vice-president, secretary, treasurer for local budget, treasurer of benevolences, and financial secretary, who generally fill corresponding offices in the Quarterly Conference. The board performs its work through the Quarterly Conference committees and such others as it may decide to elect. Its minutes are approved annually by the Quarterly Conference, and thus its action becomes Quarterly-Conference action.

The principal defect in this plan of organization lies in the large number of standing committees through which the official board functions. The following are elected in every church or charge, either by the Quarterly Conference or the official board *by order of the General Conference:*

1. Apportioned Benevolences.
2. Christian Stewardship.
3. Foreign Missions.
4. Home Missions and Church Extension.
5. Religious Instruction.
6. Tracts.
7. Temperance.
8. Education.
9. Education for Negroes.
10. Hospitals.
11. Church Records.
12. Auditing Accounts.
13. Parsonage and Furniture.
14. Church Music.
15. Estimating Ministerial Support.

16. Examination Local Preachers.
17. Church Property.
18. Finance.

In addition, authority is conferred to create "such other committees as may be thought necessary," so that frequently the list is materially longer.

It is clear that many of these committees are supposed to represent the General Boards of the denomination in the local church, presumably informing the congregation concerning their work and soliciting funds. Inasmuch, however, as this is an important part of the pastor's task, assisted by the Finance Committee, these committees almost never function. Other committees are designed to serve some actual need in the local church, but many of them function so imperfectly that duplication, friction, waste, confusion, misunderstanding, general inefficiency, and even carelessness are written large everywhere. These considerations have caused some thoughtful leaders to seek a way of coordinating the activities of the many committees and organizations without contravening the discipline.

The suggestion has been made repeatedly that the pastor should appoint a "council" or "cabinet" composed of one or more representatives from the chief organizations in the church, whose business should be the unification of the work of the several societies.[1] "This cabinet will meet and receive the program of activities of each of the several organizations, and from these compile one general program of activities for the whole church (which it is well to publish for the general information of the church membership), or it would be better still if this cabinet should suggest to all the organizations represented a comprehensive program in which all would have a part."[2] The cabinet, of course,

---

[1]So Fisher in *The Way to Win;* Cook, in *A Working Program for the Local Church,* and Tippy and Kern in *A Methodist Church and Its Work.*

[2]Warren F. Cook, *A Working Program for the Local Church,* p. 25.

would be an unofficial body. It could do nothing more than advise. But it would be a powerful agent in creating public opinion in the church which the official board would surely respect. If any complain that such a cabinet is unauthorized by the Discipline, reply may be made, "Neither is the bishop's cabinet at the Annual Conference."

Yet another method of unification might be to create several standing committees, in addition to the cabinet, to supervise the great essential tasks of the church. These are: (1) Worship, (2) Evangelism, (3) Religious Education, (4) Service, (5) Finance. The work of these committees would be to correlate and supervise the activities of all agencies at work in their respective fields. Each committee would report directly to the official board, or to the cabinet, which, in turn, would unify the programs of the several standing committees before reporting to the board. *These committees could be ordered under existing authority to create "such other committees as may be thought necessary."*[3] They might be composed, in part at least, of the membership of committees and organizations which they respectively supervise. For example, the "Committee on Worship" would absorb the committees on "Music" and "Pulpit Supply," and might include representatives from the Epworth League and Sunday school. The pastor should be a member ex officio of all such standing committees, possibly the chairman of each.

Books Recommended for Further Study

Fred B. Fisher, *The Way to Win.*
Albert F. McGarrah, *Modern Church Management.*
Warren F. Cook, *A Working Program for the Local Church.*
Tippy and Kern, *A Methodist Church and Its Work.*
Discipline, Methodist Episcopal Church, 1920.

[3]See Discipline (1920), 112: 2.

Diagram of Proposed Plan of Organization Through Committees and Pastor's Cabinet

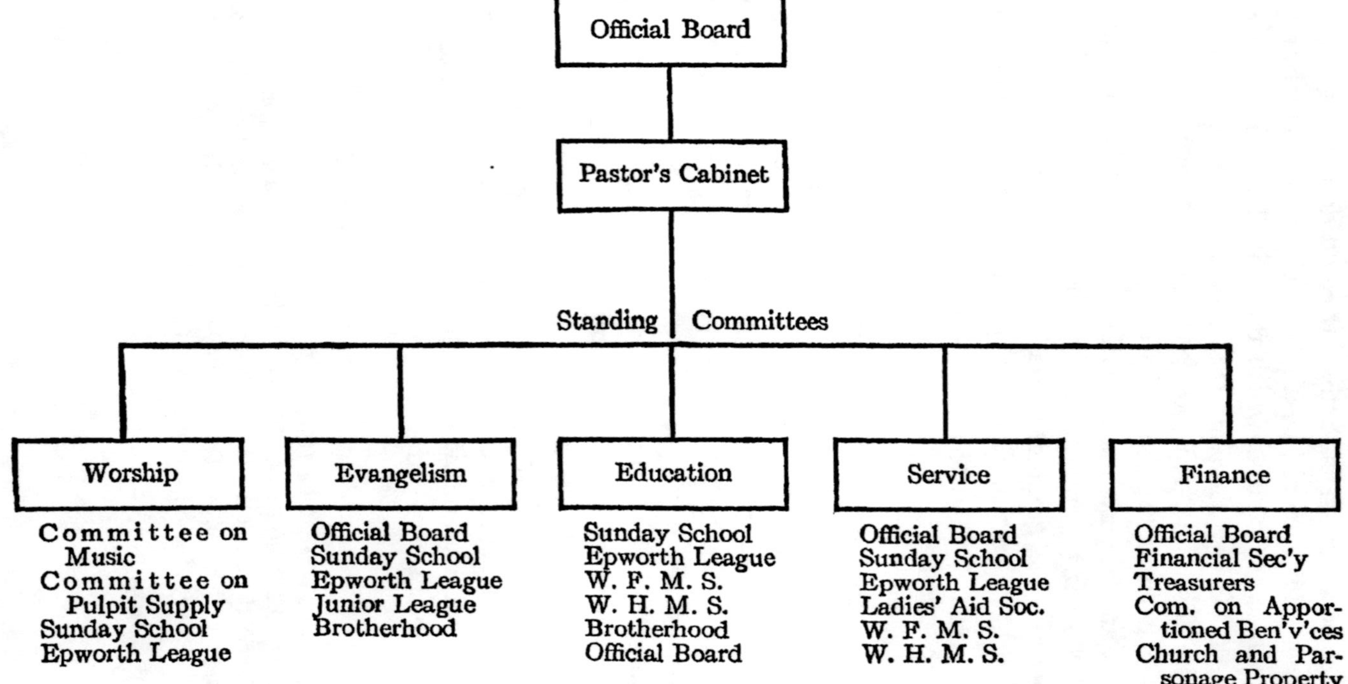

Note—The Pastor is a member ex officio of all Committees

CHAPTER XIII

THE ADMINISTRATION OF WORSHIP

THE present chapter will deal briefly with the subject of worship from the general point of view of the administrator rather than the specific point of view of the liturgist, which was presented in the first section of this book.

1. *The Standing Committee on Worship* should be composed of not more than six besides the pastor. These might well be the chairman of the Music Committee, the chairman of the Pulpit Supply Committee, the organist, the choirmaster, the Sunday-school superintendent, and the president of the Epworth League. The scope of their activities would include all that has to do with the enrichment of public worship in the church service, the Sunday school, and the Epworth League. Their judgment should be secured before new hymnals and songbooks are purchased, and before singers, organists, and directors of music are employed. They should make, from time to time, constructive criticism to the official board looking toward the improvement of the worship of all organizations in the church. Moreover, they should, by every means in their power, encourage private and family prayer throughout the membership of the church. They should cooperate with the Epworth League in promoting the "Morning-Watch" idea and recommend worthy books of devotion for individuals and manuals for domestic worship.

2. *The committee might request the pastor to use a whole service occasionally for instructing the congregation in the ideals and principles of public worship as set forth in the first section of this book.* The disorder that mars much free worship is not due to conscious irreverence, but to the unhappy fact that many people have never been taught to worship. They have gone to church all their lives "to hear

the sermon," and have not understood that they were themselves expected to make a contribution to common prayer. This instruction should be given as early in the life of the child as possible. But it will be helpful, too, to instruct the adults in the public congregation if they are unenlightened concerning ideals of worship. One of the notable memories in the life of a certain minister has to do with a Sunday morning when he took the congregation into his confidence, showing how important were the contributions of the congregation itself, the choir, the ushers, and the janitor as well as that of the minister to common prayer.

The best opportunity for teaching social worship in the average church is to be found in the Sunday school. A few superintendents understand that the introductory service is not merely a mechanical way of beginning the work of the school. But not many. The average Sunday-school orchestra may serve some useful purpose in holding the interest of the players to the school, but it seldom induces the worshipful mood. Noise, "pep," "jazz"—sometimes because it pleases the leader, and sometimes because it is supposed to have a disciplinary value on restless pupils—constitute the ideal of many superintendents for the "opening exercises." It should be a vital part of all true religious education to teach boys and girls to worship. The time to do this is in the early part of the service. "To bring each person in attendance into the conscious presence of God for a few moments every Sunday is one of the splendid privileges presented to officers and teachers of the school."[1]

3. *Every consideration which can be urged in behalf of graded instruction in the church school may be urged likewise in behalf of graded worship.* The absence of children from public worship is generally remarked upon with regret. Can it be expected, however, that active young human beings will enjoy sitting for an hour or more through a service that was never designed to meet a need of which they are

[1]Van Oosterzee, *op. cit.*, p. 445.

conscious? Everything is arranged for the adult section of the congregation—hymns, prayers, anthems, and sermon, all beyond the understanding of boys and girls. Have we any moral right to insist upon or expect the children to attend public worship unless the service is adapted to their needs? They are not "little men and women," as we sometimes declare. They differ from adults as radically in mental and spiritual matters as in physical. They are *sui generis*. Adult religion no more fits them than do adult clothes. Forms and methods of worship must be designed to meet their peculiar spiritual needs. They must be trained to worship. But they will never learn to worship by simply looking on while older people worship. Opportunity must be given them to express directly their own feelings, as is not and cannot be done in the ordinary service of worship. Respect for personality will eventually compel us to concede the principle of graded worship and provide such opportunities for the expression and development of the child's faith as are adapted to his several stages of growth.

Many pastors are experimenting with the "Children's Church"—an organization modeled after the ordinary church, but composed entirely of children, transacting its own business and conducting its own services of worship, often at the hour when the adults are met for formal worship. The success of this experiment always depends, of course, on the personality of the adult leader who is in charge. Others are attempting to convert the "Opening Exercises" of the Sunday school into "Junior Worship." Where the several departments of the Sunday school are independently organized and meet in separate rooms it is easily possible to have worship adapted to the ages which are found in each group. Still others bring the Sunday-school children into the public worship of the church and introduce elements into that service, such as a children's song and a short children's sermon, which will appeal especially to them, dismissing them before the moment has arrived for the usual sermon. Each of these methods has something to commend it.

4. *There is no doubt that the cause of social worship is greatly served by having the place of worship kept sacred for that particular purpose.* It is true that play may be as legitimate as prayer. Nevertheless many find it difficult to enter into a worshipful frame of mind in a room which is open to all causes. A minstrel show in a church is incongruous, but not much more so than many other things that are admitted. If there is but one room for all purposes, of course one must do the best he can. But when it is possible to arrange for concerts, lectures, plays, etc., in some other than the room used for public worship, let it be done by all means.

Books Recommended for Further Study

Hugh Hartshorne, *Worship in the Sunday School.*
Weldon F. Crossland, *The Junior Church in Action.*
Charles E. McKinley, *Educational Evangelism.*

CHAPTER XIV

THE ADMINISTRATION OF EVANGELISM

1. The Standing Committee on Evangelism should be composed of representatives of all the organizations which attempt definite evangelistic work in the local church, together with the pastor and one or two members of the official board. The committee will supervise and coordinate the evangelistic work of the several organizations. Not later than October first it should present a unified program of evangelism for the succeeding twelve months.

2. Principles of Evangelism. There is no single term that will more accurately describe the total task of the church than the word "evangelism," *provided it be interpreted broadly*. In specifying the principles of evangelism we are only trying to define the idea in such a way as to include its larger meanings.

a. Evangelism is not primarily a matter of delivering the Christian message, as was represented in a widely circulated book some years ago called *The Evangelization of the World in this Generation*. Dr. John R. Mott, the author of this helpful volume, distinctly affirmed that by "evangelization" he did not mean the conversion of the world, but merely such a general proclamation of the gospel that every person in the world should have the opportunity to hear of Christ and so to accept him. Knowledge of Christ must precede devotion to him, but there must be no complacency over having proclaimed his gospel in a professional fashion. *To be saved* is not identical with *thinking,* or *acting,* or *feeling* a certain way. In its highest sense it means conscious fellowship between a man and the Infinite God. To prevail upon others to establish that fellowship it is necessary to live sacrificially as well as to speak eloquently and informingly.

b. Evangelism must be adequate in its motive. Some years ago a young minister at a camp meeting, in concluding a hearty sermon, invited any who would to confess publicly their discipleship. He had failed to note that few, if any, of those present were irreligious, and acted as though a considerable number were well outside the Kingdom. His invitation was earnest but perfunctory, and evoked no response. Nevertheless, he turned from section to section until he had completed the semicircle of pews; then, buttoning his coat about him, exclaimed, "Well, I have delivered my soul!" That statement revealed the motive which impelled him in his evangelistic work. Conscious of a certain duty, he went through what he conceived to be the appropriate motions, but with as much real enthusiasm as Jonah manifested in going to Nineveh. Not to save our own souls, not to add a certain number to the church, but the feeling that men are miserable, and poor, and blind, and naked if they do not walk in fellowship with God constitutes a motive really adequate for the work of evangelism.

c. Evangelism must not be identified exclusively with exceptional and irregular methods of work To many minds the term suggests only *revivalism* of the type so popular in recent years. Revivalism is, indeed, one highly accredited method of doing the work of evangelism. But a wise evangelist will not limit himself to a single method or time if there are other agencies and occasions that may be utilized to advantage. To regard the "special meeting" and the "special man" (the professional evangelist) as the instruments *par excellence* for redeeming life, expecting little or nothing from the "regular services" and the customary ministrations of the pastor, is to fall into the error of believing that God is in the irregular in a way that he is not in the ordinary and the commonplace. It is beyond all question true that God has worked through "the revival" in a notable way. But he does not come to men exclusively through that channel. If one can have a revival, let him have it by all means! But do not be cast down if this is impossible. The primary matter is to do the work of evangelism, if not by one method, then by another. If one cannot utilize the revival, then try personal evangelism and religious education. The slower process may be less spectacular but is equally effective—indeed, it is the only one that will be effective in dealing with certain groups.

d. The scope of evangelistic endeavor should not be limited to a single phase of the evangelistic task. The program of evangelism will include all persons and classes that are in need of the spirit of God, and will have to do with the whole range of Christian experience.

(1) *Evangelism will concern itself with young people and children.* Here the problem will be rather preventing the contagion of sin than curing the disease after it has been contracted, applying the prophylactic rather than the therapeutic power of the gospel. In the nature of the case the revival method is not very valuable in this type of evangelism. Opportunity must be made, of course, for the child to come definitely to spiritual consciousness, choosing for himself to follow Christ. And in the sense that such a decision should be made publicly, the revival meeting, frequently called "Decision Day," in the Sunday school will be helpful. But even so, it will only supplement the better method of educational evangelism by which in the home and church, ideally at least, an atmosphere quickeningly religious has been created in which through months and years of training and oversight the decision made in the evangelistic meeting has been slowly ripening. In dealing with young life, the matter cannot be concluded once and for all. There must be the most careful instruction and nurture if the plant is to grow straight and strong to full maturity. Religious education rather than the revival will be our best reliance here.

(2) *But the work of evangelism must be directed toward adult as well as child life.* It has been said conversions rarely occur after the age of twenty, and that the great

opportunity for recruiting the membership of the church is to be found among the young rather than the older people. This emphasis has had an unfortunate effect in so far as it has made the church hopeless concerning the spiritual redemption of adult life. The gospel yet possesses curative as well as preventive value. The novelists, the poets, and the dramatists are ever asserting the fact of spiritual renewal for life that has become brutalized.[1] This is not an appropriate time, then, for the church to surrender its faith in the "recoverability of human nature at its worst." We must seek to save lost men and women as well as to keep boys and girls from becoming lost. No pastor is discharging his full duty unless he includes both these classes in the scope of his evangelism. The revival method is more helpful in work with adults than in dealing with young people. But in most instances even here it must be supplemented by diligent personal evangelism and intelligent religious education.

(3) *Evangelism has to do with the whole range of Christian experience—with later stages as well as with the beginnings of Christian living.* It is here that the revival meeting seems to render its largest service to-day—as an occasion for interpreting to people already religious in at least a formal sense the deeper significance of faith and trust in God. Few "outsiders" attend such meetings. Even the great tabernacle meetings in American cities attract chiefly persons who are already members of churches. Instead of complaining that this is so, one should seize gladly the opportunity to enrich and stabilize the faith of these believing ones by setting forth the doctrines of assurance, regeneration, and sanctification in wholesome terms and endeavoring to lead them into the reality for which these great words stand. What a pity that few except unreflective extremists are saying anything to the modern church about these vital matters! For this reason, if for

[1]For example, Tolstoy's *Resurrection* and Masefield's *Everlasting Mercy*.

no other, special meetings should be held in every church every year.

(4) *Evangelism must concern itself with the collective as well as the individual life of men.* It must seek to accomplish a social as well as a personal redemption. This means specifically that the principles of Christian ethics must be recognized as binding upon groups as well as individuals, and that the divorce between morality, on the one hand, and business, industry, politics, and diplomacy on the other, shall be done away. The fact of current ethical dualism can hardly be denied. We have one standard of action for some relationships and another for others. Toward his own wife and children, a man will act generously and unselfishly as though nothing were of consequence but the great human values, never once thinking of exploiting them economically. But the same man, scarcely aware of what he does, may deliberately act according to very different principles toward other men's wives and children who work for him. These have precisely the same fundamental right to human consideration as his family—yet he regards their welfare and happiness as distinctly subordinate to his own personal profit. We have been told that religion cannot be mixed with business or politics. That only means that Christian principles of action cannot be applied to these matters. The object of social evangelism is to extend the authority of Christian ethics over all relationships, and exalt the same standard for public and social conduct as admittedly controls for private and individual action. It is primarily a problem in regeneration—to transform the spirit of our collective life until it may be said that Christ dwells in the heart of the group as well as in the heart of the individual.

It is obvious that evangelism of this kind must employ the educational method. The ideal must be taught, patiently, kindly, but consistently, throughout the whole year, by every teaching agency in the church—the pulpit, the Sunday-school class, and the brotherhood organization, etc., not to the exclusion of other important matters, but according to its proper desert.

e. Evangelism must not be set over against religious education, or social service, or scholarship in a false antithesis as though inherently antagonistic to them. Let it be said again that these are as certainly instruments for doing the work of evangelism as is the revival. The aim of all true religious education is not primarily to impart instruction but to produce the believing soul. The purpose of all true social service is to create an environment in which it will be easier to be good, an atmosphere more congenial to spirituality. The end of true scholarship is that the workman may be better furnished for his task of saving men—not that he may be excused from it.

3. THE METHODS OF EVANGELISM. Wise pastors are using three agencies simultaneously to win men to Christ.

a. The Revival. The features of the typical "revival meeting" are familiar to anyone who is identified with the work of the church.

(1) *The time* of the meetings should be adjusted to the convenience of the largest number in the congregation. In rural sections midwinter usually is opportune. In towns and cities the fall or the spring may be as suitable as the winter. Increasingly Protestant churches are taking advantage of the Lenten season for special meetings. This custom has much to commend it. Such services seldom continue more than three weeks, and often no more than two. Palm Sunday, immediately preceding Easter, is usually set apart for Decision Day exercises in the Sunday school. Easter is In-Gathering Day when members are received into the church.

(2) *The aim* of the revival meetings, as stated above, should be kept clearly in mind. They are not the only, or even the chief agency, for recruiting the membership of the church. Probably their greatest value lies in providing an opportunity for emphasizing daily for a period the deeper aspects of religious experience to the membership of the

church, as we have already seen. Any pastor will have had a very "successful meeting" if he is able to secure the attendance of a great majority of his congregation at these services and awakens in them a desire for reality in religion. To this end he is warranted in asking certain classes and organizations to attend in a body on certain nights, and using other legitimate methods to stimulate interest on the part of the people already connected with the church. *The quickest way to win the unchurched is to make the church membership dynamic.* On the other hand one certainly should use the special meetings for anything they will do in reaching persons not identified with the church. Always in the Sunday school, the Ladies' Aid Society, the Brotherhood, and other organizations, there are some who while sympathetic have never actually taken the vows of a Christian. These should be the special objects of prayerful endeavor during the meetings.

(3) *The preaching* is always an important element in special meetings. Frequently the pastor feels that he cannot do all the other things that must be done—particularly the personal work—and preach each evening in addition. It may appear that a good solution of his problem will be to employ a professional evangelist. Without reflecting upon this class of workers, one may offer a word of caution against their frequent use in the church. They are exceedingly costly. The same amount of money could be spent in other ways to greater profit. They emphasize the extraordinary and the spectacular until the church tends to forget that God may come in quieter fashion and through less novel means. Often they are champions of extravagant doctrines which create trouble for the church after the evangelist has gone. And almost never do they possess social vision. A much safer plan every way, and generally quite as helpful in the long run, is to invite a brother pastor to assist one, offering one's own service in exchange at another time. In this way the church secures as good preaching as it would get from an evangelist, and that from one who has the

pastor's point of view. The meeting may be less spectacular, but the quality of work is likely to be finer. This will release the pastor himself for that indefatigable calling and earnest personal work without which no meeting can succeed.

(4) *The music* should have careful consideration. It may be well to employ a competent person to take charge of the singing. A good chorus may be organized. The better type of gospel song is generally preferred to the church hymn for congregational use in such services.

(5) *Preparation for the meetings* is exceedingly important. Revivals have never broken out magically. Some one, consciously or unconsciously, has always made earnest and intelligent preparation for them. Cottage prayer meetings are usually helpful, provided the leadership is competent and the idea of the meetings is kept to the fore. The membership of the church should be urged to prepare personal prayer lists and undertake such personal work as they may feel impelled to do. At this time the organization for personal evangelism, to be described later, should be in perfect condition. The several societies of the church should be asked to lay aside all activities during the meetings which would prevent their members from attending the services. The object in all this is to induce a prayerful and expectant mood upon the church.

The pastor himself will find it especially helpful to read, in the weeks preceding the meetings, the biographies of great evangelists, together with descriptive volumes on the subject of the revival. These will be very suggestive as to methods and his heart will be warmed to the task. Let him be assured that he will need all the enthusiasm he can muster, for a revival calls for an enormous expenditure of energy on his part. The fire must begin in his own heart before it spreads to the congregation. They will look to him for leadership in all things. However much personal work he may prevail upon others to do, he must do more than they all. A series of special meetings, however, that succeeds in deepening the religious life of the church membership is worth the cost and remains a very precious memory.

(6) *Union Meetings.* In recent years a union meeting of all the churches in the community in some central place, frequently a temporary tabernacle erected for the purpose, has become familiar in all parts of the country. Such a meeting doubtless does some good. But experience is making the church critical of this method of evangelism. It does assemble great numbers of people for religious purposes and bring together the several denominations, cooperatively engaging in the performance of a common task. And possibly it touches an occasional person who will not go to church. But the tabernacle meeting does not cultivate the church-going habit, as Professor Hannan suggests in his excellent chapter on this subject.[2] Moreover, the work in such crowds must be impersonal and superficial to a high degree. Very frequently it appears that false names and addresses are registered on the declaration blanks; that the great majority, some say ninety per cent, of the audiences are composed of Christian people; that the statistics employed for advertising purposes are generally misleading, five hundred cards, for example, being reported as five hundred conversions, whereas four hundred of them may represent people already members of churches; that the manner in which the alleged "free-will offerings" are worked up is very disillusionizing for those on the inside of the organization. It is generally required that the cooperating churches suspend their regular activities for the period of the meeting. The resulting demoralization is too big a price to pay for the good accomplished. Better than one "Big Meeting" are meetings held simultaneously in all churches. Beyond all question the aggregate results usually are much greater. If a union meeting be desired let it be one conducted by the several pastors who take their turns at preaching, and who collectively retain authority over the service.

[2]F. Watson Hannan, *Evangelism*, p. 100f.

b. Personal Evangelism. A second method of evangelism, and an indispensable aid to successful revivalism, is personal evangelism. Moreover, it is a method whereby evangelism may be made continuous throughout the year, bringing some people into Christian fellowship each month. Many pastors who have no conspicuous success as revivalists are very successful in the more quiet and sustained work of personal evangelism.

The name is highly fitting. Religion in the Christian sense is the establishment and deepening of fellowship between two persons—a man and God. Personal evangelism ideally means one person introducing another person to the Infinite Person. And that can be done every week in the year, not only in the service of public worship but any place two people can meet for quiet conference.

(1) *This is preeminently the work of the pastor himself.* With the same steady purpose that characterizes a life insurance agent in following up his prospects the minister should keep in mind particular individuals whom he covets for Jesus Christ. Of course it is understood that his work will be intelligent. He will not "nag" them—only keep his purpose steadily before him and be ready with suggestion when the opportunity shall open for conversation on religious subjects. On the other hand, he should not be too fearful of being tactless. Better a blundering attempt at personal evangelism than no attempt at all. The sincerity of purpose which shines through the awkward movement may redeem it and make it the power of God unto salvation.

(2) *But the pastor alone cannot do all that should be done. He should associate with himself in this work a group of persons in his church* with whom he counsels frequently, providing them with names and addresses of men and women upon whom they are to call, and asking them to report the results of their visits. These personal workers should be selected with considerable care, for unhappily some who would most quickly volunteer for this service are least effective. It is unwise to give great publicity to the

existence of this group of helpers. Their work may be more vital if unofficial. They should be especially active preceding and during special meetings, but their work should continue after the meetings have ended.

(3) *The "Constituency Roll" is the list of prospective members and believers in whom the "Personal Workers" are interested.* The list is usually made up about as follows: (a) Contributors who are not members of the church; (b) husbands of wives who are members; (c) wives of husbands who are members; (d) members of the Sunday school and other organizations who are not members of the church; (e) attendants who are not members; (f) new people who may be members of our church elsewhere; (g) most of the people living in the community who do not belong to the membership or constituency of some other church.

c. Educational Evangelism. In its true sense, educational evangelism, the third method generally accredited in doing the work of evangelism, would include the whole task of religious education. In this place, however, the meaning is deliberately restricted to the days of crisis in the educational work of the church when something like the revival method and atmosphere prevail, supplemented by special instruction in preparation for church membership. We mean here what others mean by Sunday-school evangelism. The purpose is to supplement the work of teaching by giving the pupils in the Sunday school an opportunity to announce publicly their purpose to follow Christ. Sunday-school evangelism in this sense merely reaps the fruit of months and years of sowing and cultivating through the regular educational agencies of the church. The administrative problem involves thorough planning for such special meetings—usually called Decision-Day services—as may be useful, and the organization of training classes later in preparation for church membership.

(1) *Decision Days.* At least two such days should have a place in the calendar of the Sunday-school year—one in the

autumn, before Thanksgiving, and another in the spring, before Easter. They should never be held suddenly or with inadequate preparation. The pastor and Sunday-school superintendent should take the whole force of teachers and officers into their confidence several weeks previous to each service, for the success of the enterprise turns more upon the cooperation of the teachers than upon any other single factor. Each teacher of a class above the Junior Division should concentrate upon the matter of winning every pupil for Christ and visit them personally to that end.

On the day of the service, and on the Sabbath preceding, the pastor should meet the whole Sunday-School Board for prayer and conference that no detail shall be overlooked. When the hour has arrived the teachers and officers should be in their places promptly, that there be no needless delay in marking rolls and receiving the offerings. Special music may be helpful preceding the address—likewise a good congregational hymn designed to induce the mood of worship. The address as a rule should not be more than fifteen or twenty minutes in length, and should conclude with an invitation to the pupils to make public their confessions of discipleship. Some pastors provide teachers with "Declaration Cards" which are distributed to their respective classes at this point, the declaration frequently being double, expressing (1) a desire to be known as a Christian, and (2) a wish to unite with the church. Others prefer to ask those who will do so to confess their newly formed purposes by coming to the platform to join them in a session of prayer, the names and addresses being taken at the close of the service by the teachers. The latter method has a touch of reality which the former seems to lack.

The foregoing method is advisable in dealing with pupils in the Intermediate, Senior, and Adult Departments, collectively or by departments and classes. Something less formal and less intense is desirable for pupils in the Junior Department (nine to eleven years). A better plan here is for the pastor, on the Sabbath preceding Decision Day, to announce simply, but earnestly, that on the following Sunday he wishes to organize the children into classes preparatory to church membership, and urge each child who may wish to join the church to secure the consent of his parents to do so. There should be an understanding with the teachers of the department that they shall visit the parents during the week to explain clearly what is contemplated and ask their cooperation. For nothing is gained by opposing the parents in a matter of this kind. On Decision Day a brief service of prayer and consecration with this department to itself will suffice, in which the children who will join the preparatory classes make that fact known. The important problem will be found later in conducting the training classes in such fashion that the children come to reality in prayer and worship.

(2) *Training Classes.* No person should be received into full membership in the church who has not been personally instructed in the meaning of religion and church membership, whether young or old, whether won by the revival method or by personal work. In the work of such classes regard must be had for the principle of graded instruction. It will seldom be possible to organize all probationers into a single class because of the great difference in ages. Moreover, it is desirable from an educational point of view to keep these classes small. Thus the instruction may be adapted to the several types of understanding and made personal.

It cannot be emphasized too strongly that responsibility for this instruction rests squarely upon the pastor, whoever he may be, however large his congregation, and whatever other obligations he may feel. *Nothing takes precedence in importance over this work.* Any energetic minister can, and should, teach two classes besides his work of preaching and shepherding. They should be *"The Teacher Training Class"* and *"The Probationers' Class."* Thus he can determine the type of instruction in his Sunday school and the beliefs of those coming into church membership. In the event that it seems best to organize several groups to meet simultaneously, he must call to his help intelligent men and women—his paid assistants, if there are such, otherwise volunteer workers. These classes should meet regularly throughout a period of several weeks, or even months.

The constant aim of the teachers should be to bring candidates for church membership to the point of reality in Christian experience, interpret effectively the fundamental beliefs of Christianity, and explain the history and polity of the Methodist Episcopal Church. The materials for such instruction may be gathered from the Bible, church history, the more popular statements of Christian doctrine, the literature of missions and social service, and the *Discipline*. Several "Manuals" are available, but the teacher must work over for himself all the material he handles so that he may present it in his own way.

Besides instruction, there should be expression on the part of the several members of the class—*training in activity*. This should consist in acts of devotion, teaching them to worship aloud through prayer and testimony. The value of attendance upon public worship should be inculcated. Suggestion should be made as to different ways in which service of a practical and humanitarian sort may be rendered to the church and the community. But above all else it should be made clear that an ethical life at home, on the playground, and in business is the greatest service which the Christian can render. Thus "church work" becomes identified with daily living.

4. A Comprehensive Program of Evangelism. The unified program of evangelism which the committee will report to the official board for the church year might look somewhat as follows:

1. October
   - *a.* Revision of Constituency Roll and organization of Personal Workers' Groups.
   - *b.* Special evangelistic meetings of the Epworth League.

2. November
   - *a.* Decision Day in the Sunday school.
   - *b.* Organization of Probationers' Classes.
3. December
   - *a.* Take advantage of Christmas season to create evangelistic atmosphere at some of the regular services.
   - *b.* Watch Night Service.
4. January

   Week of Prayer for the church in all phases of its work.
5. February
   - *a.* Utilize some of the regular services for evangelistic purposes.
   - *b.* Plan for special Pre-Easter services, arranging for cottage prayer-meetings, etc.
6. March-April
   - *a.* Pre-Easter meetings.
   - *b.* Palm Sunday—Decision Day in Sunday school.
   - *c.* Easter
     - (1) Reception of Probationers into full membership.
     - (2) Reception of new group of probationers.
7. May-June

   Organization of new Probationers' Classes.
8. The first Sunday of each month to be a special day for the reception of new members by transfer and on probation. This will give an objective which the Personal Workers group can keep in mind.

Books Recommended for Further Study

Charles L. Goodell, *Pastoral and Personal Evangelism, Pastor and Evangelist, Heralds of a Passion.*

F. Watson Hannan, *Evangelism.*

Edwin H. Hughes, *Letters on Evangelism.*

L. M. Edwards, *Every Church Its Own Evangelist.*

Washington Gladden, *The Christian Pastor,* Chapter XVII.

Henry C. Mabie, *Method in Soul-Winning.*
Harold Begbie, *Twice Born Men.*
H. W. Beecher, *Yale Lectures,* Second Series, Chapters VIII-XI.
Frederick L. Fagley, *Parish Evangelism.*
William S. Mitchell, *Elements of Personal Christianity.*
Fred B. Fisher, *The Way to Win.*
H. C. Trumbull, *Individual Work for Individuals.*
John T. Stone, *Recruiting for Christ.*
W E. Biederwolf, *Evangelism.*
Bertha Condé, *Human Element in the Making of a Christian.*
J. H. Jowett, *The Passion for Souls.*
Frederick D. Leete, *Every Day Evangelism.*
C. G. Trumbull, *Taking Men Alive.*
John T. Faris, *The Book of Personal Work.*
Charles E. McKinley, *Educational Evangelism.*
W. H. Burgwin, *Practical Evangelism.*
A. W. Leonard, *Evangelism in the Remaking of the World.*

CHAPTER XV

THE ADMINISTRATION OF RELIGIOUS EDUCATION

WHOLE alcoves have been added to the libraries of our colleges and theological schools in the past dozen years on the subject of religious education. This literary productivity indicates that there is no subject in which the church is more interested. The pastor should make himself familiar with this new body of literature. Some of it is included in the Conference Courses of Study. In addition, the books listed at the end of this chapter should be read and kept near at hand for ready reference, and to loan, perchance, to Sunday-school workers. Only a few pages may be devoted to the subject in this volume where the outlook is upon the whole task of the church rather than upon a single phase of its work. We shall attempt nothing more than to note briefly the chief factors in the administrative problem, leaving the questions of practice and method for special study.

1. THE COMMITTEE ON RELIGIOUS EDUCATION. This committee should be composed of from three to seven of the leading men and women in the church interested in educational matters. It should act as the school board of the church. The present Committee on Religious Instruction might be competent for this task if its powers were enlarged so that it would sustain a more general relation to all the organizations of the church. In a general way the duties of the Committee on Religious Education would be to study the educational problems of the local church and community, to exercise supervision over all the educational work of the church with a view of avoiding duplication and waste, and to make such recommendations to the official

board as would improve the quality of religious teaching in the church.

2. The Administrative Problem. The more important elements of the problem of administration are as follows:

a. Institutions. Several institutions besides the church are engaged in the religious education of the child, namely, (1) the home, (2) the public school, and (3) the community. The church should understand the contribution of each to the common task and seek the intelligent cooperation of all.

Among these the home is supreme by virtue of the longer period in which the child is in its care, the greater intimacy of its contacts, the informality and spontaneity of its instruction, and the democracy of family life. The modern home is breaking down, however, as an institution of religious education. The endeavor on the part of the church in this connection should be to encourage family worship by urging the erection of "family altars" and calling attention to some of the valuable manuals of prayer which will be helpful to those who find prayer difficult. Moreover, the home should be continually informed by church visitors of the work which the church is doing with the children, and its sympathetic cooperation asked for.

The public school, while not officially responsible for teaching religion, nevertheless is related in a definite manner to the problem. It is interested in *moral education* indirectly, at least, through the personal contacts of teachers and pupils, and this is an important phase of religious education. In several States, notably North Dakota and Colorado, academic credit is given in the public schools for courses of instruction offered in churches which meet the standards imposed upon the public school itself. In Gary, Indiana, this cooperation has been carried much further. The children in the public school may be excused two hours each week, at the request of parents, to receive religious instruction in their respective churches on school time. Thus the church and state cooperate in their common task without trespassing on each other's special field.

Not least significant is the general atmosphere that pervades the community as a whole. The church and the home and the public school may work in perfect harmony but to little purpose if community ideals of recreation, business, education, and politics are low. On the contrary, if these ideals are high, the church and home and public school will have in the community a friendly ally in their work.

Finally, the church must not deceive itself concerning the defects which mar its own educational activities. While the public school requires the presence of the child several hours each day under trained instructors who are provided with adequate material equipment to teach arithmetic, spelling, geography, etc., the church has been trying to teach religion through untrained teachers who have the child one hour each week and who work with inferior equipment. Small wonder that we have a generation of untaught and confused Christians in our churches who can give no good reason for the faith that is in them!

b. Aim. At the present time there appears to be much uncertainty about the true aim of the church in its educational task. "To teach the Bible," some say. "To create socially efficient persons—that is, persons who have learned how to live with other people to their mutual profit," say others. "To increase the membership and benevolences of the church," yet others suggest, by their action if not by their words. It may be that any one of these aims, properly interpreted, would be sufficiently comprehensive. As ordinarily stated, however, each leaves much to be desired. Religion is essentially an attitude toward God—a fellowship with the Infinite, and to teach religion effectively cannot mean less than to induce men to take this attitude, establish this fellowship. Instruction in Bible and doctrine is given, but only as a means to an end. That end is to produce, we insist again, the believing soul—to lead the student to make the great adventure of faith and lay hold of God at first hand for himself.

But religion tends to organize for itself certain institutional forms which are necessary to the propagation of religion. The church is one of these. Religious education, then, must concern itself with training for the work of the church as well as with the development of the religious life. The following definition includes both objects: "The functions of the church school are, (*a*) to develop intelligent and efficient Christian lives consecrated to the extension of God's Kingdom on earth, and (*b*) to train efficient leaders for all phases of church work."[1] This end must ever be kept in view by all who are charged with administrative responsibility for religious education, for the purpose of the organization will determine necessarily its form and program.

c. Program. The aim of religious education being what it is, the program of the church school must provide for (1) worship, (2) instruction, and (3) service, for true education addresses itself to the total personality. Of course it is impossible to isolate one phase of personality from all others, but, in general, it may be said that worship is designed primarily to cultivate the religious emotions; instruction, to inform the mind with religious knowledge; and service, to enlist the will so that religious action may become habitual. To plan intelligently the details of this triple program and to distribute them properly among the several agencies of the church, constitute the heart of the administrative problem of the pastor and the Committee on Religious Education.

The volumes recommended at the conclusion of this chapter contain valuable suggestions touching this matter.

d. Grading. In the Sunday school we are dealing with persons in every stage of growth. The graded character of the student body requires that the school shall be graded

---

[1]W. S. Athearn, *The Church School*, p. 1.

as to (1) organization, (2) worship, (3) instruction, and (4) activities. Some little respect has always been paid to this principle. No school puts babies into the older people's classes. Until recently, however, it would have been difficult to make an affirmation more specific, for personal preferences of the pupils and personal attachments between pupils and teachers had more to do with determining classes than any other consideration.[2]

(1) *Grading the organization* means the grouping of the pupils into classes, and classes into departments on the basis of age and development, and providing for the promotion from lower to higher levels.

(2) *Grading the instruction* has to do with both the matter and method of teaching. It implies that lesson materials should be selected with the thought of their adaptability to particular groups in mind, and not with a view of presenting in all classes the same subject at the same time. Grading the method implies the same truth as to the manner of presenting the lesson material.

(3) *Grading the worship* assumes that no one order of worship is adapted to all ages any more than one type of lesson material. So far as possible the worship of the Sunday school should be by departments. The "general assembly" may have value for special days, but is not good for regular occasions.

(4) *Grading the activities* is as important as grading the instruction, for these two are one flesh. Activities are necessary that the pupil may learn the truth by *doing* it as well as by hearing. By this means the pupil is led to *express* as well as receive knowledge by *impression* from the teacher. But children do not express themselves as adults. For a comprehensive treatment of "the graded school," every pastor should read the books recommended at the close of this chapter.

e. Officers and Teachers. The problem of the admin-

---

[2]Burton and Mathews, *Principles and Ideals for the Sunday School,* p. 123.

istrator is well-nigh solved when he has selected and trained competent associates to assist him, and distributed responsibility intelligently among them. In the Methodist Episcopal Church the selection of leaders for the church school unmistakably devolves upon the pastor. No teacher can be nominated to the Sunday School Board without his concurrence, and it would be difficult to secure the confirmation of a superintendent by the Quarterly Conference in the face of his opposition. The most frequent lament heard among pastors deals with the dearth of lay leaders or their unwillingness to serve. But the work must be done with the human material that is available. The only solution of this problem is for the pastor to take his teaching office seriously. If he ministers to a large church, he may secure an expert to whom he can turn over all responsibility for the educational work of the church, called usually a director of religious education. But not one church in fifty is prepared to employ such a teaching pastor in addition to the preaching minister. *The only alternative is for the one pastor to give himself to the task of training officers and teachers for the church school.* A few teachers may be induced to take a Correspondence Training Course under the Board of Sunday Schools at Chicago. In many larger towns and cities Community Night Schools of Religious Education are doing excellent work in training Sunday-school workers. But only a few leaders in each school are thus reached. Such agencies do not take the place of training classes in the local church. *The development of these classes should be the pastor's chief concern.* It may be pleasanter to teach the Brotherhood Class, or lead the Boy Scouts, but his general relation to the school as a whole forbids his pouring himself out exclusively over a few when all need his guidance. The way he may most directly minister to all is to fill his subordinate leaders with his ideals and spirit, who, in turn, will pass them on to others. *Every pastor can and should teach two classes, as mentioned previously*—(*1*) *the Teacher Training Class and (2) the Probationers' Class. In this way he can determine in a very few years what a whole church shall believe.*

The first step in the development of a competent staff of workers is to invite those who are already teaching in the school, but have had no training for their work, together with a selected number of young people who seem to be potential teachers, to join such a training class. Arrange an hour for meeting that will be convenient to the greatest number. Speak of the ideals you hold and the opportunity for the investment of life that is afforded the conscientious Sunday-school teacher. Then outline the course of study covering two or three years, having consulted the Teacher Training Department of the Board of Sunday Schools previously as to methods and materials. The course of study should include at least four fundamental subjects:

(1) *The pupil, his nature and development at different ages, and the way his mind works.*

(2) *The materials of study, such as the Bible, church history, Christian missions, etc.*

(3) *Principles and methods of teaching.*

(4) *Organization and administration of the school.*[3]

If the pastor can secure others more competent than himself to take charge of this class, well and good. If not, then he should not shirk the responsibility. If he is not ready, he must get ready by reading and study.

f. Finance. The administrative problem includes the element of finance. At the present time the Sunday school is a very profitable "side line" for the church. It not only pays all its own expenses but, in addition, it makes generous contributions to the benevolent work of the church—all of this without being a charge against the general budget of the church. Would it not be more ideal, however, if the church included the expenses of the Sunday school in its

---

[3]See *Organization and Administration of the Sunday School,* Cuninggim and North, p. 47.

regular budget, and then asked the Sunday school to make a contribution toward the expenses of the church? *Is not the educational work of the church as deserving of support by the whole church as the work of the choir and the work of the minister?*

In formulating a financial policy for the Sunday school, it must be remembered that *giving* should have educational value. It is an *expressional* activity, supplementing instruction by requiring the pupil to *act* upon the truth as well as hear it. Giving that is truly educational is, first of all, (1) *intelligent.* It is prompted by a rational appeal in which exact information is presented, and never based primarily on thoughtless impulse. If the pupils can be induced to ask questions or discuss the proposed object of benevolence, so much the better. (2) Again, this giving must be *real.* That is, it should be something that is of value and belongs to the child himself—not something for which he cares little or which he has received for the asking from another. (3) Moreover, this giving should be *unselfish.* Much so-called charity is actuated by motives that are un-Christian. Even in the church the appeal to denominational pride and ambition crowds aside the unselfish appeal to give without hope of personal or denominational reward. (4) And, finally, this giving should be *systematic and regular.* Only so will the church have adequate funds to carry on her work without embarrassment.

Many schools divide the total offering into three parts. The first is contributed toward the local expenses of the church; the second is set apart for missions and other stated benevolences; while the third is kept as a fund from which special appropriations are made, from time to time, in support generally of local community institutions. This fund should be safeguarded by a committee whose recommendation shall be necessary before any appropriation can be authorized.

g. Pupils. Another important factor in the administrative problem of the church school has to do with securing and holding a student body. Ideally every member of every family should be enrolled and active in some department of the school. This ideal is difficult to attain, nor can it be even approximated except by the most diligent application.

(1) The first duty is to hold what we already have. This can be done only by making the school a *good* school. For this it is not necessary that it be large, but only that its teaching be worthy. "Many a school that is blaming the people for their lack of spirituality needs to lay the blame for its empty benches on its own sloth and lack of ability." It is altogether possible for a Sunday school to deserve no pupils.

(2) But not all the students can be retained. Death and removal, if no other influences, will continually deplete the enrollment. Moreover, the community is always growing by birth and by the coming of new people from other communities. The obligation to serve these strangers as well as the need to replace the natural losses makes it imperative that new pupils shall be recruited intelligently and systematically. The following methods are generally approved:

(a) Let the school understand just what its field may be. A map of this field should hang in the room where teachers' meetings are held.

(b) A careful census should be taken of this area at least once a year, noting the names, ages, sex, and Sunday-school affiliations of all who live here.

(c) After the names of all prospective pupils as revealed by the census have been tabulated or catalogued, a persistent effort should be made to secure their enrollment in the school. Let personal invitations be given by parish visitors, teachers, pupils, and members of the church who live in the vicinity. Let these names be put upon a mailing list of persons who receive regularly bulletins from the church and school. Do not be satisfied with a single invitation. Secure the names of all children under three for the Cradle Roll. Do not be betrayed, however, into the folly of conducting a "color contest," dividing the school into rival camps of "reds" and "blues," each endeavoring to secure the larger number of students. The last state of a school which adopts this method of increasing its enrollment is nearly always worse than the first.

(d) A wholesome school spirit should be cultivated. This can be done by making the work of the school so much worth while that students cannot but be proud of it.

h. Plan of Organization. The Sunday-school administrator must ever be working over his plan of organization. The school includes persons of all ages and both sexes, sometimes in larger and sometimes in smaller numbers. And the plan of organization will vary according to these several factors. A little school of ten or twelve would probably have two classes and two teachers, the teachers acting as officers. A school of fifty, according to Fergusson, would organize five classes, under five teachers and two officers, a superintendent and a secretary; a primary, junior, intermediate, senior, and adult class. Each of the classes would expand into a department corresponding to its name as the enrollment increases to one hundred, five hundred, or a thousand, with such additional classes, teachers, and officers as the larger enrollment may require.

The departmental organization generally approved for the larger school is as follows:

(1) A General Superintendent, together with an additional superintendent for each department.

(2) A General Secretary, together with an additional secretary for each department.

(3) A Treasurer, with such assistants as may be needed.

(4) Teachers and classes grouped by departments—

- (*a*) Beginners'—3 to 5 years inclusive.
- (*b*) Primary—6 to 8 years inclusive.
- (*c*) Junior—9 to 11 years inclusive.
- (*d*) Intermediate—12 to 14 years inclusive.
- (*e*) Senior—15 to 17 years inclusive.

(*f*) Young People's—18 to 23 years inclusive.
(*g*) Adult—over 23 years.
(*h*) Extension Department with Superintendent and Visitors.
(*i*) Cradle Roll and Home Department.

(5) Organists, choristers, and ushers as may be needed for the general and departmental assemblies.

(6) In many classes in the Senior, Young People's, and Adult Departments, the stability of the group has been increased by class organizations with officers and committees. Such organizations provide new opportunities of service, and promote "class spirit."

(*i*) *Cooperation.* The Sunday-school administrator must continually strive for cooperation on the part of all engaged in the educational task.

(1) This has to do with the relation of his school to other Sunday schools in the community. It has been charged that while the public school is a unifying force, the Sunday school is a divisive force, setting group against group in mutual hostility. This need not be. It is entirely possible for the several schools in a community to regard themselves as fellow workers on the common task of religious education, so dividing the work and the field that no one shall be overlooked and the rights of all shall be respected.

(2) Moreover, it has to do with the public school. There should be no censure of the State school as godless. The same standards of grading should be followed as far as possible in the two schools. And the child should not find his teacher on Sunday denying the things that were taught him in the public school during the week.

(3) Again this concerns the spirit of his own organization. Every officer and teacher, every department and class should have the same attitude and share in the common enthusiasm. This state of affairs can never obtain if an individual or a small group makes out the program and demands that the majority shall give unquestioning obedience. School spirit and loyalty come only from full and

frequent discussion, in the most democratic way, on the part of the officers, teachers, and pupils, so that whatever decisions may be reached or plans made appear to be the outcome of the collective thought of the whole group.

(4) Finally, an effort should be made to correlate into a unified program all the educational work that is done by the several organizations in the local church. This does not imply that all study classes shall meet at the same hour, or that no organization shall conduct classes except the Sunday school. It only means that an intelligent effort shall be made to avoid duplication of classes and subjects. It is hard to see why the Epworth League should conduct Bible classes in addition to those conducted by the Sunday school. It is confusing to have several small mission study classes when one good class would be better every way. Moreover, unity, as it applies to the curriculum, requires that no important subject shall be overlooked as well as that there shall be no waste through duplication.

j. Building and Equipment. The careful administrator will realize that good educational work cannot be done without proper physical equipment and a building adapted to school work. The ideal thing would be to have a house constructed especially for the Sunday school, providing separate rooms for all departments and for most of the classes, and completely furnished with the necessary tools for teaching. A few churches approximate this ideal closely. Most of them fall far short of it, and it will be an important part of the administrator's work to secure better housing and equipment for his school.

The least he can plan on as to housing will be separate rooms for the Beginners', Primary, and Junior Departments respectively. If necessary, the Intermediate, Senior, Young People's and Adult Departments may meet together for worship, but separate classrooms should be provided as far as possible for the several classes. The Board of Sunday Schools of the Methodist Episcopal Church maintains a bureau of architecture and will gladly submit plans and suggestions to any pastor or superintendent contemplating a new building or remodeling an old one.

Good equipment can be secured by any school that really desires it. This means, first, that the rooms shall be airy and clean. A few good pictures can be hung upon the walls. Small chairs and tables can be provided for the younger children, maps and blackboards for such teachers as will use them, musical instruments and good song books as may be necessary to lead in song, and materials for manual work, such as sand-tables, clay, crayons, blocks, drawing materials, etc.

k. Records. Finally, the importance of careful accounting of personnel and funds will not be overlooked by the careful administrator. Careful records of all receipts and disbursements must be kept by the treasurer, and his accounts regularly audited. And the secretary must work out such a system of records as will account definitely for everyone who comes in the school and for every absentee. The Methodist Book Concern will gladly provide a full system of records at little cost, and the Board of Sunday Schools will be pleased to advise all persons interested in improving Sunday-school accounting.

Books Recommended for Further Study

John E. Stout, *Organization and Administration of Religious Education.*

W. S. Athearn, *The Church School.*

Burton and Mathews, *Principles and Ideals for the Sunday School.*

H. F. Cope, *Efficiency in the Sunday School; Religious Education in the Family; The Week-day Church School; School in the Modern Church; The Modern Sunday School in Principle and Practice.*

E. M. Fergusson, *How to Run a Little Sunday School; Church School Administration.*

Howard J. Gee, *Methods of Church School Administration.*

Hugh Hartshorne, *Worship in the Sunday School.*

W. N. Hutchins, *Graded Social Service for the Sunday School.*

Marion Lawrance, *How to Conduct a Sunday School.*

Franklin McElfresh, *Training of Sunday School Teachers and Officers.*

H. H. Meyer, *The Graded School in Principle and Practice.*

Margaret Slattery, *Talks With the Training Class.*

George H. Betts, *The New Program of Religious Education.*

George A. Coe, *Education in Religion and Morals; Social Theory of Religious Education.*

A. A. Lamoreaux, *The Unfolding Life.*

Albert H. Gage, *How to Conduct a Church Vacation School.*

Charles W. Brewbaker, *Sunday School Management.*

Herbert F. Evans, *The Sunday School Building and Its Equipment.*

Dan B. Brummitt, *The Efficient Epworthian.*

CHAPTER XVI

THE ADMINISTRATION OF SERVICE

The Church Family

All true worship, evangelism, and religious education create the spirit of service. Those charged with administering the church as an organization should plan intelligently for the wise expression of this spirit. Generally speaking, these activities will be directed toward a threefold object:

The Church Family.
The Local Community.
The World Community.

It will be impossible in practice always to distinguish sharply between these several types of service. Each will shade imperceptibly into the other. The distinctions, however, serve a purpose if they help us to clear thinking about the whole task of the church.

1. The Standing Committee on Service probably should be larger than the other great committees, for its field is so broad that it may be necessary to distribute its work among several subcommittees. It should be composed of representatives of all the major organizations in the church which seek to minister to human welfare in some vital and consistent manner. These usually are the official board, the Sunday school, the Ladies' Aid Society, the Epworth League, and the local auxiliaries of the Women's Missionary Societies.

A physician, a deaconess (if one is employed by the church), at least one philanthropically disposed person who is informed about the principles and methods of modern charity, and an educator should be additional members of the committee.

The function of the committee is to unify the various programs of service which are outlined by the several organizations within the church so that waste may be avoided, on the one hand, and no worthy object be overlooked, on the other; to nourish the spirit of service by making it intelligent and comprehensive; to assist in providing such equipment as may be needed if service is to be efficient; and to develop such a system of records as will tell quickly and accurately the story of service rendered by the church.

The division of labor within the committee would naturally be determined by the several objects of service, and permanent subcommittees might be appointed on (1) Local Church Relief, (2) Community Service, and (3) Missions. The work of this standing committee is necessarily related intimately to that of every other committee, and joint meetings should be held as frequently as necessary in the interest of perfect cooperation.

2. SERVICE IN THE LOCAL CHURCH. This service embraces every activity that is designed to maintain the local organization in good working condition, and to promote Christian fellowship among the members of the church as distinguished from non-church members in the community. This is not its only duty, but certainly the church is under an obligation to care for its own in every possible way.

a. One thinks first of the duty toward *dependent members* of the church. These would include the unemployed, the sick, the aged, and all who are infirm for any cause. The obligation here requires that provision shall be made for their systematic care, and for the comfort that is afforded by friendly interest and personal visitation. It is disgraceful for the church to permit one of its members to become a charge upon public charity. If the resources of the local organization are not adequate to meet the situation, then the matter should be laid before the district superintendent with a view of securing help from other churches of the denomination. Of course the aid given should never pauperize the beneficiary. The social workers on the committee should formulate a plan for the rehabilitation of the sufferer, if that is possible; otherwise for his regular support. And whatever is done should be done intelligently and in the spirit of Christian love. Quite probably an important part of the task will be to control the interest of several church organizations so that the object of their regard shall not suffer from too much attention at one time and too little at another.

b. The next great opportunity for service to the church family is found in the need of all, old and young alike, for recreation and amusement. In most of the Christian centuries play has been looked upon by the church "as a more or less permissible sin rather than a natural, right, and beautiful expression of the human spirit." The last thirty years, however, have witnessed a change that is very like a "renaissance." Teachers have come to regard play as the chief instrument of physical, mental, and moral growth for the young. There is larger appreciation too of its value for adults in its power to renew the jaded spirit. Indeed, the "amusement problem" within the church is only a part of the larger problem of community play to which the church sustains a definite relation, and of which we shall speak later. That problem is positive rather than negative in character. It does not mean primarily standing guard over young people to see that they refrain from certain amusements forbidden by the church. *It is, rather, the much more difficult task of providing all people in the church and community with such opportunities for play as are indispensable to a full, rich life.*

No simple and final answer can be made to the question, "What shall be the social and recreational activities of the church?" That will depend upon (1) the provision that the community as a whole makes for play; (2) the type of community in which the church is located; and (3) the financial ability of the church. For example, if the community supports a well-equipped Y. M. C. A. with competent directors of social work and physical education, it is not necessary for the church in that place to duplicate this equipment. Or where the community supports regular exhibitions of moving pictures, it is not quite clear that the church should render a similar service, even for its own people. The wiser plan is to cooperate with each agency that is doing well some special work, giving it financial and moral support in return for the service which it is willing to render the church. On the other hand, if the community is not providing for the play life of its citizens, and cannot be induced to do so, the church, up to the measure of its ability, is obligated to engage in this special form of service. Again, a church located in an industrial community may be expected to supply a special ministry that is not required of a church in a rural village or in a suburban town. Or, again, it would be folly for a church composed chiefly of wage-earners to attempt the achievements of a church of wealthier people.

Certain ideals should control the church in serving the need of its own family for wholesome recreation. First, it is not often imperative that the equipment be elaborate. The organized Sunday-school class, the Boy Scout Troop, the Camp Fire Girls' Patrol and other such organizations are well designed to meet the requirements of the "gang spirit" of youth without spending large sums of money. After a comfortable place for regular meetings has been provided, the resourcefulness of active young people will usually supply whatever more may be needed. Generally, the pastor and his wife will do much better to train others to lead such groups than to undertake that work themselves. This is especially true in the Methodist Church, where the pastor is subject to sudden and frequent removals. Among the simpler forms of amusement within the reach of any church the following may be mentioned:

(1) Athletic teams for boys and girls—baseball, basketball, tennis, etc.

(2) Social activities of organized classes.

(3) Camping trips, hikes, outings, etc.

(4) Boy Scouts.
(5) Camp Fire Girls.
(6) Reading Circles.
(7) Amateur dramatics, pageants, etc.
(8) Socials, entertainments, lectures, dinners, etc.

The second ideal that should be controlling for the church in this matter is respect for the educational value of play. Certain institutions may be warranted in thinking of amusement as an end in itself. This cannot be true of the church. It recognizes the play instinct as of divine origin, but an instinct which makes for growth. Any attempt to satisfy this instinct should be intelligently designed to promote moral and spiritual development. An illustration of the wrong use of play by the church may appear in athletics. A baseball team in the Sunday school might seem desirable because it would advertise the school. To do this well the team must be a "winning team." To create such a team the school authorities are tempted to blink at questionable practices; for example, make it worth while for good ball players to come to Sunday school to play ball rather than to receive education in religion and morals. All the trouble starts from the wrong use of play. If an athletic team is organized in a Sunday school, it should be because such an agency is desirable educationally. Baseball easily lends itself to religious and moral training if the end be honest, sportsmanlike fun rather than to win a game at any cost. Otherwise, it may educate in the wrong direction. To select the team out of the regular members of the Sunday school, who come winter and summer; to teach them to play the best game possible, but always an honest game; to train them to despise evasions, insincerity, ungentlemanliness, and to learn such self-control that they are "good losers"—this is to utilize play for educational purposes.

(3) A third principle is implied by the second. To have educational value, all play must be supervised. This does not mean that some one must prescribe in detail all that young people may do. It does mean that a wise senior shall

be at hand to guide and direct the play activities so that only good may come of them. This is of especial concern to those who may be planning better equipment for play, such as a gymnasium, without thought of employing a competent person to superintend it. Let nothing—not even a Sunday-school picnic—be planned in the way of recreation unless it is properly supervised. The young of the race must play, but they cannot play by themselves without danger to themselves.

c. A third specific service which the church must render to its own membership is to train them in and for Christian work. Obviously, much of this training is accomplished through worship and instruction. But these must be supplemented by activities designed to serve a threefold function, namely, (1) to express and deepen the faith of the believer; (2) to make the organized church an effective instrument for redeeming life; (3) and to support every agency in the community which helps to make the world a decent place in which to live.

Ideally, every member of the church should be responsible for doing a worthy and specific task that will call forth constantly his best efforts. It is a commonplace, however, that the work of most churches is done by "a faithful few," and that pastors find it difficult to increase their volunteer staff because of the reluctance of church members to enlist for active service. By giving the matter careful consideration, nevertheless, some have been able to approximate the ideal of "a task for everyone." They have exalted in pulpit and private conversation the dignity of church work. They have classified the things that were to be done about the church in an *Opportunity Book,*[1] and asked each member to place a check opposite the service in which he was most interested. And they have refused to limit Christian service to "church work." It includes, they insist, a helpful social ministry through community organizations,

[1]Send ten cents for the one prepared by the Fourth Presbyterian Church, Chicago.

and the application of Christian principles in the daily routine of life, as well as doing specific tasks assigned by the church. It will never be possible to put everyone at work in the narrower sense. Many members are children; others are housewives and mothers who do their own work and cannot assume responsibilities outside their families; still others find that the demands of everyday work interfere with "church work." But it is quite possible that the proportion of active workers is much larger than is generally supposed if the broader view of Christian service be taken into account. The "Unit System" of the Methodist Episcopal Church, by which each member of the church is assigned to a group called a "Unit" in charge of a "Unit leader," is a device for putting everyone at work.

In the average church some such list of tasks and needed workers as the following may be made:

(1) *Evangelistic*

- Mission workers.
- Personal workers.
- Singers in the choir, etc.

(2) *Educational*

- Sunday-school teachers and workers.
- Leaders for boys' and girls' clubs.
- Officers and committees of organized classes.
- Leaders of mission study classes.

(3) *Church Organizations*

- Visitors, canvassers, ushers, etc.
- Officers and committeemen.
- Clerks to assist in keeping records, etc.

(4) *Social*

- Friendly visiting for local charity organizations.
- Social settlement workers.
- Leading local corn, pig, potato, and other community clubs.
- Representing the church in law-enforcement organizations.
- Assisting the unemployed, etc.

Conducting farmers' institutes and fairs.
Holiday celebrations.
Hospital supplies.

Some of these workers may be enlisted by a public appeal for volunteers. For the important tasks, however, the principle of the "selective draft" must be employed if the best workers are to be secured.

In training these workers, the wise pastor will utilize the best literature that has been published and, when possible, hold local training conferences. Moreover, he will send each year as large a group as possible to the nearest summer institutes conducted by the Board of Sunday Schools, the Epworth League, or other church organizations. The local church can well afford to pay the expenses, in part, or wholly, of all such delegates.

Books Recommended for Further Study

E. T. Devine, *Misery and Its Causes; Principles of Relief; The Practice of Charity.*

R. C. Cabot, *What Men Live By,* Part II.

J. V. Thompson, *Handbook for Workers with Young People.*

H. F. Cope, *Principles of Christian Service.*

Dan B. Brummitt, *The Efficient Epworthian.*

Christian F. Reisner, *Social Plans for Young People.*

Jessie H. Bancroft, *Games for Play Ground, Home, School and Gymnasium.*

Luella A. Palmer, *Play in the First Eight Years.*

Mary E. Blain, *Games For All Occasions.*

Leader's Manual for Boy Scouts Movement.

Allan Hoben, *The Minister and the Boy.*

CHAPTER XVII

THE ADMINISTRATION OF SERVICE

The Local Community

The church is obligated, however, to render a wider service than to its own membership. It belongs to the community and must participate in all that concerns the community.

1. Definitions. It may be well to begin this section with a few definitions.

a. "What is a community?" The authorities are generally agreed that a community consists of a group of people, living in a single locality and having common interests by virtue of that fact. This describes equally well several kinds of communities—the home, the school, the township, the village, the municipality, the state, and the nation. The term will be used here to designate that circle of social relationships just outside the family group in which are to be found the principal satisfactions and interests not supplied by the home.[1] The geographical radius of this circle varies greatly in length. For the villager, the community will be identical with his home town. For the city dweller, it may mean only a section of the city in which he lives—his "neighborhood." For the countryman it will mean, as a rule, "that territory, with its people, which lies within the team haul of a given center." The motor vehicle is stretching this radius very rapidly.[2] The community always includes those families and persons who have common social, educational, economic, political, and religious needs and is the medium through which these needs are met.

---

[1]Warren H Wilson, *Evolution of the Country Community,* p. 92.
[2]*Id.,* p. 91.

b. "What is community service?" Obviously, any ministry to a community need. It may be rendered by many persons and institutions, the physician and the hospital, the teacher and the school, the business man and the institutions of commerce and industry, the officials and machinery of government, the minister and the church.

c. "What is a community church?" Let us say that it is a church which takes account of every kind of community need and endeavors to organize its activities in such a way as to minister intelligently and systematically to those needs. It may, or may not, be the only church supported by the community. It may, or may not, have denominational affiliations. All or only a part of the community may participate in its management. The determinative fact is its spirit and breadth of vision. It must be committed to the social conception of the Kingdom which insists that the Kingdom is outward as well as inward, present as well as future, and embraces the life that now is as well as the life that is to come.

There are three types of community churches, each possessing advantages and disadvantages:

(1) The Federated Church, in which two or more congregations worship as one while maintaining respectively their denominational integrity.

(2) The Independent Church which has no denominational affiliations.

(3) The Denominational Church with a Community Program.

For Methodists this ideal of service as varied as human need is a return to Wesleyan ideals. John Wesley was the chief of all eighteenth-century evangelists and at the same time one of the greatest of social reformers. John Howard was not more deeply stirred than he over the filthy jails and brutal penal methods of his day. He was among the first to agitate for the abolition of slavery, and the very last letter that he wrote was addressed to William Wilberforce bidding him, "Go on, in the name of God and the power of his might, till even American slavery, the vilest that ever saw the sun, shall vanish before it." In the face of great opposition he preached on political themes since politics had to do with such matters as war, slavery, the regulation of industry, education, disease, and crime. He established loan funds and dispensaries in connection with his chapels, and converted the society room at "the Foundry" into a place for carding and spinning cotton. In 1743 he made a "social survey" of London, mapping the city out into twenty-three districts and assigning two volunteer workers to each to care for the poor of his societies. He ministered no less enthusiastically to the intellectual than the spiritual needs of his people, establishing schools and editing cheap editions of good literature for them.

The utter futility of attempting to redeem the individual without evangelizing the social conditions in which he lives is vividly illustrated in the story of *Six Thousand Country Churches in Ohio,* by Gill and Pinchot. This is largely a story of eighteen counties in southeastern Ohio where churches are more plentiful in proportion to the population than in any other part of the State and also where illegitimacy, illiteracy, tuberculosis, venereal disease, corrupt politics, and superstition are most in evidence. The reason is not to be found in bad economic conditions, for poor soil itself cannot deprave a whole population. It is due to the prevalence of a type of religion which exhausts itself in excessive emotionalism without relating itself to matters of conduct. "For the most part the farm people of these eighteen counties are very religious. This is attested not merely by the large number of churches but also by the frequency of well-attended revival services, held in spring, summer, autumn, and winter. (In Pike County, for example, no less than fifteen hundred revival services were held in thirty years, or an average of fifty each year.) Yet a normal, wholesome religion, bearing as its fruit better living and all-round human development, and cherished and propagated by sane and sober-minded people, is rarely known. . . .

Officials of denominations to which more than two thirds of the churches belong encourage or permit the promotion of a religion of the excessively emotional type, which encourages rolling upon the floor by men, women, and children, and going into trances, while some things which have happened in the regular services of a church in one of the largest denominations cannot properly be described in print."[3]

2. COMMUNITY INTERESTS. In approaching community problems it will be noticed that all of them "hang together." Pick up the problem of industry, for example, and the problems of sickness, dependency, delinquency, education, and politics come up with it. For purposes of thought, however, we may make a logical separation of these interests and consider the more important of them as though they were unrelated. It scarcely needs to be said that within the limits imposed upon us, it is impossible to do more than suggest these problems in outline and hint at the contribution which the church can make, as a rule, to their solution.

a. Religion. In the light of what was said concerning worship, it must be clear that the most important collective interest which any community has is religion. Current criticism of religion from the standpoint of the community makes two serious charges. First, the type of religion that is generally taught is too subjective to establish any but the slightest relations with the present world. Second, many believe that the divisions and strife within the church itself render it incapable of bringing to mankind the boon of salvation. There are high-souled idealists outside the church who, far from expecting any help from the church, regard it as a part of "the social problem," and have set for themselves the task of Christianizing the church! This criticism is not always careful to appreciate the wholesome influence which the church is now exercising in society, but there is a good deal in it nevertheless.

[3]Reprinted by permission of The Macmillan Company, from *Six Thousand Country Churches*, p. 21, by Gill and Pinchot.

The question of religion as a community affair requires, then, that the church shall teach a type of religion that is socially valuable, relating itself helpfully to the whole of life. This does not mean merely that the church shall render "social service," binding up the wounds of those who are hurt in the on-going of the social order. It means, rather, that the church shall make an ethical appraisal of the order itself, inquiring if the reason so many are hurt may not be due in large part to the prevalence of non-Christian methods and motives in the order as a whole. This is primarily an educational task, and the agencies by which it is to be accomplished are the pulpit and the class-room.

In the next place, it will be necessary for churchmen to practice this gospel as well as teach it. An important factor in the present social confusion is that some of the staunchest defenders of prevailing methods in business, finance, and diplomacy which work hardship on many, are conspicuous laymen and ministers in the church. No individual can be held accountable for things being as they are. We are all caught in a scheme of things which no one person can change, and many are compelled against their will to "play the game according to the accepted rules." But there is no need that Christian men shall defend these rules as ideal. They can admit their pagan character and work earnestly for a change.

Furthermore, the church must become social toward its several parts and be filled with the spirit of cooperation toward all other community institutions. It must learn to think of itself, not as an end, but as a means (and not the only means) of Christianizing society. It must lose the self-consciousness which has exalted denominational interests above the kingdom of God, and be willing to disappear from a given community if that will unify the religious forces and promote the cause of religion. For it is quite conceivable that in some communities there would be more religion if there were fewer churches. Moreover, it must regard any agency which contributes to human welfare as its natural ally, not an enemy. The redemption of life is a task so formidable that we should welcome all possible assistance from the lodge, the school, the grange, the business club, and give our best to them in return. That may mean that the church assist in keeping them true to their highest ideals.

b. Recreation. The amusement situation in America is characterized by three unfortunate features—*professionalism, commercialism, and immorality.*[4] Professionalism is the result of the American habit of taking recreation by watching others play. Witness the vicarious play of 20,000,000 people at the motion-picture theaters every day, of probably 50,000,000 baseball "fans" congregated about the bulletin boards and newspapers when diamonds are inaccessible during the baseball season, of as many as 70,000 persons crowded into a single stadium watching the struggles of twenty-two men in the center. Is this the best that a great civilization can do in providing recreation for the multitude—employ professional entertainers to play for them? Is there no way to get the people to stretch their own muscles and exert themselves?

Commercialism follows directly upon professionalism in play. The community depends for its amusement upon the promoter who, however valuable his services may be, exploits the normal instincts for play in the interest of commercial profits. Mr. R. H. Edwards observes: "In no phase of our whole great modern struggle against excessive profits for the few and in favor of human values for the many is the battle any keener than in this 'superficial' question of popular amusement. As the congestion of city life thickens and the daily struggle for a living wage grows sharper, the human need for release through real recreation becomes sharper also. . . . If spontaneous, wholesome, and well-ordered play is a profoundly educative and moralizing force, then the substitution of cold, profit-seeking amuse-

[4] R. H. Edwards, *Christianity and Amusements,* p. 12.

ments, artificial and often nasty, can but exercise a correspondingly profound effect for demoralization."[5]

And out of these two comes the third, immorality. Who is not familiar with the struggle in every community to keep the theaters free from indecent suggestiveness; sports free from gambling; and the dance halls and public parks free from vice? Professor Rauschenbusch's generalization is not too sweeping—that pleasure resorts run for profit are always edging along toward the forbidden.

The particular responsibility of the church in connection with this matter would seem to be, first of all, the creation of an intelligent body of public opinion on the subject of play, developing in the community a sense of collective obligation to provide adequate facilities for recreation for young and old. This is another part of its educational task to be accomplished through the pulpit and the class. Besides this educational work, the church may insist upon the strict supervision by the community through proper officials of all public amusement places. Unsupervised parks, playgrounds, gardens, theaters, dance halls, are a menace to the moral health.

In the event that no other institution in the community has a major responsibility in the matter, the church should make of itself the center of social and recreational activities. The church in the country or the small village often has an exceptional opportunity to do this. The play life of the community is thus brought under the direct control of the church and no one will be to blame but the church itself if the social atmosphere is uncongenial to spirituality. To make itself thus the center of social life will require a considerable expenditure of money for buildings, equipment, and additional workers. For the pastor cannot become the director of boys' and girls' clubs and at the same time do all that he should do as preacher and shepherd. And however many salaried workers may be employed,

[5]*Christianity and Amusements,* p. 17. Reprinted by permission of Association Press.

they must have tools to work with. It is advisable, then, for the church to make sure that some other institution cannot do this work more effectively and economically before entering upon such a program of service. In that event, as indicated above, the obligation of the church would be to cooperate with such an institution rather than enter into competition with it, supplying it with financial resources and leadership, and keeping its ideals of service true.

c. Industry. Concern for its own interest, if no higher motive, would impel the church to relate itself to the problems of workaday life in the community which it serves. If the present industrial order is giving us a depleted manhood and womanhood, that means a depleted church. For "the church cannot thrive where society decays." And if the church is indifferent to these which are the paramount interests to a majority of the people, the alienation of great industrial groups is inevitable. As a matter of fact, this alienation is already an accomplished fact in many industrial and agricultural communities.

The chief contribution expected from the church in the solution of economic problems is not mere remedial activity, such as the maintenance of relief agencies which will make tolerable the misery of those who feel acutely the pressure of these problems. It is more important that the church should deal directly with the great causes of this misery and exalt a new set of ideals which, if permitted to control, would Christianize industry. Its work will be largely educational. The aim must be, not to change industrial and social forms, but to put a new spirit into whatever industrial organization is approved by society.

(1) In her teaching the church will interpret certain great ethical ideals exalted by Jesus. The first of them is *respect for personality.* Jesus put human welfare above every other consideration. Men were of more value to him than things, such as grass, birds, lilies, oxen, and sheep. The religious institutions of his day were made for them—the law, the temple, the Sabbath. Children were precious,

for of such is the kingdom of heaven. Womanhood was reverenced even though it had been ravaged by man's lust. Human life was regarded so highly that he made it his one business to nurse it back to strength after it had been enfeebled by sin, disease, superstition, and ignorance. A thoroughgoing application of this principle of respect for personality would correct every social wrong against which the workers of the world protest.

(2) A second principle that must be emphasized by the church as essential to an ideal economic order is *cooperation*. Competition and coercion stand thoroughly discredited as instruments of social advance. The champions of the doctrine of the "survival of the fittest" never were able to defend it from the standpoint of Christian ethics. Jesus' gospel of love is utterly at variance with any philosophy of force. The doctrine was justified scientifically by reliance upon a misinterpretation of Darwin's theory of the development of life. The great Englishman himself pointed out that there were two factors which explained the survival of life in its various forms—*struggle and mutual aid*. Popular thought seized upon the first and magnified it until the second was lost to view. Before his death it became clear to Darwin that his message would be hopelessly misrepresented. "I am beginning to despair of ever making the majority understand my notions. . . . I must be a very bad explainer," he said.

Obviously, the effort of "social Darwinians" to justify the principle of competition in trade and politics was wholly misguided. Commerce and industry are saving themselves in our day only by turning away from this principle to that of cooperation. Employers do not regard each other any longer as enemies to be devoured, but as friends to be helped. Hence, the development of the trust, and employers' associations. Laborers, likewise, refuse longer to eat each other up in bloody competition, and now associate themselves together in mutual helpfulness in trade and industrial unions. Industrial peace waits only upon the further application of this principle. Competition now is between classes rather than individuals. Producers combine together against middlemen, and middlemen against producers. Laborers unite against employers, and employers against laborers. *And both groups are capable of working together in exploiting the consumer.* The Christian ideal requires that all groups having to do with the production and distribution of wealth shall learn how to work together, not in the interest of one or two parties, but in kindly helpfulness to all people.

(3) Another ideal upon which the church must insist is that the *Christian motive of service shall be substituted for the pagan motive of self-interest.* To the uncontrolled desire for gain can be traced all the chicane and iniquity of modern trade. It tempts the merchant to take advantage of the ignorance of the purchaser. It prompts the producer at times to curtail production and at other times to surpass the economic needs of society. It impels the "middleman," the distributor, to gamble in the necessaries of life, and even to destroy vast quantities of food and goods for personal gain. It sends a bargain-hunting public racing after shoddy goods that have been produced by "sweating" their fellow man under intolerable conditions. It drives "big business" to do some very small things—secure monopolies that are protected by law, make industrial accidents a charge upon the community, especially upon the family of the unfortunate worker; pay wages so meager that workers have to get free board and lodgings at home or supplement their earnings by sin. And it has sometimes caused an organized group of laborers to violate contracts for no other reason than they had the power to do so.

If the practicability of service as a motive in industry be called in question, let the fact be remembered that long since all the great professions have passed under its control. Evidence of the predatory spirit in the minister, the teacher, the physician, and the lawyer is punished swiftly by a loss of caste among his professional peers. Any legitimate form of business is a service to society, and can justify itself only on this ground. By what right, then, does business ask exemptions from the control of an unselfish motive while the professions gladly acknowledge the obligations of service? Business must "professionalize" itself!

The church may employ several methods in performing this work of education. The pastor should often call attention to these great principles from the pulpit. It is understood, of course, that he will not speak until he has informed himself fully concerning them, and that he will not lose his sense of proportion so that he comes to have nothing but a "social message." Besides this, it may be possible to organize study groups in connection with the Sunday school or the midweek service for the consideration of social and industrial themes. Some pastors conduct "forums" for the candid discussion by competent persons of any matter vital to the welfare of the community. These discussions are held frequently on Sunday afternoon or on a week night. Often they are substituted for the Sunday-evening service of worship. Their value lies in the fact that an opportunity is given for questions from the floor and everyone has a chance to express himself who cares to do so.

Individual churches may find it possible to supplement this educational work with activities designed to advance the economic interests of the community. For example, many rural churches promote "pig" and "corn clubs" among the boys and girls, and cooperate with agricultural colleges in conducting fairs and institutes which bring the whole countryside together. Many city churches organize vacant-lot garden clubs and establish industrial departments which give employment to large numbers of persons. The "Good Will Industries," which are fostered by the Board of Home Missions of the Methodist Episcopal Church in a number of cities, are illustrations in point.

d. Poverty. Every community, rural and urban alike, must reckon with the fact of poverty in larger or smaller degree, for there are always some who do not have sufficient income to maintain themselves in health and physical efficiency. Before the World War the average wage-earner and his family in America lived constantly on the brink of poverty. A prolonged illness or a considerable period of unemployment brought them face to face with actual want. And in spite of the higher wages received by all classes of workers at the present time, it is a question whether they are relatively better off, for the increase in wages has hardly been proportionate to the increased cost of goods. If the average wage-earner is living all the time on the poverty line, there are many who live constantly below that line. Not all of them are paupers, that is, dependent upon public or private charity, but all of them are underfed, insufficiently clad, and badly housed. For them a period of sickness or unemployment means such a degree of want that they are pushed over the line into pauperism. In 1904 Robert Hunter estimated that there were not far from 10,000,000 persons living in poverty in the United States. At the time many regarded this as an exaggerated statement. Later researches, however, have confirmed rather than discredited it. Ward declared in 1915 that 4,000,000 persons in the United States were living in destitution.

Until a recent period poverty was generally regarded as a regrettable, but unavoidable fact. Modern leaders in social reform, however, are convinced that it is both curable and preventable. A fresh study of the prophets and the teachings of Jesus has discovered that in both the Old and New Testaments the biblical ideal is, rather, to remove the causes of poverty than mitigate the evil by mere almsgiving. The church cannot but indorse this new view, which turns out to have been an old one, and cooperate enthusiastically with all agencies which address themselves to *the prevention* as well as the relief of misery.

As in the case of the economic problem, so here, the principal service which the church can render is educational. It may see to it that the community is informed concerning the great causes of poverty. These are, in part, *personal.* Mental and physical defects, shiftlessness, intemperance, gambling, delinquency, and crime are responsible for much misery among workers. In other part these causes are *social* and of such a nature that the worker has no power over them. Sickness is most frequently the immediate occasion for charity, and often is the direct result of the nature of the work in which the toiler engages. Unemployment figures as the next most common cause of poverty. Forty per cent of all wage earners suffer some unemployment every year and the loss in wages is from twenty to thirty per cent of the total amount of what their earnings would be if they were employed constantly. The relation between a small uncertain income and poverty is unmistakably clear.

Furthermore, the church must regard it as her particular task to develop in the community a sense of collective responsibility for the welfare of the poor and to generate the moral power necessary to the relief and prevention of poverty. A message that is calculated to make employers socially minded and to secure a fairer distribution of the product of labor will contribute directly to this end. It is the particular privilege of the church to create an atmosphere in which social workers shall find their faith strengthened and to build up a body of public opinion which will provide adequately for the work of charitable organizations supported by the community.

In addition to this educational service designed to remove ultimately the causes of poverty, the church must concern itself actively with remedial measures. Nothing that the churches can do in this connection will be more important than such a ministry to the spiritual life as will transform the shiftless, the intemperate, the impure man into a new creature in Christ Jesus. The regeneration and sanctification of the individual life will go far to remove the purely personal causes of poverty.

Besides this, however, most churches will find it necessary

to minister material relief to distressed families. All service of this kind should be controlled by the principles of charitable relief now universally approved by the most successful social workers. First, all such help should be given intelligently and systematically. Injudicious and impulsive almsgiving is little less than criminal. The initial step in all relief work should be investigation of each case. Second, on the basis of facts uncovered by the investigator, a plan of aid should be worked out which will help the applicant to help himself. Third, reconstruction is essentially a spiritual process. By friendly visiting and personal interest the discouraged person or family must be brought into a spirit of faith and hopefulness. The power to carry cheer and win the confidence of the poor is more essential to a social worker than money.

The relief work of the church will be directed toward two classes of poor: those who are, and those who are not, members of the church. To the former, the church is under a special obligation to provide all that is necessary for their care, as has been pointed out previously. In the case of the latter, the obligation of the church is shared by the whole community, and the church should cooperate with other organizations in caring for them.

The word "cooperate" should be emphasized heavily in community relief. It is very common to find charitably disposed persons and organizations contributing to dependency by helping, independently of each other, the same families without knowledge of what other agencies are doing. This is especially likely to happen in a large community at festival seasons of the year. The moral effect of such haphazard charity upon the poor is worse than the poverty which it is supposed to relieve. Vagrancy becomes more profitable than labor, and many drift into beggary as a profession. All this implies that the pastor shall discover what relief agencies are at work in the community and establish working relations with them; and that he shall discourage well-intentioned but wholly inefficient methods of relief by the church itself, such as ostentatious distributions to the poor at Christmas and Thanksgiving.

The standing committee on service should supervise all the relief work of the church and should be the medium by which the church cooperates with every other agency, private and public, in meeting its total community obligations.

e. Vice and Delinquency. As no community is free from poverty, so there is none, however small or remote from populous centers, that is free from vice. In the larger towns and cities it may be strong enough to defy the law. In villages and the open country it may be clandestine and give little sign of its presence. But wherever human beings associate together in large or small numbers immorality always appears. Every community has its wild boy, and its vicious man; its incorrigible girl and its immoral woman; and some have thousands of them.

Every important study of this subject in recent years has reached the conclusions that the great causes of vice are social rather than personal, that wayward boys and girls are the victims more than they are the enemies of the community. Behind their delinquency appear poverty, lack of parental care, confused family situations, degenerate parentage, ignorance, neglect by the school and the church, and neglect by the community which has failed conspicuously to provide wholesome recreation, supervision, and instruction, and which has handed over its youth, questioning, adventurous, emotional, to commercial interests hostile to youth.

The solution of this problem involves at least three things: (1) suppression of the evil, (2) the reconstruction, physical and moral, of its victims, and (3) the restriction of supply of fresh victims. This division of labor is very clear to thought, but in actual practice one type of work shades imperceptibly into another. In abating these evils there is need of the fullest cooperation of all persons who have responsibilities therewith. Such persons are parents, teachers, ministers, social workers, physicians, the press, and municipal officials.

The work of suppressing vice when it has become flagrant falls properly to the administrative and court officials of the community, who are under oath to enforce the law. The militant type of minister is sometimes tempted to become an unofficial policeman with a view of making himself a terror to evildoers. This temptation is especially strong if he is morally certain that there is an alliance between the police officials and the underworld. Occasionally a minister has rendered a real service by this kind of work. As a rule, however, such experiments have accomplished little except to furnish the community with a brief sensation in watching the fevered antics of a "fighting parson." Often it ends disastrously for the minister who, inexperienced in the ways of corruption, becomes involved in embarrassing situations created for him by the forces opposed to him. It is equally unwise for the ministers of a community to denounce officers on hearsay evidence for failure to enforce the laws.

The best contribution which the minister can make toward the suppression of vice is to become acquainted with responsible officials and go to them privately whenever he feels that there is reason to believe that the law is not being enforced, stating his grievance and citing the reason therefor. This will not give a congregation any oratorical thrills, but generally it will make a favorable impression upon the officer. If it should be necessary, go again, this time with a group of influential citizens, encouraging him to do his duty and assuring him of the support of the best elements in the community if he will enforce the law. If he does a good thing that calls for courage, speak of that in the public congregation. But criticism is not justified unless it is absolutely certain that the law is being openly violated and that the proper officials will not do what the majority of people want them to do. If they do not enforce the law, it is because they believe the community does not care to have its laws enforced. Create a body of public opinion, however, demanding law enforcement, and they will have great regard for their oath of office. If it should seem necessary for the minister as a private citizen to proceed against the vicious elements, let him organize around himself a group of other citizens and let the action of the whole group be guided by their best collective wisdom.

The duty of the minister in the matter of reconstructing lives that have been broken by vice is fairly clear. The futility of the ordinary raid on places of evil repute is that it does not put out, but only scatters the fire throughout the community. Sound social policy demands that the victims and purveyors of vice shall be seized, not for punishment but for treatment. What purpose is served by arresting a prostitute, assessing a heavy fine upon her, and then discharging her to prey once more upon the community, scattering loathsome physical and moral contamination wherever she goes? Again, what purpose is served in seizing immoral women while the men, who make them what they are, move among their fellows with perfect liberty? Obviously, every person, man or woman, who has contracted a venereal disease, innocently or sinfully, is so great a menace to the community that he should be held for medical treatment. Physicians should be required by law to report every such case, and the community should provide hospitals and other institutions where regeneration of body and soul may be accomplished.

The minister can render an indispensable service in this connection by creating an intelligent public opinion concerning this matter, and helping remove the popular ignorance and prejudice which now obstructs enlightened action. In an American city of more than a quarter million of people, an appropriation was long since made for the construction of a hospital for venereal disease but it is impossible to proceed further because no section of this city wants such an institution in its midst.

The same method should be followed in dealing with

juvenile delinquency. To arrest repeatedly wayward boys and girls only to punish them in ways that will confirm them in their delinquency, is the greatest social folly. They should be put under instruction and in an environment that is designed to redeem them from their sin. If the community does not provide such institutions, the church must awaken it to a sense of its obligation.

The restriction of the supply of victims depends more largely upon educational than repressive means employed by police officers. Dr. Prince A. Morrow, in his treatise on *Social Diseases and Marriage,* speaks very positively concerning this matter: "The true remedy, the most effective remedy available to modify or lessen the appalling evils, moral and physical, which flow from venereal diseases is the general dissemination of knowledge respecting the dangers and modes of contagion of these diseases. It is by the persuasive force of enlightenment, by combating the dense ignorance which prevails among the laity, especially among the young, upon whom the incidence of these diseases most heavily falls, that these evils can be diminished." The United States government instituted a great propaganda during the Great War to inform soldiers and civilians of the dangers of sexual immorality, and in cooperation with State Boards of Health through their Educational Departments continues its fight on vice by instruction concerning vice.

The church can throw itself into this educational work with the greatest enthusiasm, for no program of religious education can be called complete which overlooks sex hygiene. It may cooperate with physicians and government officials in spreading a wholesome knowledge of sex-life and of the train of evil consequences that follows the irregular indulgence of sexual appetites. But its distinctive appeal will be to moral and spiritual motives. It will be less appalled by what vice does to the body than to the soul of a man. It will remind the youth of the community that the body is the temple of God, and this temple must not be defiled. It will urge the control of a single standard of morals for both sexes. It will appeal to men and women to keep themselves pure against the day of marriage that the next generation may not be handicapped by an evil inheritance, physical or moral. And it will urge the spiritual dynamic that religion affords for personal discipline and self-control in the moment of temptation. The methods to be employed in promoting this instruction should be carefully determined by conference with the wisest physicians, social workers, teachers, and parents in the community.

f. Politics. It is one of the principles of democratic government in America that state and church shall be independent each of the other. Some have inferred from this that the church must have nothing to do with politics. No such inference is warranted. Separate though they are, the functions of the church and the government are identical within broad limits, and while each must respect the independence and importance of the other, there should be the fullest cooperation between them in realizing their common aims. Moreover, the church is composed of citizens of the commonwealth who must give political expression to their moral and religious ideals. Their prayers are not to be canceled but, rather, answered by their votes. The church that is in "political exile" is already smitten by death.

The nature of the political service to be rendered generally by the church is determined by the demand of a democratic government for a favorable public opinion. This demand is as great as that of the lungs for air. Neither a "bad" nor a "good" government long can function in the absence of popular support. The church is one of the great agencies for creating public opinion. Its independence of state control makes it possible to criticize as well as support the administration. Whether it shall censure or approve will depend upon the regard which the administration has for policies that are admittedly ethical. It will insist that the state is under the control of morality, and the very essence of Christian morality is to serve the highest welfare of the many rather than the selfish interests of the few. The church, speaking unitedly, can thus make it "politically safe for a man occupying a high public position to perform his duties fearlessly" and also "politically unsafe for any public official to be false to his trust."

But mere criticism of a bad administration is not sufficient to secure good government. We sweep our political house clean to little purpose unless care is taken to obtain proper tenants thereafter. These tenants, that is, office-holders, are selected primarily by small political groups and ultimately by the ballots of voting citizens, and good government waits upon the wise use of these agencies by good citizens. Because the membership of the church represents every political view, the church cannot indorse *partisan* programs. More fundamental to good government than party platforms is the ethical obligation of its members irrespective of party affiliations to see to it that good men are nominated for office on every ticket. When a great moral issue is involved it may be necessary for the churches to form a special organization through which they can function. The Anti-Saloon League is a conspicuous example of the church acting politically. The method employed generally by this organization was to secure the nomination of the best citizens by all parties rather than enter the field as a "third" party. The conspicuous success of this method in securing constitutional prohibition should commend its use in other great reforms.

It is the business of the church to make good citizens, and every program of religious education should provide for training in civic matters. That excellent little book, *The Church School of Citizenship*, by Professor Allan Hoben, is rich in suggestion as to ways in which this training can be given through church agencies to children, adolescent youths, and adults, in rural as well as urban communities. The approach, of course, will be from the ethical and religious points of view.

g. Education. According to an old definition, the essential meaning of education is "to draw out" the undeveloped capacities of the young. Ideally it has to do with the total personality—the physical, the mental, the volitional, and the emotional powers. In every American community the educational task is divided irrationally between the state and the church, the former being restricted to the physical and cultural aspects of the task, the latter to the moral and religious phases. The state may teach the child to think, the church is supposed to teach him to trust. The state may make him strong and alert, and the church is to make him good. It is not strange that some young Americans feel that religion has nothing to do with knowledge and power.

This division of labor, regrettable as it is, at least leaves us in no doubt about the contribution which is expected from the church to this community interest. It must give itself most enthusiastically to that part of the educational task which the state leaves untouched.

But it is under an obligation also to cooperate with every other educational force in the community. One thing that can be done is to make such an interpretation of religion as will not deny the science that is taught in the schools. Another would be to offer courses in biblical subjects which conform to the public-school standards, so that credit may be given for this work by the public schools, after the so-called "North Dakota" and "Colorado" plans. Yet another would be to cooperate with other churches in establishing "Community Night Schools of Religious Education" and "Vacation Bible Schools." Such schools can be started by two churches as well as by a dozen. In a community where educational ideals are low and public school equipment is inferior, the church can develop a public opinion that will support the demand for better things. One country pastor in Illinois agitated for four years for a township high school and at length got it.

h. Health. Good health is yet another great community interest. Once more the chief contribution which the average church can make to this matter is educational.

Physicians are *teaching* people how to keep themselves strong, and the church can cooperate with this teaching program by securing competent persons to address special groups and classes on the subject of personal and community hygiene. Moreover, it can support by its gifts local hospitals and dispensaries for the care of the stricken. In exceptional instances it may be that the church itself may establish a hospital department.

Finally, it will be in order for the church to emphasize the curative value of a genuine religious faith, as has been suggested in the first chapter of this book.

Books Recommended for Further Study

SOCIAL INTERPRETATION OF RELIGION

Walter Rauschenbusch, *Christianity and the Social Crisis; Christianizing the Social Order; A Theology for the Social Gospel.*

Charles Ellwood, *The Social Problem; Reconstruction in Religion.*

Committee Report, Federal Council of Churches, *The Church and Industrial Reconstruction.*

E. A. Ross, *Sin and Society.*

W. N. Clarke, *The Ideal of Jesus.*

R. H. Tawney, *An Acquisitive Society.*

H. F. Ward, *Social Evangelism; The Social Creed of the Churches.*

H. S. Coffin, *In a Day of Social Rebuilding.*

RECREATION

R. H. Edwards, *Christianity and Amusements.*

H. S. Curtis, *Education Through Play; Play and Education.*

Rural and Small Community Recreation, by "Community Service," 1 Madison Avenue, New York.

Joseph Lee, *Play in Education.*

N. E. Richardson, *The Church at Play.*

Warren T. Powell, *Recreational Leadership for Church and Community.*

LaPorte, *A Handbook of Games and Programs for Church School and Home.*

Jane Addams, *The Spirit of Youth and the City Streets.*

INDUSTRY

J. A. Hobson, *Incentives in the New Industrial Order.*

Walter Rauschenbusch, *Christianizing the Social Order.*

Committee Report, Federal Council of Churches, *Church and Industrial Reconstruction.*

Harry F. Ward, *The New Social Order: Principles and Programs.*

POVERTY

E. T. Devine, *Misery and Its Causes; Principles of Relief; Practice of Charity.*

H. F. Ward, *Poverty and Wealth.*

Robert Hunter, *Poverty.*

John Spargo, *The Bitter Cry of the Children.*

THE CHURCH AND THE COMMUNITY

P. M. Strayer, *Reconstruction of the Church.*

W. M. Tippy, *The Church a Community Force.*

R. B. Guild, *Community Programs for Cooperating Churches.*

R. E. Diffendorfer, *The Church and the Community.*

Walter Burr, *Rural Organization.*

J. M. Barker, *The Social Gospel and the New Era.*

E. L. Earp, *The Rural Church Serving the Community; Rural Social Organization.*

Warren H. Wilson, *The Church at the Center.*

Richard Morse, *Fear God in Your Own Village.*

L. H. Bailey, *Country Life Movement in the United States.*

E. deS. Brunner, *Country Church in the New World Order.*

K. L. Butterfield, *Country Church and the Rural Problem.*

T. N. Carver, *Principles of Rural Economics.*

P. L. Vogt, *Introduction to Rural Sociology; Church Cooperation in Community Life.*

Fred B. Fisher, *The Way to Win,* Chapter III.

A. F. McGarrah, *Practical Inter-Church Methods.*

CHAPTER XVIII

THE ADMINISTRATION OF SERVICE

The World Community

The service of the church may never stop at the geographical boundaries of its immediate neighborhood. Its sympathy and helpfulness must go out to all men everywhere. This is required by the great Head of the church who himself came to redeem a world community. "God so loved *the world* that he gave his only begotten Son." Practical expediency, however, would impel the church to become missionary even if there were no specific direction from its Master. Saint Paul likened the church to an organism, the human body, and declared that when any part suffered, the whole body suffered with it. This figure is quite as applicable to society as to the church. The Great War through which we have just passed emphasized afresh the fact of social solidarity. Modern inventions, such as the steamboat, the telegraph, the submarine cable, the telephone, the aeroplane, make it impossible for any social group to live in isolation. Whatever happens anywhere is of immediate consequence everywhere. Opportunities for friction and misunderstanding have been multiplied a thousandfold. It is inconceivable that society can hold together if the old selfishness continues to dominate the life of the world. Further advance in civilization waits upon the creation of a larger body of good will than now obtains. And the church itself, which is a part of society, will be involved in the general catastrophe that must certainly follow a refusal to bring the world community under the control of Christian ideals.

This world community begins where the local community leaves off. It ends only with the last person in the uttermost parts of the earth. That portion of the world community which lies within the United States is generally called home-missionary territory, and that lying outside the homeland is designated as the foreign-missionary field. But it is all one service. We cannot choose between them. We are bound to minister to both.

The primary aim, of course, in all mission work is to teach the religion of Jesus and apply the saving power of his gospel to all the ranges of life. This requires not only the maintenance of a corps of evangelists in the mission field but the establishment of educational institutions, medical dispensaries, homes, hospitals, and trained technicians of all kinds, such as agriculturalists, chemists, biologists, engineers. Ultimately the purpose includes the Christianization of all social, industrial, and international relationships.

To serve the world community the church must provide (1) *workers* and (2) *money*. The administrative problem consists of devising means to awaken such missionary interest in the church that there will be no lack either of persons willing to invest their lives in this service, or of equipment to permit them to serve effectively. And this interest must be permanent, not spasmodic. *It should be such as to make every member of the church an intelligent missionary, in spirit and intention, though possibly not engaged professionally in missionary service.* This is the problem of the important subcommittee on missions of the great Committee on Service, which must "unite and correlate every parish interest which pertains to the propagation of the gospel at home and abroad."

1. Interest in any matter that is sustained and abiding must rest upon knowledge. The first great item in the missionary program of the local church, then, will be "*Missionary Education.*"

a. There are *several institutions* through which this educational work may be accomplished in the average church —(1) The Woman's Home Missionary Society and subsidiary organizations among the young people, such as the Queen Esther Circle, Home Guards, etc.; (2) the Woman's Foreign Missionary Society and subsidiary organizations, such as The King's Daughters, Little Light Bearers, etc.; (3) the Sunday school, which, according to the law of the church, must be organized as a missionary society; (4) the Epworth League, with its Department of Missions; (5) the organized Bible Class; and (6) the pulpit. It will appear at a glance that it is unnecessary to set up any new organizations for this task. The real problem with so many collaborating institutions is that of coordinating and distributing the work so that there will no waste or needless duplication of effort.

b. The materials of missionary education consist of (1) historical matter concerning the great periods of missionary expansion in the growth of the Christian Church, beginning with the story of the early church in the Acts of the Apostles; (2) biographies of great missionary leaders; (3) habits, customs, history, and ideals of races and national groups which are the objects of missionary endeavor; (4) the social aspects of mission work as appears in its influence on education, science, industry, and politics; (5) the study of particular mission fields and current events in those fields; (6) the great non-Christian religions of the world, for example, Buddhism, Mohammedanism, Taoism, Shintoism, Confucianism, etc.; with particular reference to the points at which they resemble, and differ from, Christianity; (7) the theory and practice of missions, explaining the great policies adopted by mission boards and the methods generally employed in missionary endeavor; (8) the history and success of the more important Protestant mission boards. The Missionary Education Department of the Methodist Episcopal Church, 150 Fifth Avenue, New York city, will be glad to suggest suitable textbooks on these subjects, such as have been issued from time to time by the Missionary Education Movement of American Protestantism.

c. The methods which have been employed successfully in many churches in presenting this great body of material include the following: (1) Sermons, lectures and addresses by the pastor and other informed persons, particularly missionaries engaged actively in the home field or returned on furlough from the foreign field; (2) the distribution of missionary literature and periodicals; (3) the organization of mission study classes; (4) creating a missionary atmosphere by hanging on the walls of the church the pictures of persons who have gone out from its membership into professional religious work as ministers, deaconesses, foreign missionaries, etc.; (5) correspondence with these and other workers in the field; (6) amateur theatricals and pageants dealing with missionary subjects; (7) institutes and conferences.

d. A unified program of missionary education might have some such appearance as this, taking into account the organizations, the materials, and the methods that are usually available:

I. *Sermons, Addresses, Stereopticon Lectures*

1. The Pulpit, once each quarter.
2. The Sunday school, once a month if possible.
3. The Epworth League from four to six times a year.
4. The Woman's Organizations as frequently as can be arranged.

II. *Study Classes,* conducted by the following organizations, no two covering the same subject or appealing to the same group:

1. Woman's Home Missionary Society.
2. Woman's Foreign Missionary Society.
3. The Epworth League.
4. The Sunday school, in all departments taking certain Sundays for missionary lessons.

NOTE. Competent leadership is all important. It is better to have one class with a strong leader than several led indifferently. The best results are secured when the class can meet weekly, perhaps in connection with the mid-week service.

III. *Missionary Literature*

1. Distributing such free literature as may be prepared by the benevolent boards of the church.
2. Subscribing for church papers and missionary periodicals and textbooks.
3. Calling attention occasionally to important articles and books on mission subjects and fields, published by the secular press.

IV. *Entertainments, Pageants, etc.*

Two or three each year given cooperatively by the young people of the church who are members of several missionary organizations.

e. The aim of all true missionary education is to produce the "missionary person," one who is filled with the missionary spirit. This spirit will express itself in many ways. Such a person will always *pray* for missions. Intercessory prayer has ever been a most important factor in extending the Kingdom.

Again, the "missionary person" will always *give himself*—his time, and thought, and service—up to the full measure of his ability. A good program of missionary education should keep a stream of people going from the strong to the weaker churches in a spirit of helpfulness. More particularly, it should develop a corps of volunteer workers for distinctly home missionary tasks. The type of missionary interest that becomes enthusiastic over the Chinese in Peking but despises the representatives of that same race who populate our American "Chinatowns," may well be suspected of unreality. Genuine missionary interest seizes upon the opportunity that lies nearest at hand. And out of the many who are willing to engage in part-time service, an occasional young man or woman will be prompted to consecrate a whole life to this special task. Always the pastor and lay leaders of the church should be alert to advise and encourage, or to restrain, perhaps, such young people.

Finally, the "missionary person" will give of his means to make it possible for others to do what he cannot do—give his whole time to missionary work. The subcommittee on missions will seek constantly to increase the missionary giving of the church. This matter of finances will receive more attention in a later chapter devoted to that subject.

It appears, then, that the program for recruiting and giving must be supplemented by another program of missionary education, and the two articulated into a single great world program:

Missionary Recruiting and Giving

I. *Prayer*
   1. Individual prayer for missions.
   2. Organizing bands of intercessors.

II. *Recruiting*
   1. Life service conferences in the local church and at summer institutes.
   2. Constant attention by the pastor and others to the matter of personal guidance in life-work decisions.

III. *Giving*
   1. Stewardship Campaigns.
   2. Financial canvass for support of the Benevolent Boards of the church.
   3. Supporting the mission work of local organizations.

Books Recommended for Further Study

H. P. Douglass, *The New Home Missions.*
R. E. Diffendorfer, *Missionary Education in Home and School.*

Louise Creighton, *Missions: Their Rise and Development.*
E. C. Moore, *The Spread of Christianity in the Modern World.*
George A. Miller, *Missionary Morale.*
A. J. Brown, *Rising Churches in Non-Christian Lands.*
J. E. McAfee, *World Missions from the Home Base.*
C. H. Patton, *World Facts and America's Responsibility.*
E. W. Capen, *Sociological Progress in Mission Lands.*
W. H. P. Faunce, *The Social Aspects of Foreign Missions.*
R. E. Speer, *Missionary Principles and Practice; The Gospel and the New World.*
Fred B. Fisher, *The Way to Win,* Chapter IV.

CHAPTER XIX

THE ADMINISTRATION OF FINANCE

As an administrative officer the pastor must give faithful attention to church finance. This cannot be left entirely to the laymen. He will not be officious or dictatorial, nor will he assume entire responsibility for raising the budget. But he should know the exact financial condition of the church every month and be ready with helpful suggestions concerning a wise financial policy. If the money is to be used for spiritual ends, then money-raising is quite as religious as preaching.

If American churches find difficulty in managing their finances generally, it is not because the members of the churches are poor. "Probably not more than two or three per cent of the churches secure all the funds they should in order to perform their duties," says one expert in church finance. "According to the religious census of 1906, investments in church property in America are less than one per cent of the national wealth, and the annual income of American churches for buildings, equipment, salaries, and all other purposes equals scarcely one per cent of the national income."[1] Nor is it because they are unwilling. The United Presbyterian denomination is composed chiefly of small churches, many of them located in rural communities and the open country, but their average giving is $20.90 per member, including the children. In Iowa they averaged over $30 per member in 1914. We have a right to assume that they are not at heart more devoted than the members of other communions.

The more common embarrassments in church finance are

[1]McGarrah, *Modern Church Finance*, p. 27f. By permission of Fleming H. Revell Company.

(1) delay in paying salaries and current bills, thus annoying the minister and other creditors; (2) the accumulation of deficits year after year until the total is overwhelming; (3) many separate appeals for money, in public and in private; (4) dependence upon socials and entertainments to raise funds that should be contributed outright by the church membership; (5) the expectation that a few persons in the church shall assume obligations that should be distributed throughout the whole body; (6) careless handling of funds, making possible great waste and loss through inaccurate bookkeeping, or failure to audit accounts annually; (7) inadequate budget through lack of vision and parsimony; (8) the major obligations, missionary and benevolent, of the church as a whole made impossible of attainment through the competitive solicitation of funds by minor organizations within the church; (9) complacency over past achievements and unwillingness to give up to the level of real ability; (10) the apologetic spirit in which money matters are approached before the congregation; (11) no single individual responsible for the purchase of supplies; (12) no financial secretary to receive moneys before they are handed over to the treasurer; (13) the diversion of funds contributed for one purpose but used for another. In the light of all this, success in church finance must imply:[2]

(1) The honest and prompt payment of all bills and obligations.
(2) Avoiding deficits and debts.
(3) Adopting budgets that are sufficiently ample to be truly economical.
(4) Securing funds by methods that are both Christian and business-like.
(5) Democracy in giving.
(6) Handling all moneys in business-like ways.
(7) And raising all that should be raised.

---

[2]Summarized from A. F. McGarrah, *Modern Church Finance*, pp. 11-18. By permission of Fleming H. Revell Company.

1. The Committee on Finance. Responsibility for working out a sound financial policy rests upon the Finance Committee. The *Discipline* requires that this committee shall consist of from three to seven persons. It is customary to make the financial secretary and the treasurers members because they are better informed usually on financial conditions in the church than others. The pastor should meet with them frequently in an advisory capacity. The duties of the committee are stated very definitely: (1) Before the close of the fiscal year it shall "prepare an estimate of the current expenses and benevolences for the ensuing year. This estimate shall include the amount necessary for ministerial support, viz.: pastor's salary and house rent, district superintendent, bishops, and Conference claimants; also the amount deemed necessary for current expenses, such as interest on indebtedness, heat and light, music, insurance, repairs and supplies, telephone, printing and postage, janitor, and miscellaneous items; also for benevolences as apportioned to each charge by the Committee on Conservation and Advance. (2) When approved by the official board or Quarterly Conference, immediate steps shall be taken by a personal canvass of the entire membership of the church and congregation to secure pledges to meet these expenses by weekly payments, so that the result may be known on the last Sunday of the fiscal year, and payment of these pledges begin on the first Sunday of the new fiscal year."[3] Moreover, the General Conference has prescribed a plan, in great detail, for raising these budgets, which has been approved by the experience of many denominational bodies over a period of many years. It is substantially the plan described at length in McGarrah's *Modern Church Finance,* and any finance committee that will work this plan exactly as set forth in the *Discipline*[4] will be happy over the results. Time would fail one to tell of half the

[3]See *Discipline* (1920), ¶ 112, § 2.
[4]*Id.,* ¶ 111.

churches which have been rejuvenated by this all but perfect device.

2. Preparing the Budgets. In preparing the budgets, the committee should not ask, "How little can we get along with this year?" but, "How much should we raise in order that the church may be able to do all its work creditably and effectively?" Moreover, the total budget should always be large enough to tax the church to something like its full capacity if spiritual results are to come from giving. A church composed of wealthy people should probably average from $50 to $100 per member, including children. A church of modest means should average from $20 to $40 for all purposes.

a. The Local Budget. The first item in the local budget will be *pastoral support,* which includes the claim not only for the pastor and his associate, if there be one, but also those for the support of the bishops, the district superintendent, and the Conference claimants. The obligation requires that all these claims be fully met. Any deficit must be shared proportionately by all. Every year, if possible to do so in justice to other demands, a church should increase the pastor's salary. The largest salaries are only sufficient to permit a standard of living that is enjoyed by most of the people in the church. And many, many ministers receive less each year than carpenters and blacksmiths. The inferior preaching in some pulpits is due to the fact that the minister's income does not permit of anything but the narrowest range of experience. He cannot enrich his mind by travel, or even by books, for he is unable to purchase them. The church that will take these things into account in estimating the salary will find itself abundantly rewarded in the increased effectiveness of its pastor. Moreover, the committee should ask itself if the pastor should not be relieved of a load of burdensome details in keeping church records and attending to other small matters that could be performed by a secretary or clerk. Is it wise economy to pay a pastor a good salary and then expect him to do work that another will do quite as well for eighteen or twenty dollars per week?

Fuel, light, repairs, music, supplies, printing, insurance, are other fixed charges that necessarily appear against the local budget. It is impossible for those responsible for the expense items to estimate some of these exactly, because prices change and consumption varies from year to year. But the average for a period of three or five years may be taken as a safe guide.

Interest charges on borrowed money must, of course, be provided for, and if there is a *debt,* the easiest way to pay it is to insert a substantial sum each year into the budget for its gradual reduction.

To avoid a number of appeals later in the year from other committees and organizations for their special work, the Finance Committee would do well to ask from each a careful estimate of the amount needed to carry on its work. Then an appropriation can be made for each organization, and the members of the church may be asked fairly to give to the church budget as much as they have been in the habit of giving for all purposes. This is particularly true of the Sunday school, whose expenses should be borne by the church and whose gifts should be made to the church budget rather than independently of it. And to guard the treasury, the Finance Committee should insist that a single individual shall be "purchasing agent" for all supplies bought in the name of the church, and his approval necessary to the payment of bills. In this way the control of expense and income may be unified, and also appeals for funds. It will make for clear understanding if, in estimating the expense for the coming year, the actual expenditures for the current year and the year preceding be noted in parallel columns. In this way the subscribers can tell at a glance where the budget has expanded and contracted. A detailed estimate of receipts should accompany the estimate of expenditures.

In establishing the limits of a fiscal year, it is usually

better to select October 1, January 1, April 1, or July 1, than "Conference time," which is a movable date.

After the budget has been prepared with great care, it should be submitted and explained to the official board for their adoption.

The local budget for a church of 500 to 800 members will appear somewhat as follows:[5]

BUDGET OF LOCAL EXPENSES METHODIST EPISCOPAL CHURCH

Estimated Expenditures

For the Fiscal Year Beginning October 1, 1923.

Pastoral Support (Pastor, Dist. Sup. Bishops, Conf. Cl.)	*1921*	*1922*	*1923*	*Increase+ Decrease−*
Pastoral Support (Pastor, Dist. Sup. Bishops, Conf. Cl.)	$3,390	$3,390	$3,590	$200+
Secretarial Help	......	......	600	600+
Janitor	720	720	720	
Janitor Supplies	50	60	50	10−
Fuel and Light	620	620	620	
Music	1,200	1,200	800	400−
Insurance	75	75	75	
Repairs	800	2,000	500	1,500−
Printing, Postage, etc.	425	425	425	
Telephone	60	60	60	
Interest	900	750	750	
Reduction of Debt	2,500	......	2,500	2,500+
Telephone	60	60	60	
Sunday-school	900	900	900	
Miscellaneous	300	300	300	
Total	$12,000	$10,560	$11,950	$1,390+

Estimated Receipts

Expectation from unpaid, 1922, pledges	$600
Pledges renewable at 10 per cent increase	9,750
Pledges from new members	1,000
From Sunday-school for local Budget	750
Total	$12,100

[5]See McGarrah, *op. cit.*, for suggestions.

The budget for a church of 250 to 300 members would probably be somewhat as follows:

ESTIMATED EXPENDITURES

For the Fiscal Year Beginning October 1, 1923.

	1921	*1922*	*1923*	*Increase+ Decrease−*
Pastoral Support.........	$2,360	$2,470	$2,583	$113+
Clerical Help............	......	100	150	50+
Janitor	300	300	300	
Fuel and Light............	250	250	250	
Insurance	50	50	50	
Music	100	100	100	
Repairs	600	300	500	200+
Printing, postage, etc......	100	100	100	
Interest	350	300	250	50−
Reduction of Debt.......	1,000	1,000	1,000	
Sunday-school	400	400	450	50+
Miscellaneous	200	200	200	
Total	$5,710	$5,570	$5,933	$363+

Needed to pay all bills $114.11 each week.

Estimated Receipts

Weekly pledges from		
5 members at $3.00 per week..........	$15.00	
10 " " 2.00 " "	20.00	
15 " " 1.00 " "	15.00	
15 " " .75 " "	11.25	
40 " " .50 " "	20.00	
60 " " .25 " "	15.00	
30 " " .20 " "	6.00	
25 " " .10 " "	2.50	
		$104.75
From the Sunday-school for local expenses...		5.00
Expectation from unpaid pledges, 1922, average per week..............................		5.00
Total		$114.75

b. The Benevolent Budget is somewhat simpler, the items being received, for the most part, from the district superintendent. It includes (1) *the Apportioned Benevolences* ordered by the Committee on Conservation and Advance for the support of the great boards of the General Church; (2) *the apportionments ordered by the Annual Conference* for educational and philanthropic work within the Conference; (3) *the benevolences ordered by the Official Board of the local church* for the support of community enterprises, such as City Missions, Educational Institutions, Anti-Saloon League, Associated Charities, etc.

It will relieve the pastor of much embarrassment often if the official board will adopt a rule that no public appeal shall be made from the pulpit for funds without the consent of the board.

The items in this budget should be set forth in orderly fashion and added to the local budget. The total will be the amount which must be raised by the congregation during the year. Ideally the Benevolent Budget should equal the Local Budget. *"As much for others as ourselves."* At least half of the gift from the Sunday school should be credited to the Benevolent Budget.

3. THE FINANCIAL PLAN. There are six features in the financial plan recommended by the General Conference, and each is indispensable. (See *Discipline.*)

a. Education. After the two budgets have been approved by the official board, a campaign of education covering a month should be instituted for the purpose of informing the membership accurately concerning them, the reasons for enlargements, and the plan adopted for raising the money. The methods usually employed in this educational work are:

(1) *Form Letters* sent to all members setting forth essential facts briefly.[6]

(2) *Church Bulletins* where such are printed.

(3) *Full explanation from the pulpit.*

(4) *Special dinners and social gatherings.*

(5) *And instruction in Christian Stewardship and Systematic Giving throughout the year.*

---

[6]See McGarrah, *Modern Church Finance,* for good sample letters.

After the plan has once been put into operation, the educational work will be less arduous in succeeding years.

b. Every-Member Canvass. (1) Canvassers are selected from among the most capable men and women in the church, and in sufficient numbers that no one will need to visit more than twenty persons, fewer, if possible. After careful training they make their own pledges—then go two by two to every member of the church, securing a subscription from each, children as well as parents. It is an *"every-member"* —not an *"every-family"* canvass.

(2) It is generally best to limit the canvass to a short period, preferably between certain hours on a given Sunday afternoon. The members of the church will expect the visitors and be prepared to make their pledges without much argument. Many congregations give a sacramental character to the canvass by commissioning the canvassers in a season of prayer at the altar of the church in the morning service preceding the canvass. Of course such persons as cannot be seen on the day set apart will be visited as soon thereafter as possible.

(3) In distributing the names of persons to be solicited it is generally well to permit the canvassers to select, as far as possible, those whom they can approach most easily. The remainder may be assigned arbitrarily. The name of each prospective giver should be placed upon a card containing the amount paid the preceding year and the amount that the committee feels may reasonably be expected on the new budget. This is given the canvasser for his information. It is not an apportionment—merely a suggestion.

c. Weekly Offering. The pledge is a weekly pledge to be divided between the Local and the Benevolent Budgets according to the wish of the giver.

d. Envelope System. Each subscriber is provided with a set of fifty-two duplex envelopes which he is expected to use in paying his pledge week by week. These can be secured from The Methodist Book Concern.

e. Two Budgets and Two Treasurers. To avoid confusion and diversion of funds, the official board is asked to elect two treasurers, one for the Local and the other for the Benevolent Budget. Moreover, a financial secretary is to be chosen who shall receive all moneys, keeping an accurate account with each subscriber, then turning the moneys over to the respective treasurers, receiving their receipts therefor. Thus church funds are handled in a businesslike manner." The treasurers shall pay out this money by check and only on the authority of the Finance Committee or the official board.

f. Monthly or Quarterly Remittance. The Apportioned Benevolences should be sent each month or each quarter to the Committee on Conservation and Advance. This will make it possible to reduce the interest charges of the several boards. Other benevolences should be sent directly to executive officers of the respective beneficiary organizations, or deposited with the Conference Treasurer, by the pastor, at the next session of the Annual Conference.

Books Recommended for Further Study

A. F. McGarrah, *Modern Church Finance.*
F. A. Agar, *Modern Money Methods; Church Finance.*
F. B. Fisher, *The Way to Win,* Chapter VIII.
Discipline, Methodist Episcopal Church, 1920.

CHAPTER XX

CHURCH RECORDS

An important part of the work of administration is to keep accurate records of all transactions. In a great department store every sale, however small, is recorded in such detail that, years after, the management can quickly discover the nature of the sale, the date, and the clerk who made it. All that comes in and goes out is carefully checked —whether goods, cash, or employees—so that at the end of the year everything and everyone is accounted for. Only by giving attention thus to accurate accounting is it possible to carry on any organized business. While this is being written, a man, reputed two years ago to be a multimillionaire, is going into bankruptcy in Chicago *unexpectedly to himself!* He says he thought he was making money until a few weeks ago. This ignorance on his part is due primarily to his failure to keep proper records.

Ideally, the local Methodist Episcopal Church is supposed to have a good accounting department. "Are the church records properly kept?" is an inquiry made annually in the Quarterly Conference. A Committee on Church Records is appointed and required to report annually on the condition of all record books (not financial) of each organization in the church. Furthermore, an Auditing Committee is required to audit the accounts of all financial officers. But these seldom function or tell the whole truth when they do attempt to discharge their duties. So "church records" have come to be a symbol for confusion and unintelligibility. Church reports and statistics can almost never be taken at their face value. If the State were to call for such an accounting from religious organizations as is demanded of banks and life-insurance companies, the community is rare indeed, that would escape without an ecclesiastical scandal. Such carelessness puts a sore temptation in the way of church officers charged with the care of *church money*. And to be careless in accounting for *the people* intrusted to the church is a greater sin!

The General Conference of 1920 gave careful consideration to records, and approved certain forms for Quarterly Conference and official-board business. The official board is responsible for (1) church members, and (2) church funds. The pastor represents them in caring for the former, and the financial secretary and two treasurers for the latter. And the General Conference is very clear about the kind of records that are to be kept by every such officer in any Methodist Church. No better investment of money can be made than to secure from the nearest depository of The Methodist Book Concern these new forms if they are not already in use in the local church.

1. Records to be Kept by the Pastor.

a. A Permanent Membership Roll which constitutes the fundamental record of *personnel*. The names should be arranged *alphabetically* and *grouped by families*. The only way this record can be kept up-to-date without rewriting frequently is to use a *loose-leaf* book. A page should be given to *each name*, the lower part providing for the names of other members of the family. In case of death or removal, the leaf can be taken out of the active list and reinserted in the same book under the guide *"Removed,"* or *"Died."* The data should be very full, including head of family; occupation; business address; telephone number, family and Christian names; state in life; official position in the church; when, how, where received; when, how, where removed; other members of family; baptized children; birthday (if under 21); organizations in which active, as Sunday school, Epworth League, W. F. M. S., W. H. M. S., etc. This roll should contain the list of preparatory and nonresident members as well as those in full resident membership.

b. Card Index.—Membership and Constituency Roll. The permanent loose-leaf roll is not practicable for daily reference. A *card index* should be prepared containing the names of *full members, probationers,* and *constituents.* Cards of different colors may be used for different classifications, for example, full members, *white;* probationers, *yellow;* constituents, *blue.* This index will be in use constantly in pastoral and evangelistic work. It also has great value as a *"mailing list"* for circularizing the church. The data may be much less full than on the permanent roll, including only such facts as are especially useful in everyday work and experience—full name, residence and business addresses, telephone number, organizations in which the individuals are shown to be active, official relation, for example, steward, trustee, president Ladies' Aid, teacher in Sunday school, etc.

c. Historical Record. Certain matters of permanent interest, not provided for above, should be recorded in a *bound volume* of board covers. This book should contain (1) A history of the local organization, brought up to date annually; (2) A record of pastors and terms of service; (3) The official members from the time of organization; (4) The statistical and benevolent reports made yearly to the Annual Conference; (5) Baptisms; (6) Marriages; and (7) Deaths.

d. Calling List. In addition to the card index, the pastor should have a "street list" of members and constituents in compact form which he carries with him constantly. This should be revised frequently and left with his successor on removing from the charge.

2. OFFICIAL BOARD RECORDS.

a. Record Book for Secretary of the Official Board containing full minutes of all actions by the board.

b. Record Books for Secretaries of Boards of Trustees and Stewards, respectively, when separately organized, containing full minutes of proceedings.

c. Financial Secretary's Record, containing (1) Detailed weekly account with each individual subscriber to the two budgets, and a (2) Weekly summary of cash received on subscriptions and special collections, and deposited with the two treasurers.

d. Record of the Treasurer of Benevolences should contain (1) The amounts apportioned for the several causes; (2) Cash received, source and purpose; (3) Cash disbursed, and vouchers for the same; (4) Blanks for yearly report to the Annual Conference with carbon copies for permanent record.

e. Record of Treasurer of Local Expense Fund should contain (1) Cash received from subscriptions and special collections; (2) Cash disbursed, and warrants for same; (3) Ledger accounts with the pastor, district superintendent, janitor, and others as necessary; (4) Monthly summary and report.

3. SUNDAY-SCHOOL RECORDS.

Great variety is found in the matter of Sunday-school records. A large school, closely graded by departments and classes, will necessarily work out a system of accounting more complicated than is desirable for a small school. It would appear, however, that the following records are essential in any school if people and money are to be accounted for satisfactorily:

a. Sunday-School Secretary—

(1) *Permanent Register* in which every new member is enrolled on joining the school, containing name, address, date of birth, date of enrollment.

(2) *Card Index* of officers, teachers, and pupils, arranged alphabetically by departments and classes, with fuller data than is asked for in permanent register, such as members of church; baptized; attendance (by month or quarter); parents or other members of family; activities, when, why, and how removed, etc.

(3) *Class Books* containing names of teachers and each

member of the several classes to mark attendance, collection, study of lesson, etc.

(4) *Summaries* of attendance and collections by week, month, quarter, and year.

b. Sunday-School Treasurer—

(1) Weekly Record of cash received by classes.

(2) Cash disbursed—warrants and vouchers for same.

4. Other Organizations.

The Secretaries of other organizations, such as the Epworth League, Ladies' Aid Society, and the Women's Missionary Societies, should keep (1) accurate *membership records* of their respective organizations and (2) complete *minutes of all meetings.* These should be submitted to the Committee on Church Records for inspection each year.

The Treasurers of these organizations should keep careful records of all moneys received and disbursed by them, and submit their accounts to the Auditing Committee of the official board annually, as well as reporting to their own organizations. For the official board has responsibility for their oversight by virtue of the fact that all these organizations have representation in that body.

Note: The necessary books and supplies are all obtainable from The Methodist Book Concern, 150 Fifth Avenue, New York city.

CHAPTER XXI

CHURCH PUBLICITY

THOSE engaged professionally in the advertising business complain that they are unable to overcome the conservatism of the church as to publicity. As a matter of fact, the church for many centuries has practiced publicity diligently. The church spire, setting the church building apart from all others in the community and visible from afar, has been for centuries an excellent device for advertising religion; and the cross on the spire and the gable-ends commonly suggests certain denominational viewpoints in religion.

The most that can be said truthfully is that the church is only conservative in adopting certain *new methods of publicity*. The inertia of an old and established institution is, in part, responsible; in other part, it is due to the control of an old ideal in all the great professions that disapproves undue self-assertion on the part of professional workers in attracting attention to themselves. It is not quite obvious that the bizarre methods employed in getting a certain brand of chewing-gum or cigarettes before the nation are in good taste for lawyers, physicians, and ministers. A newspaper may shamelessly declare itself "the Greatest Newspaper in the World," but such a legend emblazoned above the door of the church is so at variance with the spirit of humility as to arouse the suspicion that the church, through pride and self-conceit, has ceased to be Christian. On the other hand, the professional worker must believe in his cause or he will never succeed. Self-confidence is indispensable, so long as it stops short of egotism. And he must find a way to establish new personal contacts, thus widening the range of acquaintance. All this applies to the church and the minister as certainly as to medicine and the physician. It would be stupid for any religious worker to say, "I do not believe in publicity." But a wise man will be cautious about the publicity methods which he employs.

No final answer can be made to the question, "What is legitimate?" Whatever will appeal to the imagination of the community, without cheapening religion or offending good taste, is in order. But communities differ greatly in their standards touching such matters. Moreover, a man must be true to himself, doing nothing that will harm his self-respect. This implies that he must constantly examine the motive that actuates him in his desire for publicity. Does he seek a crowd for a crowd's sake? to gratify his conceit? or is he honestly desirous of reaching unselfishly a larger number of people for the good he can do them? Within these limits the largest liberty must be accorded ministers and churches.

It is quite possible that in another twenty-five years churches generally will employ devices which now are used only by a very few. Let it be said, however, that modern advertising has become almost an art. And one who contemplates the use of new methods should read many volumes on the general subject before committing himself to a unique program of publicity. And he should read everything that has been written by the pioneers in these methods as applied to churches. The more helpful volumes will be found listed at the close of this chapter.

But the publicity methods which are most open to criticism are probably least valuable for the work of the church. After all such are eliminated, there remains a multitude of devices which are generally approved, whose power does not derive from novelty and is not affected by frequent repetition. And every pastor should use them in his work.

1. Well-Kept Church Property. The condition of the building and grounds always advertises the church, sometimes for better and sometimes for worse! Some congregations would find new people coming to their services if they would only spend a little money on paint and keep

the lawn well watered and neatly trimmed. And an attractive exterior must be matched by a clean and inviting interior. The stranger in the community instinctively feels that a church which keeps its property in good condition probably has other worth-while ideals. On the contrary, if the first impression made by the property be one of untidiness and general decay, he does not expect much helpfulness from its spiritual ministry. Experience too often justifies this estimate.

2. BULLETIN BOARD. A bulletin board on the outside of the church is a useful publicity device, provided it is neat in its appearance and announces simply and briefly the services to be held, together with the name and address of the pastor. One that is in need of paint or repair, or on which the announcements are hastily scrawled with crayon, is of questionable value. If an announcement is worth making, it should be made in such fashion as to attract—not repel. Many churches in recent years post a "wayside sermon," consisting of a single short sentence, on their bulletins, thus rendering a helpful ministry by dropping a great thought into the minds of those who read.

3. WORTH-WHILE SERVICES. No church has a right to large numbers in its congregation unless it is doing everything in its power to make the services worth while. By novel publicity methods it may be possible to induce people to enter the church for a single service, but if they get nothing, they will not return a second time, be the publicity agent ever so clever. "Have something of value to advertise before you advertise," is a word of caution needed by many congregations and ministers. To conduct their services of worship more skillfully and make them more dynamic, to improve the quality of their educational work, to give Christian fellowship more significance would be the finest possible "ad" for many congregations.

4. PRINTING. The printer's art can be of great help in spreading information about the work of the church.

a. A congregation which can afford it should publish a

"*weekly calendar*" containing all announcements for the next week. It is better than making oral announcements, for the calendar may be taken home for reference. It should be paid for, as is true of all printed matter issued by the church, out of the church treasury and never contain anything except church news. No official board should permit the pastor or any organization in the church to solicit advertisements with the view of compelling the business men to bear the cost of such publications. This is a deliberate exploitation of commercial institutions, and it is disastrous for worship. While the minister attempts to lead the minds of the congregation in prayer, the bulletin, thus prostituted to secular ends, is reminding them where they may secure groceries and clothing most cheaply.

b. Paid "*display ads*" in the newspapers are becoming increasingly common. The writing of them so as to be impressive is a difficult matter.

c. Better than these are "*news letters*" about the churches of the community, which the editors are glad to publish frequently without cost if prepared by a minister who knows how to write newspaper English.

d. For special meetings or unusual occasions, *window cards* are valuable.

e. Neatly *printed invitations* sent through the mails or carried by church visitors to individuals make a good impression generally. The mechanical work of all printed matter issued by the church should be excellent and on good paper.

5. Personal Touch. The most valuable publicity is that which costs nothing—the commendation of those who are pleased with what they have found. This is *personal* and *voluntary*. When the members of the church express spontaneously great happiness in the fellowship and worship of their church, that church will have congregations whether they employ unique methods of advertising or not. Let church members form the habit of talking their church up—not down. It will always be possible to find some fault

if one is so disposed; but, on the contrary, there is nearly always more to commend than condemn if we choose to find it.

a. Pastoral visiting. The systematic visitation of all persons on the membership and constituency rolls of the church *by the pastor* is a very fine method of publicity, to say no more concerning it. It suggests that the chief leader of the church is personally interested in the people of the community, and makes an irresistible appeal. However large the membership, and however many paid workers there may be on the ministerial staff, every pastor should "visit from house to house."

b. Personal Canvass. An organized canvass of the community for persons, similar to a canvass for money, in which members of the church carry invitations to other persons, individually, is immensely rewarding.

c. Letter-writing. The writing of letters, where calls cannot be made, will often serve equally well.

d. Telephone. A pastor in Denver had his church so perfectly organized by the "Unit System" (though not a Methodist church) that by using the telephone, the whole constituency could be informed of any important matter in two hours, without anyone calling more than six or eight persons. The pastor would call his ten "captains"; each of these, five or six "lieutenants"; and each of these, six or eight persons or families. "In rural communities, one person can notify all the families on a given telephone line."

6. COOPERATIVE PUBLICITY. In many communities the churches advertise cooperatively through the press, by billboards, and other devices. The occasion is generally some special event or campaign, though it may be intended merely to call attention to the regular services of the church. The "Go-to-Church Sunday" is a familiar example.

7. THE ADVERTISING COMMITTEE. Many churches have an advertising committee composed of from three to five persons whose judgment and zeal in such matters are worth while. The pastor should meet with them frequently to

suggest and guide—sometimes to save himself embarrassment resulting from the personal exploitation of his gifts by the committee. For an unrestrained publicity committee will almost certainly proclaim from the housetop the virtues of their pastor in a way that is painful to a modest man. *Advertise the church, but not the pastor!*

8. MISCELLANEOUS METHODS. The resourcefulness of such committees is very great. Among the devices which have been employed successfully have been (*a*) parades, (*b*) billboards, (*c*) broadcasting from radio-stations, (*d*) blotters in schoolrooms and the writing rooms of hotels, (*e*) electric crosses and signs on the church, (*f*) street-car bulletins, (*g*) musical programs, (*h*) doorknob tags, (*i*) stories of community service rendered by the church, (*j*) lead pencils with name of church upon them, etc. The literature of this subject is growing rapidly and is very suggestive for those contemplating new methods.

BOOKS RECOMMENDED FOR FURTHER STUDY

E. E. Elliott, *How to Advertise a Church.*
Christian F. Reisner, *Church Publicity.*
Charles Stelzle, *Principles of Successful Church Advertising.*
William C. Skeath, *Building the Congregation.*
A. F. McGarrah, *Practical Inter-Church Methods,* pp. 199-335.
Fred B. Fisher, *The Way to Win,* Chapter VI.
Francis H. Case, *Handbook of Church Advertising.*
Roy L. Smith, *Capturing Crowds.*

CHAPTER XXII

CHURCH BUILDINGS

Buildings ill adapted to the needs of a religious organization are responsible for much inefficiency in the church. Sometimes this is the result of poverty. The congregation may not be able to afford a better house. But often it is due to ignorance on the part of the pastor, influential laymen, or the architect. The congregation may supply money in abundance, but those responsible for spending it may create a pile of brick and mortar that would serve as a railway station or a factory quite as well as a church. A church was built in Illinois some years ago whose total cost approximated $100,000, and the acoustics were so bad when it was finished that the worshiping congregation beyond the first few rows of pews could not understand what the speaker was saying. That was a defect for which the architect was to blame. Within five years the only church in a community of a thousand people was built in Kansas at a cost of $30,000. This organization is responsible for the religious education of three or four hundred young people and for the money which they provided at great sacrifice they got a building of four rooms—a large and a small one above ground, and these were duplicated in the basement. Almost in the center of the large basement room, a huge hot air furnace was installed, reducing the serviceability of that room by at least fifty per cent. The responsibility for this fearful blunder must rest upon the pastor and the building committee, for the structure does not show that they had any proper knowledge of the work which a modern church should undertake. Another building committee in Iowa was persuaded that an architect's fee of $200 would be a misappropriation of funds, and, with the assistance of a local contractor, drew their own plans, and spent

$12,000 in erecting a building. When finished the church proved to be unsafe for a public assemblage. Poor ventilation, crude interior decoration, and inadequate heating facilities are other very common defects, which cannot be charged to poverty. All this is said to emphasize the fact that much is needed besides money to provide properly for the housing of a congregation. Just as some persons are better dressed on a small income than others who are not compelled to practice economy, so many congregations, because they were led by men of intelligence and insight, possess a more serviceable church building than others, and at a smaller cost.

We do not have space, even if we possessed the ability, to write a treatise on church architecture. A few considerations, however, may be emphasized as important for all who contemplate remodeling or building new churches.

1. Neither size nor cost necessarily determines worth in a church building, but fitness to serve the religious needs of the community. The three great activities of the church are worship, education, and service, and every church should be adapted to this threefold function. It is remarkable what excellent service can be rendered with limited equipment in the hands of an imaginative pastor. A single room seated with movable chairs placed in rows, is a place of worship. With these chairs rearranged in circles or semicircles and concealed from each other by portable screens, it is a schoolroom in which the church performs its educational task. Another arrangement of chairs and screens, and it becomes a social center promoting good will and fellowship. The chairs pushed back against the walls —the room is a gymnasium in which basket-ball, volley-ball, and captain-ball are played by the young people. Arranged in rows again facing the platform, it is an "opera house" in which are held amateur theatricals, farmers' institutes, and other neighborhood meetings. Of course, this is not at all ideal. But if it is the best the community can afford, it can be made very usable.

2. As rapidly as increasing wealth permits the people to have better homes, they should have a better place of worship to comport with the new standard of living. In planning for the new church, let the demands of *worship* and *education* have the right of way over everything else. Do not build a larger main room than is needed for *the ordinary occasions of worship*. Probably some allowance should be made for growth, but to provide seating capacity for eight hundred when no more than two hundred usually come is a mistake. Remember too that the Protestant ideal requires intelligibility throughout the service. *Acoustics* should be such that a speaker may be heard easily in every part of the room. *Ventilation* is all-important. It should be possible to get a fresh supply of air into the room constantly without a draft blowing on any person in the congregation. The *heating system* should warm the room to sixty-five degrees in cold weather without an extravagant outlay for fuel. The *interior decoration* has much to do with creating atmosphere in a place of worship. The best taste in these matters declares in favor of simple lines and light colors, and against somber tones and mural decorations in the form of figures, or even verses of Scripture.

The building should be as well adapted to modern ideals in religious education as worship. Warm, well-ventilated, cheery rooms, large enough to accommodate respectively the Beginners', Primary, and Junior Departments of the Sunday school, are needed. The other departments may assemble in a larger room for worship, but as nearly as possible each class should have its own room for study and instruction. Some of the rooms used by the elementary departments may well be furnished as parlors for social and fellowship meetings of other organizations in the church.

Rooms designed primarily for service, such as game-rooms, club-rooms, gymnasium, etc., should be included in the plan only after *a careful and prolonged study of the relation of the church to the needs of the community.* It is to be feared that such rooms sometimes have been built because they were supposed to be "up to date" rather than because they were sorely needed. This service entails an increased budget for special workers and maintenance of plant. Unless all this is clearly understood and provided for by the Finance Committee, it is much better to keep these out of consideration. Not a few congregations which possess this kind of equipment wish they were rid of it.

3. All of which leads to the following suggestions.

a. No plans should be made for a building enterprise until the needs of the community have been studied carefully, and specific conclusions reached, in conference with lay leaders, concerning the exact nature of the service to be undertaken by the church.

b. The financial resources of the church and its constituency should be estimated as accurately as possible and some decision reached as to the maximum amount that can be raised for this purpose.

c. The committee should then consult with the architects who are specialists in planning church buildings. One may be competent to design an office building and possess no ability to draw plans for a church. The Board of Sunday Schools, the Board of Home Missions and Church Extension, and the Committee on Conservation and Advance have organized cooperatively an excellent Bureau of Architecture, employing only those draughtsmen who are experts in designing buildings for public worship and religious education. This bureau will be pleased to submit several plans to any inquiring official board, at a small fraction of the usual architect's fee, on being informed of the number of persons to be accommodated, the exact nature of the services to be rendered by the church, and the total cost which the congregation can afford.

d. Great care should be taken in selecting a suitable building site. We do well to follow the example of the Roman Catholics in locating churches where they will be accessible to the majority and on conspicuous sites. The unfortunate location of many churches makes it impossible for them to serve effectively.

Books Recommended for Further Study

E. deS. Brunner, *The New Country Church Building.*

Herbert F. Evans, *The Sunday School Building and Its Equipment.*

P. E. Burroughs, *Church and Sunday School Buildings.*

CHAPTER XXIII

THE CHURCH SURVEY

THE policies of the local church and the form of the organization should be determined by scientifically observable *facts*—physical, personal, industrial, social, and religious—which appear in the life of the community. Some of these may be seen at a glance. Others are discovered only after diligent search. The device employed for uncovering them is commonly called a *social survey*. It is in some disfavor for the moment because of abuse by "faddists" who do nothing about the data which they assemble by ostentatious effort. In principle, however, the survey is absolutely sound. No pastor or church can do its work properly without taking "a calm, clear look into the community to see what is there."

This is probably the place to say that one should not form his notion of a survey entirely from the elaborate findings of the Russell Sage Foundation, or other agencies which in recent years have made exhaustive studies of community life. The average pastor has neither ability nor time for such microscopic social analysis. Nor is it necessary. For the most part, such facts as are important for him may be observed quietly as he performs the routine work of the parish. On occasion he may institute an organized canvass in which he should have the assistance of other pastors and competent laymen. But even here the aim of the study should be so clear and definite that nothing irrelevant shall emerge to produce confusion. It is better to make several simple surveys than attempt a more comprehensive study which embraces a bewildering body of facts. Let the surveyor be very certain what specific things he desires to know, and then go about it in the most direct fashion to discover them.

1. The Religious Census. In general it may be said that church surveys usually take one of three forms.[1]

1. The first is not properly a sociological survey at all, but merely a *census* in which the enumerators list all persons in the community with reference to their religious affiliations, noting such facts as will be helpful to the churches in serving them. When every house is to be canvassed, all religious organizations in the community should participate. If the work is done by a single organization, scrupulous care should be exercised in notifying other denominations of those who prefer their ministry. Such a canvass is necessary before a complete constituency roll can be prepared and will supply a list of prospective members for evangelistic and Sunday-school campaigns.

A card which can be filed in an index for permanent record is filled out for each member of the family. The information usually asked for includes the following:

Name; residence; business address; telephone number; age; married; unmarried; widowed; church membership; church preference; Sunday school attended, etc.

It is possible to increase the number of questions, but these are sufficient to locate the individuals. Other information may be collected later by church visitors. *In communities where the population is constantly shifting, this canvass should be made annually.*

Accuracy on the part of the enumerators is very important. The pastors should meet them for training several times previous to the census. When possible, they should go in pairs. In small communities, the pastors themselves can do the work without assistance from the laymen. Prepared forms may be secured from certain agencies, but it is better to make out the particular blank desired and have it printed locally.

The importance of such a census cannot be doubted. It is a systematic search for the unchurched, and renders it

---

[1]See Fisher, *The Way to Win*, p. 131ff.

impossible for any religious organization to be unaware of its obligation to minister to certain people. Of course it is of no value unless an effort is made to bring the church into touch with those who have become dissociated from it. In cities it will be necessary to confine the canvass to the particular geographical area for which the cooperating churches are primarily responsible. Likewise in the open country. In villages and towns the canvass should embrace the whole community.

2. THE COMMUNITY SURVEY. The community survey proper has a very different aim. It is a study of environment, and seeks to note and classify every factor in the environment which influences human well-being.

a. Scope. (1) *Physical conditions* such as climate, soil, rainfall, housing, sanitation, water supply, community health, etc., are always an important part of such a study.

(2) Since a good material foundation is indispensable to the life of the spirit, the inquiry will carry into the field of *economics*. Does the community depend chiefly upon agriculture or manufacturing? If manufacturing, under what conditions do the workers toil? What wages are received by different classes of workers? Number of hours in the working day? Women in industry? Children in industry? Unemployment? Welfare work? Cost of living? What proportion of the workers receive sufficient income to enjoy a fair standard of living? Are workers organized? etc. In an agricultural community the investigation will concern itself with questions of tenantry, absentee landlords, marketing, crop production, etc.

(3) The survey will give careful consideration to the *sociological structure* of the community, for race, nationality, sex, family life, inbreeding, immigration, etc., have profound significance for the spiritual life.

(4) *The educational agencies* will be scrutinized. Number of schools? Graded? Centralized? High schools? Number of pupils per teacher? How many young people are in college? How many evening schools? libraries?

What per cent of the pupils finish the eighth grade? The high school? Are there vacation schools? Parent-teachers' associations? etc.

(5) Again, it is vital to know accurately what agencies serve the instinct for *play and recreation*. How many parks are there and what facilities do they afford for baseball, football, bathing, boating, tennis, and other out-of-door games? How many pool-rooms? theaters? movies? dance halls? Where do the young people congregate? Is there a Y. M. C. A.? Y. W. C. A.? What are their social activities? Do the churches and public schools make themselves social centers? etc.

(6) *Community morals* cannot be overlooked in such a study. How many arrests annually by the police and for what offenses? Gambling? Drunkenness? Prostitution? Juvenile crime and delinquency? Jail conditions? How are child offenders treated? etc.

(7) And all *philanthropic institutions* will come in for investigation. What organizations assist the needy, such as organized charities, lodges, churches, etc.? How many dependent families cared for by each? Are their methods modern and scientific? etc.

(8) *Religious institutions* will be surveyed. Number of churches? Membership of each? Amounts raised by each for current expenses? for benevolences? attitude toward evangelism? religious education? community service? missions? Service rendered to social and recreational life of their own young people? of the community as a whole? Do the pastors give full time to their church work? Do the churches cooperate with each other? Is the community overchurched? underchurched? etc.

The suggestions made under the several headings are by no means exhaustive. The number of inquiries in each case could be multiplied indefinitely. They merely suggest the vast scope and prodigious labor involved in a comprehensive study of this kind.

b. Method. (1) The first step in making a community

survey consists in determining *its scope.* It may be very elaborate. For ordinary purposes the simpler study which takes account of the more important factors in the community life, and these only perhaps one at a time, is the more valuable. In any case the initial step involves the preparation of the questions which are to be asked. The same inquiries will seldom be appropriate for two communities.

(2) *The geographical area* must be defined very accurately.

(3) *Who shall make it?* In the open country, or in a rural village or town, *the pastors* themselves can do the work better than other persons. In larger towns and cities the survey may be made a community achievement by securing the cooperation of business clubs, lodges, the Board of Health, the Board of Education, the Woman's Club, and other organizations. In this event, the survey should be put under the direction of an *Executive Committee* composed of representatives of the participating groups.

(4) *Assistance from the outside.* In the more involved surveys, it is better generally to raise a fund and employ a trained director of social surveying to supervise the whole task. It may be that a near-by educational institution, such as an agricultural school or State university, can supply such a worker. To organize and instruct his assistants will require weeks of time, and to tabulate and interpret the data impressively will consume even a longer period.

(5) Proper interpretation of the facts is quite as necessary as skill in detecting them. The work of interpretation includes *map drawing, charting, and graphing* so that the eye as well as the ear may be impressed. A single map should not be overloaded with facts. It is much better to make three maps, for example, one showing the location of churches, another the location of schools, and another the location of social service agencies, than to crowd all into one drawing. *"Comparisons"* and *"averages"* are devices which give significance to local figures. "The fact that there are 500 children in school means nothing unless that

figure is compared with the total number of children of school age." "A death rate of 9.77 per thousand in Washington Heights is not particularly informing unless it is known that the death rate in the city of New York is 13.40 per thousand."

(6) After the facts have been discovered, the next question is, "What shall be done about them?" Frequently nothing has happened. A few years ago many American cities appropriated considerable sums for the study of vice conditions, and important findings were made. In almost no instance, however, were those surveys followed by intelligent changes in public policy with reference to social conditions, and of late there has been much fruitless surveying within the church.

Suppose that it should appear that the community is not provided with adequate facilities for play? Suppose that the school buildings are overcrowded, badly located, and poorly equipped? Or that there are too many churches? What change will that make in the program of the church? A community survey will certainly raise embarrassing issues to meet which thoughtful *policies and programs* must be adopted for a period of years. Better make no survey at all than let it end there.

3. THE CHURCH SURVEY. The third type of survey aims to discover and chart important facts about the church organization itself. It too may be elaborate or simple, dealing with many or with single phases of church activities. It may concern itself with the history of the church; its growth or decay; the benevolences, the financial policy and resources, the buildings, missions, community service, evangelism, religious education.

The materials for such a study are found largely in the records of the church and its several organizations, and may be reviewed by the pastor without much assistance from others. Fisher's *The Way to Win,* pages 153-155, contains a suggestive list of questions for such an inquiry.

Books Recommended for Further Study

Edwin L. Earp, *The Rural Church Serving the Community.*

C. E. Carroll, *The Community Survey in Relation to Church Efficiency.*

Fred B. Fisher, *The Way to Win,* Chapter VI.

Margaret F. Byington, *What Social Workers Should Know About Their Community.*

Anna B. Taft, *Community Study for Country Districts.*

Warren H. Wilson, *Community Study for Cities.*

SECTION III

PASTORAL RELATIONS

CHAPTER XXIV

THE CALL TO THE MINISTRY

In the preceding chapters we have considered the ideals and methods generally approved for making the modern church an effective instrument for Christianizing society. But the mere mastery of the technique of religious work will not of itself produce the successful church leader. Spirit, temperament, zeal, inward attitudes of soul and heart are the vital elements in the ministry, and will supply the themes for discussion in the final section of this book. Conspicuous among them is the "call" to the pastoral office.[1] In the absence of this experience, one is likely to be distinctly unhappy in the ministry, and will abandon it ultimately for more congenial employment. To interpret the meaning of the "call" is our aim in the present chapter.

1. Let us begin by asking, "Is the work of the ministry really distinguished in this respect from that of other professional men?" Undoubtedly, all work may be sanctified by the spirit of service, and the same obligation is on every Christian which is on the minister to "do all as unto the Lord." But this is not quite what is involved in a divine call—the conviction that any worthy work is God's work and that the worker stands in "living connection with the heavenly world." Take coal-mining, for illustration. There can be no doubt that it is a "basic" industry, absolutely necessary to human happiness. And the man who burrows underground to bring fuel to the surface for his fellow men is a most valuable servant of society, deserving

[1]It might be possible to distinguish between a call to the pastorate and to some other form of religious work. No differentiation of this kind, however, is made here. The term is used in its most comprehensive sense, applying to all forms of ministerial service.

much more consideration than he usually receives. Moreover, many religiously minded miners derive an inward satisfaction when they reflect upon the service which they render, and are conscious of God's sustaining grace as they toil. But the effect of this work upon the workers themselves is such that it would seem highly incongruous to declare that one has been *divinely called* to mine coal. As a matter of fact, most miners probably feel that they have been *condemned* to the mines by the accident of birth and the circumstances of their early lives. A "divine vocation" may be expected to enrich the mind and heart of the worker as coal-mining does not do. A "calling" should give such joy that the worker would not be engaged in other labor if he could! And it is difficult to think of miners feeling thus about their employment. All this applies to most hand-workers. We do not deny the social value or spiritual significance of manual labor. The only point we are making is that men usually *drift* or are *forced* into it rather than deliberately choose it. It may be glorified, indeed, by the religious imagination, and thus yield high satisfactions, but the most devout laborers would be slow to declare that their work was a divine calling.

The distinction is not so clear in the case of professional workers. The successful teacher, lawyer, physician, artist, musician, architect, and engineer must have peculiar personal fitness for their work as certainly as the minister. Many of them are very happy in the practice of their professions. In most cases professional work is deliberately adopted after other possibilities have been considered. Moreover, the work tends to enlarge mental horizons and is rewarding in rich fellowships. Finally, all the great professions have passed under the law of service. Financial gain is not the dominant motive, as in business. In these respects they do not differ from the ministry.

But the ministry is distinguished from all these in that its aim is confessedly spiritual. However noble may be the service to the physical, the intellectual, and the æsthetic needs of human life, religious work is more fundamental in that it deals with intangible values which give life its real meaning. This makes it impossible for the minister to know always how well or ill he is succeeding. But it constitutes the chief glory of his task. Blunderingly enough the work goes on, as the workers themselves confess, but where there is a reasonable amount of intelligence, imagination, and unselfishness, the awkward efforts of even an incompetent minister are singularly sanctified to the spiritual well-being of a community. If it be said that other types of professional work produce spiritual results, we still insist that they are secondary, and not primary. And this holy daring which prompts religious workers to make that the chief object of all their striving which others regard as incidental, lifts the ministry out of the rank of professions into the dignity of a divine calling because its aim is divine in a sense that cannot be affirmed of other professions.

Again, the effect of the ministry upon the minister himself sets this work apart. Ideally, labor should always enrich the personality of the laborer. One of the deplorable facts about modern industry is that men become as mechanical as the machines which they tend. Born human beings, they die mere grocers, or bankers, or mechanics. Instead of the means to a fuller manhood, work too often menaces what manhood they already possess. And to this dwarfing of personality through the performance of simple processes which require no thought or imagination, must be added the positively immoral effect of the atmosphere of strife, suspicion, and mutual distrust in which employers and workers live. All this gives abundant reason for declaring, with Phillips Brooks, that work is one of the cherubim which stand with flaming swords before the Garden of Eden to prevent man's return to happiness. The supreme test of any labor must be, not the amount of wealth, but the *kind of men* it produces. And one is not happy about the human product of our industrial organization, whether it be the masters or the workers. It is very different with the professions. All react upon their members to enrich personality to a remarkable degree. It will be found, generally, that the physicians, teachers, lawyers, social workers, and ministers are the persons of broadest sympathies in the average American community. They do not accumulate great wealth, as a rule, but they possess good private libraries and overflowing reading tables, and their friendships are usually superior. Furthermore, the ethical standards of their work lay moral responsibilities upon them not imposed upon others. The shock is always greater when a professional man breaks down at the point of goodness than when a business man or laborer falls.

The influence of the ministry upon those within its ranks is similar to that of other professions, with this difference —*the ethical effect is very much greater.* The nature of the work requires constant study, which stimulates the intellectual life. It is likewise rewarding in the opportunity it affords for social intercourse of the finer sort. But the demand which it makes upon the minister himself to live on the highest moral levels exceeds that of any other profession. In a way, of course, careless living is a disqualification for any professional work, but for the pastor it is a capital offense. And no one will hold him to as strict account as he holds himself. He will be aware of personal defects which others do not observe, and these will give him constant pain. More sharply than others he will feel the inconsistency of a moral physician becoming himself a source of evil contagion and a teacher of religion failing to exemplify in his own life the doctrine which he preaches. We are not thinking of his being self-consciously "an example to others," affecting a piety which he does not feel. That road leads to cant, insincerity, hypocrisy—offensive to God and man. Rather we have in mind the passion for genuine and transparent goodness which must adorn his own life before he can successfully transmit it to others. Nor are we declaring that ministers always become immaculate in their saintliness. As a class they are subject to the same temptations that befall other men, and often are defeated in the very "citadels of their souls." But the ethical demands of their work make it more difficult for them to yield, acting as a sharp spur, impelling them to "go on to perfection" when otherwise they might cease their striving. This superior ethical influence of the ministry upon the minister is a divine effect and supplies another reason for regarding it as a sacred vocation.

Again, most ministers testify that they entered upon their work because of an *inward imperative* which is not often the experience of other professional workers. The physician, the teacher, the lawyer, the dentist, unite generally in saying that they *like* their work, but rarely does one go so far as to declare that he undertook it because of a sense of duty. The matter of peculiar fitness apart, he could have been quite as happy in some other profession as the one he chose. Indeed, many do engage successfully in business while they practice their professions. But not so, as a rule, with ministers. They are happy in their work, but something deeper than the attractiveness of the profession drew them to it. With almost no dissenting voice they affirm that their loyalty to the best that they knew was involved in their choice of a life work. It was a highly moral experience in which they were chiefly conscious of a sense of duty. An authoritative "must" was heard from the voice of conscience —the "Thus saith the Lord" of the Old Testament prophets. Let it be confessed frankly that events have proven that some were mistaken in their interpretation of this experience. But, on the other hand, experience has justified the conclusion which was reached in a majority of cases. And it is significant that an attempt to abandon the ministry, or to engage in business as a side line, for reasons less noble than those for which one entered upon it in the beginning, results usually in great unhappiness. Religious work is a jealous mistress. "The Lord will have no driftwood for his sacrifices, and no drift men for his ministry."

These three facts, then, justify the belief that the min-

istry is a work apart from others—its spiritual aim, its ethical effect upon the minister himself, and the motive actuating those who undertake it. With more warrant than is conferred by mere poetic license, it may be thought of as a "divine calling." This doctrine should be held in great humbleness of mind, however, not in arrogant self-sufficiency. The minister will prove that his is a holy office, not by proclaiming the fact self-assertively from the housetop, but by showing in his words, and life, and work, the divine spirit of kindness, love, gentleness, forbearance, and meekness.

2. We are commanded on the highest authority to test the movements of the Holy Spirit in the hearts of men.[3] If these come from the Divine Father, investigation will only make that fact more clear. If spurious, the sooner we know it, the better. *What, then, are the evidences of genuineness in a call to the ministry?* They are gathered from various sources.

a. The first is an idealistic attitude toward life. He who is more concerned with exploiting men than serving them unselfishly is inherently disqualified for religious work! He must love men deeply and feel as his very own their misery and blindness.

b. No one is called into ministerial service who is not deeply religious in his personal life. The unseen world must be for him the realest of worlds, with which he holds commerce daily by faith and prayer. He must be very sure of God and have some power at least to make other men see God in everything. In the language of the *Discipline,* he must have "the love of God abiding in him." His religious earnestness will show itself in the conviction that the sickness of the world is spiritual—a matter of wrong inner ideals and attitudes rather than maladjustments in the social organization—and as such the only cure is a wholehearted acceptance of the gospel of Jesus in all relations.

c. An inward drawing toward the work is essential. We

[3]Phil. 1. 9, 10.

should be warned, however, that the strength of the subjective impression is not very significant in itself. Emotional temperaments may describe it as overwhelming, while less excitable persons may feel nothing more than a strong inclination in a certain direction. It frequently happens that the most successful ministers experience this call in its milder forms. If one is unable to dismiss the subject from his thought, or finds pleasure in imagining himself engaged in the work that is allotted to a minister, he has as much mystical intimation as is accorded to most. And he has all that is needed, for this inclination must be corroborated by other evidence to make sure that it is more than a human preference for the office—"a hankering after its perquisites, the position it offers, the gains and emoluments it promises."

d. The absence of peculiar physical, mental, and social fitness for the work nullifies, usually, an alleged inward call. If one is not strong in body; or if he does not possess at least average intellectual ability; or if he cannot express himself clearly and with some degree of readiness; or if he does not love people, and has little ability to enlist and organize them under his leadership, he has a right to conclude that he is not called to the work of the ministry.

e. The inward call should be confirmed by the outward. That is to say, one's personal inspirations should be submitted to the judgment of others. Dr. Gladden most wisely declares, "No minister ought to undertake the work unless he believes he has a divine vocation; but he ought to submit this conviction of his to the approval of his brethren."[4] The Holy Spirit reveals himself in the collective wisdom of the many as certainly as in the private insight of the individual. If one possesses the "gifts and graces" which qualify him for religious service, those who know him and love the church will have an opinion on the subject which deserves consideration. If their judgment does not sustain his, it is quite probable that he was wrong in his in-

[4] *Op. cit.*, p. 69.

terpretation of the subjective experience which was regarded as "a call."

f. The final test of a call is some measure of success in the actual work of the ministry. If one's efforts do not command the approval of the reflective people in the congregation under reasonable conditions, he has a right to conclude that he should serve as a layman rather than a minister.

3. The call to the ministry ultimately resolves itself into a call to a particular church. This is determined in various ways. Under a "Congregational" polity, the local church issues the invitation. The "Presbyterian" ideal requires that the choice of the church shall be confirmed by the "presbytery." In the Church of England, the "parish" has little voice in determining who the "incumbent" shall be, the right of nomination being vested in a "patron," who is, in some instances, the government; in others, the bishop or archbishop; in yet others, a dean or chapter, but generally a landed proprietor.[5] In the Methodist Episcopal Church the matter, theoretically, rests entirely in the hands of the bishop. In practice, however, this officer usually seeks the advice of district superintendents, and invites churches and ministers to express their wishes fully concerning "appointments." Among the larger churches, it is becoming customary for the bishop to approve arrangements which have been entered into by churches and ministers. The right of the church and the minister to an opinion about establishing the pastoral relation can hardly be denied, even under an episcopal form of government. They will be more seriously affected in case a mistake is made than the bishop can be. On the other hand, it is not at all certain that the average pastorate has been lengthened or the joy of the relationship increased by the self-assertion of ministers and churches.

Where large liberty is granted a church in seeking its pastor the initiative in establishing a new relationship should

[5]Recent legislation by Parliament gives the parish more opportunity to express itself than was formerly enjoyed.

be taken by the church. The denomination generally is sensitive to the indelicacy of a minister actively seeking an ecclesiastical office, whether it be a pastorate, the episcopacy, a general secretaryship, or an editorial position. Under the doctrine of a divine call to religious work, the normal state of the pastor's mind should be, "I am where I am because God has placed me here. . . . I should stay here until Providence makes it clear that I am needed elsewhere." If conditions of health or work make a change seem desirable, he is at liberty to express himself in a general way to district superintendents and bishops, but not to suggest himself for particular appointments. If approached by the committee of a particular church, he may express himself as willing to accept an invitation provided the bishop approves. It will be important for him to know whether the invitation is extended unanimously or only by a majority vote. He should be more interested in the spirit and ideals of the church than the salary which it pays. And he should decline to preach a "trial sermon." Neither minister nor congregation are likely to be at their best under such an ordeal.

The customary procedure on the part of the church seeking a pastor is to appoint a committee to consult, first, with the district superintendent and bishop, and, second, with other responsible persons who may suggest the names of available ministers. The committee should not enter into negotiations with anyone until it has satisfied itself concerning his acceptability. It is an easy matter in the Methodist Episcopal Church to discover what kind of work a pastor has done in previous charges, and this is a much safer criterion than the impression he may make in a single sermon. They should as little think of asking him to "candidate" as he should think of consenting to do so. Having satisfied themselves that they are ready to extend an invitation if he is willing to accept, they may interview him, and, if he is agreed, request the bishop, through the district superintendent, to make the appointment.

If there is a call to begin a pastorate, there may also be a call to end it. The conviction may come to the pastor that he has made his best contribution and to continue longer in the service of a particular church is unwise. Let him make sure, however, that he is not moved merely by small personal irritations, or by the desire for an increase in salary, or by sheer restlessness. Again the conviction may come to the more thoughtful members of the church, and become so strong that they feel compelled to take the initiative in ending pastoral relations. There is a Christian way of proceeding in these matters which will be taken instinctively by persons of imagination and brotherly regard. One way *not* to do it is to pass complimentary resolutions inviting the pastor to return, and then quietly send a delegation to the bishop or district superintendent insisting that he must not come back. That is unethical in the highest degree. Frankness and candor, mixed with kindly consideration, alone are justified in handling a matter so delicate.

4. Very often the call to religious work may take the form of a call to some special task or field, for example, foreign missions, foreign-speaking work at home, industrial work in cities, rural church work, or religious education. The prevailing considerations in reaching such a decision should be (1) sufficient knowledge concerning the proposed service to make possible an intelligent opinion, (2) the possession of the special abilities required for effective service, and (3) a strong inward response to the appeal of the work itself.

5. It is assumed that the call to the pastoral office is for life. The time may come, however, when the way may lead providentially into other service. It seems necessary to draft men continually from the pastorate for educational and administrative work in the denomination at large. And sometimes there are honorable reasons for withdrawing from full-time work in the ministry. For example, if it is impossible to support one's family on the salary which

the church pays, without being embarrassed continually by debt, one is justified in resigning to engage in secular employment which will afford a living. The important thing in all such changes is to be certain that one is prompted by unselfish motives such as first led him into the ministry, and not chiefly by considerations of worldly ambition and private gain.

6. Having insisted that the ministry is a divine calling, let it be said also that it is a profession, in the sense at least that special training is necessary to a high degree of success. Irreparable injury has been done by misguided persons who have discouraged young ministers from attending college and theological school. The level of general culture is rising continually in every community, and professional standards must be elevated correspondingly. It is little short of tragic that the only professional worker who has made no special preparation for his work often is the minister. It is said that out of every five men in the ministry of the Methodist Episcopal Church, only *one* has received complete training for his work; *two* others have completed the major part or all of a college course; while the remaining two have never attended a college or theological school. Anyone in doubt about the relation of training to efficiency in the ministry should write to Rochester (Baptist) Theological Seminary, Rochester, New York, for their illuminating bulletin on this subject. This training should consist primarily of a broad foundation of general knowledge such as a college course affords. Later, there should be specialized instruction in professional subjects and methods of church work, such as biblical interpretation, church history, Christian doctrine, religious education, missions, and social service, together with supervised practice in preaching, conducting public worship, evangelism, and church administration. The Conference course of study is in no sense an equivalent training. It is at best an unsatisfactory substitute devised by a church doing its work largely with untrained men, in the hope of cultivating in them habits of

study and intellectual tastes which will overcome in part the handicap imposed by insufficient preparation.

Books Recommended for Further Study

Matthew Simpson, *Yale Lectures on Preaching,* Lectures I, II.

N. J. Burton, *Yale Lectures on Preaching,* pp. 31-46.

W. Gladden, *The Christian Pastor,* Chapter IV.

Charles E. Jefferson, *The Minister as Prophet; Quiet Hints to Growing Preachers.*

James A. Hensey, *The Itinerancy—Its Power and Peril.*

Ernest Clyde Wareing, *Critical Hours in the Preacher's Life.*

W. L. Sperry, *The Call to the Ministry,* Harvard Theological Review, July, 1923.

CHAPTER XXV

THE MINISTER'S STUDY

EXCEPT in comparatively rare instances the minister's study is a combination of library, office, and place of prayer. Here he retires to enrich his mind, to do the "paper work" necessary in administering the church organization, and to worship. Ideally, the office work should be cared for elsewhere in order that the hours of study and devotion may be protected from interruption. When this is not possible, the working day must be divided so that each phase of his task may receive his whole attention in its own time.

1. THE MINISTER AS STUDENT. The growing minister must be an earnest student throughout his whole life. Unceasing intellectual effort will be required to master the truth which he is to teach, and to acquire the skill to express it effectively. This is not a denial of the fact that God may communicate his wisdom immediately to men. It is only asserting that his revelation is more likely to come to the man who is honestly using his mind to discover it than to the intellectual loafer who regards study as superfluous. The race has been strangely obsessed with the idea that the movements of the Holy Spirit are erratic and capricious, despising the ordinary instruments of knowledge and employing always unique and mysterious methods. This view identifies God with the irregular and the extraordinary, but not with the usual and the commonplace. As a matter of fact, the "natural" cannot be explained without him any more than the "miraculous," and there is much to suggest that he will not use a miracle if a sufficiently perfect natural instrument is at hand by which to communicate his will. It is sometimes asked, "Why does God speak through certain individuals and not through others?" The probable

answer is, "The primary reason why more of the Word of God has come to us through Isaiah and Paul than through other men is that the minds of Isaiah and Paul were better fitted to receive these sublime truths than the minds of other men. This fitness may have been due in part to providential causes, but it must have been largely explained by the thoroughness with which they had prepared themselves for such mediumship."[1] The pearl of great price in the parable was not discovered by a shiftless vagabond who hugged a comfortable grate-fire, but by a traveling jeweler, restless, eager, constantly searching for precious stones. The buried treasure was not uncovered by a man who never worked the field, but by the conscientious tenant who held himself to the prosaic business of plowing that soil year after year—until at last he had his reward. In similar fashion the priceless pearl, the hidden treasure of divine inspiration, is discovered, not by the man who neglects the drudgery of study, but by him who regularly and continuously applies himself to the hardest of intellectual labor. By mastering the truth which others have proclaimed about God, he is making his own mind and heart fit instruments for detecting the divine will.

The diligence with which the great preachers of the past gave themselves to hard study is instructive. Jonathan Edwards said, "My method of study, from my first beginning the work of the ministry, has been very much by writing; applying myself in this way to improve every important hint . . . when anything in reading, meditation, or conversation has been suggested to my mind that seemed to promise light on any weighty point; thus penning what appeared to me my best thoughts on innumerable subjects for my own benefit." Samuel Hopkins studied fourteen hours a day, generally rising at four in the morning, occasionally as late as five in the winter. Doctor Chalmers, in the most active portion of his life, secured five hours

---

[1]Gladden, *op. cit.*, p. 87f.

daily for study. F. W. Robertson studied German by making written translations of the best German authors. He said, "I read hard, or not at all—never skimming, never turning aside to many inviting books; and Plato, Aristotle, Butler, Thucydides, Jonathan Edwards, have passed like the iron atoms of the blood into my mental constitution." His biographer says of him: "It was his habit, when dressing in the morning, to commit to memory daily a certain number of verses of the New Testament. In this way, before leaving the university, he had gone twice over the English version, and once and a half through the Greek. . . . He said, long afterward, to a friend, that, owing to this practice, no sooner was any Christian doctrine or duty mentioned in conversation, or suggested to him by what he was writing, than all the passages bearing on the point seemed to array themselves in order before him." His idea of study was to have some plan, even if a poor one, which prevented discursiveness—in his own words, "the steady habit of looking forward to a distant end, unalterably working on until he had attained it—the habit, in fact, of never beginning anything which is not to be finished."[3]

But even if the message could be received directly through prayer and faith without mental toil, the problem of expressing it clearly would remain. And the significance which this truth has for others will be determined very largely "by the dimensions and furniture of the mind through which it is communicated." A mind well equipped with a good vocabulary of words, abundantly stored with illustrative material gathered from wide reading, and skillful at sifting out the irrelevant and nonessential, will be able to pass on this truth to others as one cannot do which is furnished with nothing but good intentions. No one has put this matter more effectively than Gladden. "Language is the instrument by which the greater part of the minister's work is done. If he has a message to deliver, it will be con-

[3]See J. M. Hoppin, *Pastoral Theology*, pp. 164-169. Reprinted by permission of Funk and Wagnalls Company.

veyed in the forms of human speech. *The Word of God must reach the minds of men through the language of men. All revelation, all inspiration, is conditioned by this fact. There can be no more revelation than there is language to convey. . . . It goes without saying that the better a man understands the instrument, the more familiar he is with its structure and its possibilities, the more perfectly he can convey his own conceptions to the minds of other men. . . .* The laws which govern the inspiration of the prophet must be in many respects similar to those which govern the inspiration of the artist. The artist must become familiar with the forms by which beauty, the beauty of which his art is the vehicle, finds its best expression. Long and painful courses of discipline are needful in order that he may gain the power of utterance. . . . We have been told that poets are born, not made; but if this implies that all their powers are the gift of nature, and that none of them is due to training, it is far from the truth. The poet, for his part, was first compelled to learn the language in which he writes; a great deal of patient training was expended on him by his mother, and his nurse, and all the household, before he was able to articulate the simplest words of our common speech. Later he was led by many tutors through the mysteries of the alphabet and spelling-book and grammar; there is no royal road even for poets through these mysteries; the knowledge must be gained by toil. After the rudiments of the language have been mastered, there is a great deal more for him to learn of the idioms and forms by means of which the spirit of beauty finds expression in language. And after the technique of his art, so to speak, has thus been acquired, if he is to be an interpreter of nature and life—and this, as we are taught, is the poet's function—there will be room for long years of patient study of nature and of life before he will be able to interpret them to any clear purpose. . . . Of every kind of art this principle holds true. The musician must prepare himself by the same kind of discipline. There is a certain manual facility which can be gained only by the most patient toil. . . . The principle is not different in the case of the minister, even when we are thinking of his prophetic function. *Prophecy is the divine word spoken by the human voice, and the voice must be trained for speaking.* Inspiration is not caprice; it must follow the law which conditions all divine intervention in behalf of men. . . . *The grace of God is not given to relieve us from effort or to discharge us from responsibility, but to supplement our powers and to stimulate our activity.*"[3]

In mastering language it is impossible to exaggerate the importance of writing. One who always speaks extemporaneously, never undertaking the drudgery of painstaking literary composition, will not make language a perfect instrument for expressing thought. Rather he will incline to wordiness which may conceal thought when it is not a substitute for it. The church suffers greatly from this "vice of extemporaneity." Words are merely symbols of ideas. Many men create the impression when they speak that there is some especial virtue in using as many symbols as possible. But if one sign by the roadside points the way clearly, why should the landscape be cluttered up with ten others? The first characteristic of good literary style is clearness, and in saying a thing clearly one will use the fewest possible words, selecting them with the utmost care so that each will convey the precise shade of meaning which the speaker intended. The extemporizer in public address does not have time to choose his words with discrimination. The demand for continuous movement forbids pausing to search for just the term he wishes. One who halts thus wearies an audience quickly. He must take the word nearest at hand, whether it is the right one or not, and unless he has expressed previously that thought in writing, searching the dictionary through for better terms than those which first offered their services, the right one will seldom

---

[3]Reprinted by permission of Charles Scribner's Sons. Gladden, *op. cit.*, pp. 86-89. Italics are the author's.

be available. The one within reach will say more, or less, than he wished to say, and it will be necessary to seize another, and another, to soften or sharpen the meaning of the first; whereas if he had written carefully in the study when he had time to wait until the word he needed came to mind, that very word would have been found lying on the surface of his mind when he called for it in extemporaneous address. And this applies to figures of speech and illustrations as certainly as to words. The "vivid metaphors," "the felicitous phrase," "the vital analogy" are seldom the product of sudden inspiration but, rather, the handiwork of the patient craftsman who wrought them out carefully on paper before he used them in public speech.

Thus the relation between writing and concise, impressive public utterance is that of cause and effect. There is no easier way to enrich one's speech. The minister should write completely at least one sermon each week for the first ten years of his ministerial life. He need not, he should not often, take the manuscript into the pulpit. The writing, nevertheless, will affect profoundly his expression. As aids in enlarging his vocabulary he should read the best literature, noting carefully the manner in which others declare themselves. New words, as well as new ideas, should attract him, and he should keep a good dictionary at hand to define accurately each unfamiliar term. To make them his own, he should learn to use these new words accurately as rapidly as he acquires them. They will seem awkward at first, but after two or three trials they become a part of his own mental equipment so that he employs them almost unconsciously. A new word a day added thus to one's vocabulary will enhance greatly his power of speech in a single year. The study of synonyms is important too in the enrichment of utterance. *Ideas* must be repeated frequently, but they should be clothed in *new words* each time they appear, to avoid a sense of monotony. The larger dictionaries give the equivalent terms of every important word. A good thesaurus or book of synonyms and antonyms should be found on every pastor's study table, and show evidence of frequent consultation.

The minister's reading should be determined by the nature of his work. He is preeminently a teacher of the Christian religion and his chief studies should ever have to do with his professional interests. In a general way it may be said that he will always be digging into the subjects to which he was introduced by the theological school or the Conference course of study. Four or five hours of every working day should be spent in this kind of toil. From four to six hours will yet remain which can be devoted to correspondence, administration, and pastoral visiting.

This implies that he should have access to books, many of which must be purchased. In this way he will gradually assemble a professional library. The limited financial resources of most pastors make it imperative that books should be selected with the greatest care. Few can afford to spend more than two hundred dollars a year on their libraries. Many are unable to appropriate more than seventy-five dollars annually for this item. *But none can afford to spend less.* If need be, the minister may do without the clothes he might wish, and reduce his diet to the simplest articles of food, but he must buy nourishment for his mind whatever physical deprivation is suffered.

The quality of a private library is not necessarily determined by its size. Some ministers' shelves are heavily loaded with worthless volumes which cost much money. Others purchase comparatively few books, but always of the finest type. A small library of choice books which can be studied profitably again and again is much better than a larger collection of inferior volumes which may be read swiftly and then forgotten. Generally speaking, the man of limited income should not purchase *sets* of theological books. While there are notable exceptions (for example, religious encyclopedias), these are made to sell rather than to inform the mind. The minister does well to buy single volumes, which should be distributed among all the major departments of theological knowledge—(1) Biblical Interpretation, (2) Christian Doctrine and Philosophy of Religion, (3) Church History, (4) Religious Education, (5) Missions, (6) Social Ethics, and (7) Practical Theology. It is unsafe in one's early ministry to buy new books without advice. Seek the judgment of the best-informed men in the Conference, and ask any theological teacher in the church to recommend authors and titles. Do not buy a book that may be exhausted at a single reading.

Since a private library is always an expression of individual tastes, it is impossible for one to prescribe for another the contents of his reading shelves. A studious elderly minister will see in his library the record of his varying intellectual interests across a period of years. At one time he was fascinated by philosophy and filled a shelf with treatises on that subject. At another he was enthusiastic over the expansion of the church and assembled twenty-five or thirty volumes of church history and religious biography. At still another he was absorbed in varying problems of biblical interpretation—the prophets, the life and teachings of Jesus, the parables, the miracles, or the life of Saint Paul—and his volumes on those subjects will remind him of that period. Thus one's library becomes a kind of autobiography of the intellect. These special interests, however, should all rest on a broad foundation of general knowledge, and it is in order to make certain suggestions about fundamental volumes which should be in every minister's library, without in the least abridging the right of the individual to his own special enthusiasms.

Because he is primarily a teacher of the Bible this book must be the object of his continuous study. He will brood over it, first, to enrich his own life, and, second, for its message concerning the spirit, confident that this record of God's dealing with the race in other years will be supremely instructive to men to-day as they seek a way to life and peace. But the Bible does not "wear its heart on its sleeve." It is not easy to understand. What we get from it will depend largely on what we bring to it in the way of principles of interpretation. The first books, then, to be purchased by the young minister as a nucleus for the biblical section of his library should be a few volumes which treat in a simple and clear way the subjects of biblical revelation, inspiration, and authority. J. Paterson Smyth's *How God Inspired the Bible,* and *The Making of the Bible;* McConnell's *Religious Certainty* and *Understanding the Scriptures;* William Newton Clarke's *Sixty Years With the Bible;* Eiselen's *Christian View of the Old Testament;* Dods' *The Bible—Its Origin and Nature;* A. S. Peake's *The Nature of Scripture;* James Orr's *Revelation and Inspiration*—these suggest the type of work we have in mind. Later, technical treatises may be added, but these more elementary volumes will suffice in the beginning. Moreover, there can be no proper understanding of biblical literature without a knowledge of the religious, political, and social background of every book; and the next most important volumes in this section will be one or two good "Introductions" such as Driver's or MacFayden's *Introduction to the Literature of the Old Testament,* and Moffatt's or Peake's *Introduction to the Literature of the New Testament,* together with Hastings' Bible Dictionary (five large volumes) and Charles Foster Kent's *Historical Bible* (six small volumes). After these general reference works have been installed one may purchase "commentaries" and "expositions" of particular parts of the Bible. At last one may secure a good one-volume commentary on the whole Bible (Peake's or Dummelow's), and there are excellent interpretive translations of the New Testament which have more value than some commentaries, for example, Moffatt's and Weymouth's. For the most part, however, commentaries come in great sets, a volume, in some instances two, devoted to each book in the Scriptures. Among the more distinguished of these in recent years are the "Century," "Cambridge," and the "Expositor's" Bibles; and the "Westminster" and "International Critical" commentaries. They are very expensive, and the several volumes in any set are of unequal worth. On the whole, it is generally better to select single volumes from all these sets as one needs them than to make a large investment in books, some of which one may not use for years. As suggested above, any minister should feel at liberty to seek the advice of any theological professor in the church, by correspondence if not by personal interview, in selecting the worth-while books. In addition to the commentaries there are numberless individual studies on special themes which are rich in expository material.

It is well to follow the same method in building intelligently the remaining departments of one's library—one or more comprehensive works which outline the whole field, supplemented by special volumes on particular aspects or periods of the general subject. The basis of the doctrinal section should be two or three standard treatises on Christian Theology such as Sheldon's *System of Christian Doctrine,* Clarke's *Outline of Christian Theology* and W. A. Brown's *Christian Theology in Outline,* together with a few reliable volumes on the philosophical ground of faith, for example, Strickland's *Foundations of Christian Belief,* or *Foundations,* by Seven Oxford Men. A knowledge of the manner in which Christian teaching has developed throughout the history of the church is important to a proper understanding of that teaching, and every minister should possess an excellent work on the history of doctrine, such as Fisher's or Sheldon's.

Throughout one's whole ministry he will add to this section single volumes on special doctrines, having respect, first, for the great beliefs that all bodies of Christians hold in common, and afterward for the doctrines of religious experience in which Methodists have been especially interested. The following titles will illustrate what we have in mind: Knudson's *Religious Teaching of the Old Testament;* Sheldon's or Stevens' *New Testament Theology;* Streeter and others, *Immortality, Prayer,* and *The Spirit;* Bowne, *The Divine Immanence, Studies in Christianity;* Jefferson,

Things Fundamental; Mackintosh, *The Person and Work of Jesus;* McConnell, *Essentials of Methodism,* and *Diviner Immanence.*

In the department of church history, the introductory work should sketch in outline the whole story of the expansion of Christianity. This is done well in a single volume by Williston Walker. If a work of several volumes is desired, buy Sheldon's *History of the Christian Church.* Later add volumes on particular periods, and biographies of great churchmen in all periods. After these a volume on the Protestant denominations and a good history of Methodism and the Methodist Episcopal Church would complete the section.

The fundamental volumes in the department of religious education will deal with the psychology of religious experience among children and adults. Next should come volumes on principles, ideals, and methods of teaching religion. And finally there should be several volumes on the organization and administration of church schools. The reader is referred to the books recommended for study at the close of the chapter on religious education (XV).

In developing the section on *Missions,* there should be, first, two or three volumes on the great ethnic faiths of the non-Christian world such as Soper's *Religions of Mankind,* or Hopkins', Menzies', or G. F. Moore's *History of Religions.* After these, historical volumes treating of particular mission fields, and biographies of great missionary leaders should be added, together with a number of texts expounding missionary ideals for the mission fields, and methods of missionary education that may be adopted in the local church.

The department of *Social Ethics* will be in many ways the most important, yet the most difficult to develop. The basis should be a few reliable volumes on social organization, interpreting the mutual relations of the individual and society, and the significance of economics for both; next, there should be several volumes setting forth the principles and methods of the more significant social movements, such as socialism, trade-unionism, syndicalism; and lastly, there should be at least a half dozen of the great statements of the ethical ideal of Jesus for social relationships. The reader is referred to the books recommended for further study at the conclusion of Chapter XVII.

The section on *Practical Theology* should contain a great variety of books having to do with the technique of church work. Some of the great expositions of the art of preaching made annually for a long period by the Yale lecturers and the great teachers of homiletics should be secured. At least one new volume of this sort should be read earnestly each year to keep one's ideals untarnished. There should be a good collection of the best sermons by preachers living and dead, not for the sake of the material they contain but for the standard they set in the matter of literary form; also a few works on hymnology, several expositions of the ideals and methods of public worship, devotional volumes for the spiritual enrichment of the preacher's own life, and many volumes on church methods and administration. (See books recommended in Sections I and II.)

The morning hours of each day should be dedicated sacredly to devotions and professional study. There will be another hour or two, generally in the evening, besides vacation periods, which may be utilized in reading general literature and periodicals. Here one may follow his own taste. History, biography, science, essays, fiction, poetry, all have peculiar values for the preacher, and in the course of a year he should read them all. History, biography, and science, being descriptions of life, will supply an abundance of the best illustrative material. Essays will suggest themes for sermons. Fiction and poetry will be recreative and at the same time cultivate the power of imagination without which the minister cannot attain to excellence in anything. Upon his reading table should be found the official weekly of his denomination, a digest of current events and news, religious periodicals like The Christian Century, the Methodist Review, and The Journal of Religion, together with at least one great magazine of general literature such as The Atlantic Monthly, The Yale Review, Harper's, or Scribner's.

One should learn the art of reading rapidly the lighter kinds of prose, both general and theological. There is in every well-written paragraph a single sentence, sometimes a single phrase, which summarizes the whole, and good readers know how, at a glance, to fasten upon these central words. To mark them with pencil makes it possible to review quickly the contents of the chapter or book with little effort.

The only way to conserve the results of one's reading is to make notes. The most interesting information, the most impressive illustrations, and the most suggestive interpretations will inevitably escape unless they are rendered permanent by writing. After Phillips Brooks' death his biographer found many notebooks filled with jottings as he had read and outlines of sermons as they had first come to him—the germs of his greatest discourses. And practically every successful minister reads with a pencil in his hand. It is possible, however, to keep one's notes in such form that they are of little value. The bound notebook and scrapbook "keep" things too literally. It is necessary to read every page of every book to find what one wants. Notes and clippings must be *indexed* in some practical and simple manner to be useful.

The following method is employed by one of the most successful Methodist pastors, with the result that all the data he has collected concerning any subject through his whole ministry is available immediately for use:

(1) All books in his library are numbered and arranged on his shelves in consecutive order.

(2) He has clipped interesting articles on every conceivable subject. These are numbered consecutively from 1 to 5,000 as they have accumulated, without any reference to subject, and are filed in folders containing fifty clippings

each; for example, Folder No. 1 holds the clippings numbered from 1 to 49; No. 2, from 50 to 99; No. 3, from 100 to 149; etc.

(3) His personal jottings have been made on separate sheets of note paper and are filed separately in the same manner as his clippings.

(4) His sermons are preserved in strong manila envelopes on each of which appears a number, the subject of the sermon, when, and where preached.

(5) All this material is indexed carefully in a card index under fewer than one hundred topics arranged alphabetically. He began with a much smaller number and developed additional topics as there was need. The following will suggest the character of the groupings: Assurance, Atonement, Authority, Bible, Church, Education, Faith, God, Holy Spirit, Industry, Inspiration, Jesus Christ, Methodists, Missions, Politics, Prayer, Press, Recreation, Regeneration, Social Movements, Sunday School, Temperance, Texts and Subjects. As he comes upon any impressive fact or suggestion in his reading he makes note of it under its appropriate topic in his index.

Under each heading there would be dozens of cards like the following on "Prayer":

Meaning of Prayer........................	B 248–43
Prayer and Daily Life......................	C 16–884
Prayer in the Life of Jesus..................	S 127
Missions and Prayer........................	B 274–123
Illustration	N 39–1962

These symbols tell him that in Book No. 248 in his library, page 43, there is a chapter on the "Meaning of Prayer," and in Book No. 274, page 123, another phase of the subject is discussed. He has also a clipping in Folder 16, No. 884. Once he preached on "Prayer in the Life of Jesus," Sermon 127; and in his Note-file, Folder 39, Note 1962, he once recorded a valuable illustration. He has a score of other cards on this same general subject, containing material enough for a dozen sermons on every phase of the subject and all within reach.

2. The Minister's Office. The minister's office work should be cared for outside of the morning hours devoted to study. If he is so fortunate as to have a good secretary, this work will seldom need more than thirty minutes personal attention each day from him. Comparatively few pastors, however, have such assistance and must be their own clerks. If this work requires more than one and a half hours per day on the average, he is justified in asking the official board to make an appropriation for stenographic help, for the pastor's time is too valuable to spend a large amount of it keeping records and running a typewriter which some one else can do better for fifty cents or less an hour. The best available time for office work probably is in the early afternoon just after lunch and before it is wise to begin his afternoon calling.

3. The Minister's Devotional Life. There is nothing more important for the pastor than the culture of his own spiritual life. His energies, constantly being drained, must, as constantly, be replenished. Happily his intellectual toil and pastoral visitation among the people of the community will often refresh his spirit if his attitude in them be prayerful. For, as Doctor Fairbairn says, "It may be laid down as a general principle that the whole of a minister's labors should be intermingled with meditation and prayer. He should never be simply a man of learning and study, for this itself may become a snare to him; it may even serve to stand between his soul and God, and nurse a spirit of worldliness in one of its most refined and subtle forms."[4] But in addition he must engage regularly in such special private exercises as are designed to make him conscious of the presence and peace and power of God in his own heart. The first of these is the meditative reading of the more devotional and liturgical parts of the Bible. The great hymns

---

[4]Quoted by Gladden, *op. cit.*, p. 105.

of the church, also, read thoughtfully and memorized, have power to nourish the spirit. Furthermore, the reading of prayers and religious poetry will help induce the mood of worship in which, finally, the soul of the man himself comes to self-expression and reaches out to lay hold of God at first hand. He who is not fully aware of the necessity for such communion is not fit to preach the gospel.

Books Recommended for Further Study

Washington Gladden, *The Christian Pastor,* Chapter V.

Frank W. Gunsaulus, *The Minister and the Spiritual Life.*

P. T. Forsyth, *Positive Preaching and the Modern Mind,* Chapter V.

Evelyn Underhill, *Practical Mysticism.*

CHAPTER XXVI

PASTORAL VISITING

To many pastors the most distasteful phase of their work is visiting from house to house. This antipathy expresses itself often in mere neglect; but occasionally, in a frank belittling of the task. It is said, "My business is not ringing door bells!" or, "I do my work with my head, not my feet!" or, "I am a shepherd, not a sheep-dog." Quite naturally attempts are made to justify this feeling on rational grounds. "Let the people send for me as they do the physician when they desire my services"; or, "A minister invites serious criticism by visiting the women when their husbands are not at home"; or, "Pastoral calling is unnecessary in the highly organized church of to-day"—these and other reasons are urged as an excuse for visiting only the sick and the troubled.

The fundamental difficulty here arises from a misunderstanding of the purpose and method of the pastoral call. If one contemplates the trying exercise described by Dr. William M. Taylor, a distinguished Congregational minister in New York in the latter part of the nineteenth century, it is better that he leave it undone. "I was first settled," he says, "over a church of about one hundred and eighty members, many of whom resided in the village in which the place of worship was situated, but a considerable number of whom were farmers scattered over an area of about six miles in length by about two in breadth. I made my visits systematically, week by week, taking the parish in manageable districts. At first I was accompanied on each occasion by an elder. It was expected that I should ask a few questions of the children, assemble the members of the household, give a formal address, and, then conclude with prayer. The presence of the 'lay brother' was a great embarrassment. I supposed that because he was with me I should have a new address in every house, and should have a prayer in every instance perfectly distinct from any which I had formerly offered. . . . So I went on from house to house, making a new address in each until, when it was toward evening, and I had walked perhaps five or six miles and made ten or twelve addresses, I was more dead than alive. You cannot wonder that, in these circumstances, pastoral visitation became the *bête noir* of my life, and I positively hated it. Thus prosecuted, it was simply and only drudgery, and, so far as I know, was not productive of any good result."[1] This kind of visiting implies an aristocratic view of the minister's relation to the members of his church. Calling is an official function, a kind of spiritual inspection tour in which he formally peeps into their souls to see that they are swept and garnished. And after the manner of official affairs, the etiquette of the occasion is prescribed in great detail. This solemn farce gave the pastor no real knowledge of his people, nor did it permit them to derive any benefit from his presence, for an atmosphere of unreality wrapped both him and them about.

But suppose that he had been actuated by the democratic motive of friendship, going forth to his calling, not because custom and tradition prescribed it, but because he sincerely desired to visit with old friends and to make new ones among young and old alike. And suppose, too, that he, in genuine friendliness, had come informally instead of formally, upsetting the routine of family life as little as possible, adjusting himself to the mood and circumstances in every home; praying here because it was perfectly natural to do so; omitting the prayer and even religious conversation there because it would have been an embarrassment to everyone; staying an hour in one place, and only five minutes in another, for precisely the same reason—that it was

---

[1]Reprinted by permission of Charles Scribner's Sons. Quoted by Gladden, *op. cit.*, p. 197f.

the wise and judicious thing for a friend to do. On this view of the matter pastoral visiting becomes a great adventure with the prospect ahead of endless variety—a fascinating game, the object of which is to secure the good will of as many different persons as there are members of his constituency and show himself an equally good friend to all. If any object that "social calling" of this sort is not religious, it is well to remember that one cannot win people to Christ until he has first won them to himself. Moreover, we have no right to regard the social call as necessarily lacking in religious value. The religious motive does not express itself exclusively in formal devotional exercises. The call which promotes unselfish fellowship, deepens human sympathy, and increases the sense of brotherhood is as certainly religious as one which definitely concerns itself with religious subjects. Bishop Quayle gives a valuable hint to the pastor when he remarks, "That every call a pastor makes should be of the revival order is simply a piece of grievous misconception."

Again, pastoral visiting has no terrors for the minister who relates it clearly in his thought to his preaching. All sermonic material is not gathered from books. Much of it comes directly from life. We have seen that, according to the Protestant theory of worship, the minister acts as the representative of the congregation, giving expression to their collective thought and striving. This is true of the sermon as well as of the prayers. But how can he know what the people are thinking if he refuses to mingle with them under circumstances which lead them to express themselves freely? We do not mean to suggest that he should show servile regard for any individual's opinion, or that he should fear to speak his mind when he differs honestly from others. The hope of lifting the congregation to higher levels of thinking and feeling and living rests largely upon the fact that the minister's thinking shall not always conform to that of others. But we read that "the spirit of a man is the candle of the Lord"; that is, God reveals himself through human beings. We are likely to find the beautiful, the courageous, the heroic, the virtuous among simple persons as well as among the most learned. And how shall we receive the inspiration of their lives if we hold ourselves aloof from them? Pastoral visiting is highly accredited as a method of gathering homiletical materials, of acquiring the truth the congregation may have for the minister.

Yet another conception of ministerial calling will convert it from an unpleasant duty into a high privilege. The auricular confession of the Roman Church rests upon a sound psychological principle—the demand of the human spirit in moments of worry, excitement, and remorse, for an opportunity to unburden itself. It seeks an ear into which it may pour its feelings. Evangelical Protestantism, for good cause, rejects the Catholic method of providing this ear, and finds in pastoral visiting a better device to serve the same end. This is in Bishop McConnell's mind when he suggests that, in visiting the people in their homes, the pastor shall seek, not so much to become a good talker, as a *good listener.* To give sympathetic heed to what others feel inclined to say to us, though it may seem trivial and commonplace; to direct conversation without forcing confidences, so that men and women and children may talk frankly about what concerns them most; to be patient while a nervous, perplexed, annoyed soul eagerly lays its fears and hopes before us—is to render, often, the greatest possible service. It may be that a word of wise counsel can be given, or that relief may be afforded through prayer. But the very act itself of discharging the load of pent-up emotion loosens the tension and relaxes the strain so that the weary soul "feels better," though the outward situation may remain just as it was.

"If a pastor shows himself willing to listen, and can listen without fidgeting in a hurry to get to the next call on his list, he will be astonished to see how thoroughly people will open to him the depths of their lives, and how often they will give him a message which is a genuine voice of humanity. A successful pastor once told me of the following experience: A member of his church suddenly met a terrible grief. For days the stricken man sat almost in silence, but when my friend called on him he was moved to talk by the rare sympathy of a skilled physician of souls, for my friend possessed such rare sympathy. The mourner talked for one hour, for two, for three, and found his way toward the light as he himself talked. For the rest of his life he held in grateful honor the memory of the pastor who listened while he talked. Now, what the mourner gained as he thus thought aloud toward the light was not less than the pastor learned. The pastor heard not just the man talking; he heard the voice of stricken humanity and a note from that voice sounded thereafter from his pulpit. One reason for encouraging people 'to talk themselves clear out' is that in the experiences which are most peculiarly our own we may find ourselves to be most like other people. Who of us has not had thoughts and feelings which have seemed so peculiarly his own that he has been afraid to mention them to others for fear of being misunderstood and perhaps laughed at? Yet who of us has not had the experience of discovering that such thoughts or feelings when actually expressed have been those that other people have seemed to understand best? Many of these most intimate experiences are most catholic in their sweep. The man who knows these peculiarly personal experiences is able to preach in widely human terms. Moreover, apart from all such intimacies, the preacher who, with a consecrated desire to serve, mingles most closely with his fellows is the one who can most genuinely utter the voice which we call the voice of humanity."[2]

Finally, it accords with the social view of the minister's relation to the church to insist that in his pastoral visiting he acts as the representative of the whole congregation.

F. J. McConnell, *The Preacher and the People*, pp. 90-92.

He is the voice through which all the members speak to each.

These considerations make pastoral visiting an all-important part of the minister's work. Indeed, they justify Vinet in his statement that willingness to visit from house to house is the final test of a call to the ministry. "Public speaking is comparatively easy and agreeable; we can only be sure of our vocation to the ministry when we feel drawn and impelled to exercise the duties of the care of souls." It would greatly simplify matters if a manual could be prepared, such as some have pleaded for[3] containing "examples and rules for the examination of the burdened conscience governing the wants of souls seeking guidance and help, and the ways for meeting them sanctioned by God's Word, the church's discipline, and the Christian experience of all the past." But the technique of pastoral oversight cannot be thus codified. Imagination, insight, and sensitiveness to moods and conditions are indispensable. Without these, rules are ineffective. With them, rules are not needed. If the pastor is not the kind of person who does the right thing almost instinctively and intuitively, he is not likely to do it because it is commanded; or if he should go through the prescribed actions, it would be in a spirit that would make them ridiculous. Nevertheless, a few general suggestions may be helpful in dealing with certain types of calls.

1. General Calling. By this we mean the regular and systematic visitation of every family in the membership and constituency of the church. The pastor may have assistance in this work, but he himself can never be excused from participating in it, however large his congregation or however numerous his helpers. No one has a right to regard himself as a good shepherd who does not plan to visit personally every family at least once a year. When F. B. Meyer, S. Parkes Cadman, Charles Reynolds Brown, and

[3]See Bishop A. N. Littlejohn, in *The Christian Ministry at the Close of the Nineteenth Century*, p. 322.

Bishop McConnell never passed a year as pastors without making at least a thousand calls (Bishop Quayle always visited every family once a quarter), others may indulge no hope of pardon for neglecting this work.

The busiest pastors have only to plan intelligently and conscientiously for this visiting to get into every home regularly each year. Let them divide the total number of calls which should be made annually by fifty-two to discover how much work must be done each week, and then see to it that as early in the week as possible the appropriate number of visits is made. If one were to spend but three hours a day, five days a week in visiting the people, he could make fifteen hundred calls in a year, allowing a half hour for each visit. In few churches will it be necessary to make a larger number, and most churches will demand less. This will leave four or five hours daily for study, and two more for correspondence and administration, provided the minister is willing to work nine or ten hours each day—and he should be ashamed to work less.

a. "What is the purpose of such calling?" First, the establishment of friendly relations between the minister and every member of every family. These relations spring up only as the result of careful cultivation. The diligent pastor will carry with him constantly a visiting list containing not only the names of the heads of the family but of every child and other person in each home, and when he calls, will inquire thoughtfully concerning each by name. He will keep a memorandum of pertinent facts about each individual. One of the great pastors of American Methodism twenty-five years ago was the Rev. Henry A. Buchtel, D.D., who is known to the church now as chancellor emeritus of the University of Denver and former governor of Colorado. On his first visit in a home he was accustomed to inquire carefully for the names and birthdays of all young people in the family. The occasion for this appeared later when the children on every successive natal day received from their pastor letters written in his own hand, and never two alike. Who could resist such overtures of friendliness? To recall that on your last visit the father was ill, to remember that James is interested in collecting stamps, and to send your regards by her mother to Mary, who is at college, may be small matters, but they do much to bind people to you. And whatever will do that is very important.

The second object of this general calling is to discover any who may be troubled, disaffected, or indifferent, and to render such individual aid as lies in one's power.

Third, this kind of calling binds the church constituency into a single spiritual unity. Like a human shuttle-cock the pastor moves back and forth through the community, carrying the same spirit and the same ideals into all homes, counseling, sympathizing, admonishing, rebuking, encouraging as each case may demand, but all to the same end. Nothing could be more valuable from the standpoint of church organization. Commercial and industrial corporations often pay welfare workers large salaries to do just this among their employees.

Finally, it should be said that in this persistent work of visiting the pastor keeps his parish maps up to date. He constantly re-surveys the field, noting new facts and faces in the community, changes of residence, and the like.

b. "What do you do when you call?" Chiefly, carry a spirit of buoyant faith and hearty cheer into the homes of the community. A sanctified imagination (common sense) will suggest the particular things which should be done. These will vary with the personality of the pastor and with the conditions which he finds. If he arrives inopportunely, say in the midst of housecleaning, or just as his hosts are preparing to go out, or when other company is present, he will make everyone happy by wishing all "good day" and leaving in a moment or two. Let him not be deceived by assurances that he must stay. A courteous mistress will always conceal, if possible, any embarrassment which a guest unwittingly may cause. Match her courtesy with another equally fine and refuse to interfere further with her plans, which are important, at least to her. "The getting away is quite as much of an art as coming," says our wise Bishop Quayle. "Many times preachers are so engrossed with their pastoral concerns that they do not get at the magnitude of the concerns of others."[4]

On the other hand, circumstances may justify the pastor in lingering long to talk. Should the home be one in which dwells a lonely soul who is largely cut off from religious and social fellowship, and upon whose hands time hangs heavily, stay as long as you choose, talking about the life and activities of the church, telling all the good things you know of persons and institutions in the community, though, of course, the conversation should never degenerate into mere gossip. If the host be devoutly minded, it will be quite in order to read a helpful portion from the Scriptures and pray briefly before leaving. This prayer may be made sitting or standing as well as kneeling.

Again, it might be appropriate to stay and *listen,* rather than talk. As previously noted, there are burdened spirits who need nothing so much as a sympathetic and attentive ear into which they may discharge their feelings. They will derive more comfort from an inarticulate pastor than one who is voluble. It is a good thing for the physician of souls to know when his silence will be more healing than his words.

Let no minister suppose that he must pray in every home. A pastor on coming to a new church let it be known that this was his ideal, and later discovered that few people were at home when he rang the bell. A wiser pastor announced that, except in cases of sickness or trouble, as a rule he was not accustomed to suggest prayer when he visited members of the church in their homes. Since the obligation of hospitality was on them, he would wait for an invitation. His own hope, however, was expressed hu-

[4] *Pastor-Preacher,* p. 139.

morously by the comment that he expected them to be well-mannered in this regard. Why should the physician of souls have but one prescription, regardless of varying temperaments and conditions? Let him be as wise as the healer of the body, who makes a careful diagnosis of each case and adapts the treatment to the disease.

Some ministers utilize the mail as a valuable pastor's assistant. The personal visits of the lamented Maltbie Babcock were very brief. Frequently he made as many as twenty-five calls in an afternoon. But he had the imagination to take in a situation at a glance, and on his return to his home often spent several hours writing notes of advice and helpful suggestion to those whom he had found in need of pastoral counsel. Dr. George S. Butters, of Boston, has followed a similar plan. In every community where he has lived men and women treasure pastoral epistles which he addressed to them at important crises in their lives, and literally hundreds of ministers in his denomination, whom he first met as theological students, preserve with great care letters which he has written across a long period of years. This use of the pen is commended especially to those who find it difficult to express themselves in speech when they feel deeply.

In cities and larger towns it is all but impossible to see the men of the congregation during the day unless one calls on them at their places of business. As a rule, laymen rather like to have their pastor hunt them up at their work, provided he does not come too often or stay too long. This kind of a call usually should be *very brief*. The object should be merely to let the man know that his pastor thinks of him and wishes him well in all that concerns him. If one plans to consult laymen on church business during the day, an appointment should be made in advance for that purpose. Men usually are appreciative of any effort which the pastor may make to visit their families during the evening. They have time then for social and religious conversation which is denied them during the day.

It is not clear that a minister should announce publicly in advance that he will call on the families who live in a certain district during the following week. There is always a possibility that he may be compelled to change his plan, and some will await his coming in vain. Moreover, it may give others the opportunity to avoid a call which they need sorely. It seems better, on the whole, to take one's chances on finding people at home, and, if they are absent, to call again.

It should be unnecessary to say that no minister should make pastoral visiting an occasion when he airs his personal grievances or works up sympathy for himself. He goes to give sympathy and not to get it.

Some ministers feel that their wives must accompany them in their pastoral visiting. When it is convenient and pleasurable for them to go, let them do so by all means. But that they are obligated to attend their husbands thus is not obvious. The minister's wife may have a unique relation to the church, but certainly it cannot be that of parish visitor. Should a physician's wife accompany her husband on his professional calls? Let the mistress of the parsonage have her own calling list independently of her husband. In many cases the same names will appear on both lists, but the lists will not be identical throughout. It may be urged that there is a type of woman in almost every community who is especially attracted to ministers, and against these their wives must protect them. In reply it may be said that almost never does a minister whose heart is pure and whose manner is above reproach get into trouble of this kind. If he needs other protection than a clean mind affords, let him take as escort a male lay official of the church or an officer of the law—or stay away.

2. Special Calling. This includes all official visiting which is required by something exceptional in the experience of individual members of the church or its constituency. It is additional to the regular visiting which should go on constantly, and, in importance, takes precedence over it.

That is to say, an individual in especial need of pastoral attention has a preferred claim upon the pastor's time, even the hours ordinarily set apart for study. This type of visiting embraces calls upon the sick, the troubled, strangers, and all who are upon the pastor's "personal work list."

a. Upon the Sick. A pastor on going to a new parish should begin his work by visiting immediately all who are ill, and he should let the congregation know that he desires to be informed in the event that any home is stricken with sickness. Nothing but ignorance of the fact can excuse pastoral neglect of any who suffer. Those who are "shut in" as the result of chronic invalidism should be visited regularly, both by the pastor and any parish visitors who may assist him. Their names should be on special mailing lists to receive all printed matter issued by the church, and good wishes may be sent frequently over the telephone.

In the case of acute and sudden illness the pastor should call as soon as he learns of the trouble, and, under ordinary circumstances, every day thereafter as long as the illness continues to be serious. Some of these subsequent calls may be made by telephone, particularly if the sickness is not of a threatening nature; but the personal visit will be more appreciated because it requires a greater expenditure of time and energy.

The pastor should have two ends in view in visiting the sick: (1) composing the spirit of the patient, and (2) being a good friend to the family. In the first instance his call may have genuine therapeutic value. The relation of the mind to disease is now generally admitted. Depression and irritability are inimical to health and retard recovery from sickness, while calmness, buoyancy, and hopeful expectancy assist the healing process greatly. The wise minister may do much to create a state of mind favorable to the restoration of health.

Nor does it depreciate the value of this service to recognize that it is accomplished by "suggestion." It is not necessary to approve all that is said in the name of a behavioristic psychology to use its method intelligently, as does the salesman in selling merchandise. The wise pastor knows what kind of a response he wishes to secure from the patient, and will plan his appeal with the utmost care. On entering the home, let him lay aside his outer garments —overcoat, hat, gloves, and rubbers. His manner on approaching the bedside of the patient should be cheery, though quiet; and sympathetic, though not solemn. He should not stay long, for sick people tire easily; nor should he talk much of his own illnesses. Let him listen, however, if the patient wishes to describe his sickness. All this is of absorbing concern and relieves the mind. Then the patient's attention may be directed away from his illness to people, things, and events of interest. Leave a book to be read when reading is possible, or flowers, either in your own or the name of the church. If you know a good story that will provoke a smile, this is the time to tell it. Let all that is said be designed to stimulate in the sufferer a hopeful, pleasant frame of mind. And, if possible, one should turn the conversation so as to suggest naturally the healing values of prayer and faith, for nothing is more potent in composing the restless mind. Thus the spirit, manner, and words of the pastor will be designed to induce an attitude which will be favorable to recovery.

If it should appear that the patient grows steadily worse and death is imminent, the pastor should be the most devoted friend of the family. This would mean, at the least, keeping in constant touch with them, and, at the most, putting himself entirely at their disposal for any service which he is able to render. One distinguished minister in Methodism well-nigh took up his abode at the home when death was expected in any family in his parish. Happy is that family whose pastor is gifted with imagination as well as sympathy so that he understands without being told how he can serve best, whether by speaking or keeping silence, by his activities or by his prayers! And this service should continue long after the funeral, if it comes to that. A certain bishop in the church is generally commended for the profundity of his thought and the simplicity of his utterance, but the sound of his name is like sweet music to one elderly woman because every day for three weeks he called at her home after a member of her family had died. He seldom stayed more than five minutes, but it was long enough to let her know that she and her loneliness were much in his mind those dreary days.

The conduct of the pastor in the face of contagious disease will be regulated largely by the laws of public health. He has no more right to consider personal danger than a physician; and his family is obligated to take the same risks should occasion arise, which are run by the doctor's wife and children. But let him be guilty of no foolhardiness. If he must expose himself to contagion in the discharge of his pastoral duties, let him consult a physician concerning protective measures which may be taken, both for his own and his family's sake. He should never be guilty of disregarding quarantines without the consent of health officials. The telephone and mails, of course, may be used to communicate with those who are isolated.

As a matter of fact, visiting the sick is always attended by more or less hazard, and the careless pastor may easily become a "carrier" of disease. He will almost certainly shake hands with the patient, and may handle articles which the latter has touched. Consider how perilous that is in a case of tuberculosis. The thoughtful pastor, then, should always be careful to cleanse his hands thoroughly after a visit to the sick-room.

The relation of the pastor to the physician should be one of cordial cooperation. Most physicians recognize the therapeutic value of the pastor's call and welcome it, except where a pastor has proven himself to be a wretched bungler who irritates more than he soothes by his coming. Generally, the minister will be admitted to sick-rooms, hospitals, and operating rooms when all others are excluded, and he may call at other than the regular hours for visiting.

But should the physician leave orders that *no one* may see the patient, or if the nurse should warn, *"Only a minute!"* he must have the utmost respect for their commands. They are in charge of the case. Let him turn his attentions to the family, who need him in such an hour more than the patient.

b. Upon Strangers. After the sick, strangers have the next best right to the pastor's attention. It is quite possible that the minister may not understand how lonely new people can be in a community. He and his family receive so much attention when they come that he may mistakenly assume that others are as cordially received. It is seldom so. Often strangers wait in vain for signs of friendly interest in their neighbors. They may even attend church without anyone inquiring for their names or bidding them welcome. For an occasional Christian (?) takes the position that he does not care to make any new friends. As soon as he learns of their presence the minister should call in the name of the church, provided, of course, that they belong to his constituency. (If they are members of another denomination, he should give their names to the pastor of that religious body.) And he should urge the members of his own church who live near by to call soon. Conscientious pastors use many devices to inform themselves concerning strangers. Blank cards are kept in the pews for reporting their names. The members of the church are asked to act as "sentinels" who notify him when he should call on new people in their block. Sunday-school teachers are trained to report the names of new pupils so that the minister may call on the parents. Ushers in the public service note the unfamiliar faces and quietly secure their names and addresses, introducing them when possible to the pastor. He, in turn, secures their "church letters," and builds them as rapidly as possible into the life and organizations of the new church.

c. The Troubled. This group would be, as a matter of fact, identical with the entire membership of the church, for trouble in some form comes to all. Here the term is restricted, however, to those who are miserable for other reasons than physical illness. It includes the wearied, the worried, the anxious, the depressed, the perplexed, the discouraged, the sinful. The amount of mental and emotional suffering in the world cannot be exaggerated. The number of persons who destroy themselves annually because life has become intolerable; the multitudes who follow after Christian Science and other cults which promise peace of mind; the tens of thousands who take "the rest cure" in sanitariums; the millions who seek diversion and self-forgetfulness in drugs, intoxicants, and extravagant amusements—these all bear witness to the far-reaching sway of unhappiness. The causes are numerous, sometimes found in external circumstances, and sometimes in psychological conditions. In part, they are due to the monotony of modern industry; in other part, to defective education in the home, the school, and the church; and, in yet other part, to the rapid pace of modern life, which gives very few an opportunity to compose themselves. Some of this misery is psychopathic, a matter for experts highly trained in the methods of psychoanalysis. Most of it may be relieved, however, by the "healing personality" of a sympathetic pastor who has the imagination to understand in how many ways the spirit of man may be burdened; and the patience to listen while the heart pours out that which has been too long repressed; and the wisdom to make helpful suggestion concerning the attainment of peace and self-control.

The nature of these suggestions will vary greatly, for different problems require different solutions. When poverty is the real source of trouble the pastor must do all in his power to find employment, or, if that is impossible, to provide for permanent relief, enlisting the interest of all persons and institutions directly concerned. When the case is one of domestic unhappiness in which husband and wife are alienated, appeal, exhortation, rebuke may all be in order, according as the facts show that one or both are culpable. No more difficult problem ever comes to the pastor than this, and, as a rule, he will do well to take with him a wise and patient layman for advice and counsel. If the troubled be young people who have blundered through ignorance or lack of self-mastery, the case is one for sympathetic reproof and constant watchfulness in the future. And if the case be one of moral obliquity on the part of a mature person in the church, the pastor may find it necessary to speak as the voice of conscience, both of the sinner and the church. But we must say again that no set of rules can be laid down for handling any pastoral problem. Only common sense, imagination, and sympathy can teach us what to say or do.

The spiritual welfare of the church membership may be increased by the pastor who emphasizes, both in the pulpit and his calling, the value of daily prayer and meditation. The discipline of Christian Science requires that a considerable portion of time each day shall be devoted to the deliberate culture of the sense of well-being by uncritical reflection upon the affirmations of "Science and Health." This practice more than anything else accomplishes the alleged "cures" of this body. But anyone who will spend at least twenty minutes each day in religious meditation, closing the mind to that which disturbs and annoys, and filling it with that which is peaceful and holy by reading worthy devotional literature and engaging in prayer, will find his mental, moral, and physical health improving. An old monk long ago called this "practicing the Presence of God." And there is no way of truly reviving the church except by cultivating this old habit.

d. The Unevangelized. A final group which has special claims upon the pastor's time consists of those who are unevangelized. The term is a broad one, embracing not merely the unchurched, but the unconverted, and all who have never ventured into the deep places of Christian experience, whether members of the church or not. Their names will compose the pastor's "Personal Work List," and none but himself and God will see it. These must be cultivated persistently and lovingly, though with tact and common sense. There should be no nagging, yet there must be constant pursuit which never abandons the holy chase. Let the pastor angle for these souls as the fisherman angles for the wary trout. He should be tactful, yet at times be ready to risk a blunder by bold adventuring. This work must go on month after month, intensified, perhaps, during special meetings, but not abandoned when meetings are done.

Books Recommended for Further Study

W. A. Quayle, *The Pastor-Preacher.*
Charles E. Jefferson, *The Minister as Shepherd.*
Washington Gladden, *The Christian Pastor.*
F. J. McConnell, *The Preacher and the People.*
John T. Stone, *In the Footsteps of a Pastor.*

CHAPTER XXVII

MINOR MINISTERIAL ETHICS

THERE is no professional worker whose service is affected more by an unethical quality in his living and conduct than that of the minister. Yet it might be possible, as Doctor Batten suggests,[1] to say that the ministry as a body has no code of professional ethics. This is true, however, only when we mean by a professional code one that has been formally elaborated and adopted by a group of workers who were empowered to speak for a whole profession. Examples of such codes are found in the canons of ethics for lawyers, adopted by the American Bar Association, and in a code of medical ethics adopted by the American Medical Association.

Several reasons may be urged for the lack of such a formal code for religious workers. The motive for entering the ministry differs radically from that of any other profession, as has been suggested in a previous chapter. It might be assumed that men acting from such a motive would not need the restraints of a formal ethical code. Again, practically all ministers belong to particular denominations. The differences separating these religious bodies are very marked. Each has its own standards for its own ministers, but it would be difficult to secure the cooperation of all in formulating a code which should be binding upon all. Nevertheless, the profession is tested by the highest standards. There are those who believe that the unwritten Constitution of England is of greater practical utility than the written Constitution of the United States. Similarly, the unofficial code of ethics for the ministry is more exact-

[1]See an article, "The Ethics of the Ministry," in Annals of the American Academy of Political Science, May, 1922, p. 147.

ing than the carefully formulated rules which govern workers in other professions. A minister will be discredited and unfrocked for private conduct which would not affect at all the professional standing of a lawyer or a physician. This is due chiefly to the fact that he stands before the community as a teacher of New Testament ethics, and by this Christian standard, which he interprets, the community inevitably will judge him.

Besides the restraints imposed upon his private and professional life by the ethics of the New Testament, the minister in the Methodist Episcopal Church is bound by a carefully written code set forth in the *Discipline* of the church.[2] It is called "the rules for a preacher's conduct." These were written first by John Wesley for the guidance of his English preachers. On the organization of the church in America, they were adopted by the ministers in the new country, and have been confirmed by each succeeding General Conference. Every minister who applies for admission into an Annual Conference is asked, "Have you considered the rules for a preacher, especially those relating to diligence, to punctuality, and to doing the work to which you were assigned, and will you keep them for conscience' sake?" Thus each candidate for our ministry admits this code as binding, in spirit, upon himself.

Formal professional codes aim to safeguard the entrance to the profession, to maintain the dignity and standing of the profession, and to assert with great care the obligation of all professional workers to be bound by the motive of service. The principles of medical ethics, as set forth by the American Medical Association, are arranged in three chapters, namely: (1) The Duties of Physicians to Their Patients, (2) The Duties of Physicians to Each Other and the Profession at Large, (3) The Duties of the Profession to the Public. The concluding paragraph says, "While the foregoing state-

[2]*Discipline,* 1920, ¶¶ 117-130.

ments express in a general way the duty of the physician, . . . it is not to be supposed that they cover the whole field of medical ethics, or that the physician is not under many duties and obligations besides these herein set forth." A similar statement might be made in concluding the rules for a preacher's conduct. These rules take account chiefly of matters of major importance. But many ministers become wholly unacceptable, not through the violation of these greater rules but through disregard of minor matters, which, though trivial by comparison, are of great consequence in the community's estimate of their efficiency. In this chapter we shall deal with these little things, many of which are not mentioned at all in the chapter in the *Discipline* on "Qualifications and Work of the Ministry," and one might even search the New Testament in vain for a statement concerning some of them. Saint Paul says, "I put no obstacle in the path of any so that my ministry may not be discredited."[3] Every minister should be equally eager to remove from his life and conduct everything, however trifling, which in any way reflects upon his office. It is impossible to make a complete catalogue of these faults. They fall into a few great groups which are not mutually exclusive. Such practical classifications as are attempted here include only the more common failings. We must repeat that which has been affirmed so often in these pages, that there is no safe guide in these matters except what is afforded by a discriminating taste and a sensitive conscience.

1. Personal Hygiene. *a.* It is so regrettable as to be painful that some ministers are untidy to an intolerable degree. The mediæval association between piety and filth is no longer admitted. No degree of sanctity, and no depth of ministerial poverty will ever excuse soiled linen, grimy hands, black finger nails, unbrushed teeth, dirty shoes, vests spotted with grease, dandruff-covered coat collars, in the minister himself. Nor will they excuse untidy housekeeping

[3] 2 Cor. 6. 3, Moffatt's translation.

or unkempt children in his home. Each of these things betrays an indifference to personal cleanliness which everywhere shocks the sensibilities of people of ordinary refinement. How can they respect the minister's judgment in spiritual things when they must apologize for him in such elementary matters as these? "I am ashamed to introduce him to my business associates as my minister," exclaimed a vexed layman whose badly groomed pastor was a constant source of humiliation.

b. But some who are meticulous in caring for the outside of the body are grossly indifferent to the inside, with the result that spiritual efficiency becomes seriously impaired through low physical vitality. The men who follow sedentary occupations must put their bodies under and provide sparingly for physical appetites. Ministers are proverbially poor, but that does not keep some of them from eating too much. Nor is it altogether a question of quantity, but also one of kinds of food. They consume too much meat and starch, and too little fruit and green vegetables. The organs of digestion and elimination are overloaded. Constipation, kidney trouble, indigestion, and foul breath inevitably result. John Wesley's demand that his preachers should fast regularly was justifiable on physiological as well as religious grounds. "Do you use only that kind and degree of food which is best both for body and soul? Do you eat no more at each meal than is necessary? Are you not heavy or drowsy after dinner?"[4] An overfed body is not an effective instrument for the soul.

c. Posture has much to do with physical efficiency. Physicians tell us that man has limb for limb, bone for bone, and muscle for muscle with other mammals. His upright position puts an unaccustomed strain on the nervous system. The weight, which in other animals is supported by the abdominal muscles, settles into the pelvis and puts pressure on new nerve centers. This strain quickly produces a

---

[4]*Discipline,* 1920, ¶ 121f.

sense of fatigue. The only way to relieve it is to maintain a good posture—head erect, shoulders thrown back, and abdomen supported by muscular effort. Yet how infrequently does one find a minister who carries himself properly! Generally he stands lop-sidedly on one foot, chest and shoulders thrown forward, and abdominal muscles completely relaxed. He thinks he stands this way because he is tired. As a matter of fact, the truth probably is that he is tired because he stands this way.

d. Exercise is important too, though not in the same sense as for the athlete. The minister does not need hard muscles. He requires only that degree of physical activity which will keep every bodily organ in good condition. Setting-up exercises morning and night, and additional exercise which will be equivalent to a five-mile walk each day, will generally suffice.

2. Good Manners. Of all men in the world, the minister should be most mannerly; yet good manners are not always in evidence among religious leaders. We are not thinking now of codes of etiquette which prescribe in detail the action appropriate to ceremonial occasions. "The words *etiquette* and *ticket* have the same origin. Formerly, the rules and ceremonies to be observed at court were printed on a ticket, and given to every person presented at court." So E. J. Hardy comments in *How to Be Happy Though Civil.*[5] Rules of this kind change, like fashions, with every wind. We have in mind, rather, that gentle bearing and consideration for others which is indispensable to happy relations among men. Edmund Burke says: "Manners are of more importance than laws. Upon them, in great measure, the laws depend. The law touches here and there, now and then. Manners are what vex or soothe, corrupt or purify, exalt or debase, barbarize or refine us, by a constant, steady, uniform, insensible operation, like the air we breathe in. They give their whole form and color to our lives. Accord-

[5] P. 13.

ing to their quality, they aid morals, they supply them, or they totally destroy them."[6]

In spite, however, of the obligation which his religion imposes upon him to be civil, and its usefulness in allaying the frictions incident to his work, the rude and ill-mannered minister is conspicuous and discredits the whole profession. This is apparent in his ostentatious disregard of proprieties on the supposition that he is proving himself democratic; in conversing with guests in the pulpit while others are contributing to public worship; in looking bored while others are speaking; in taking more than his share of time on a program when others besides himself are to speak; in self-assertively doing all the talking at a dinner party or other social occasion; in affecting eccentricities of dress and manner; in petty concern for his own prestige, anxious that proper deference shall be paid him on every occasion; in parading the affairs of his own household and the cleverness of his own children before the congregation; in improper bodily contacts with members of the congregation, jocosely slapping men on the back and sentimentally dealing with women or holding their hands in both his own as though he were their father or older brother; in carelessness about engagements; in slangy and coarse speech; in discourteous contradiction of the statements of others; in fidgeting and fussing; in planning to get before the public and see his name in print; in picking his teeth, chewing toothpicks, trimming his finger nails, and expectorating in public places; in assuming generally that the obligation to be a Christian gentleman rests upon every person in the world but himself. Of course no one minister was ever quite guilty of all these faults, but everyone knows some minister who is guilty of one or more of them. Bad manners are regrettable for any minister. They are inexcusable for Methodist ministers. Professor Hoppin, of Yale University, said, "John Wesley, plain and severe as we picture

[6]Quoted by E. J. Hardy, *op. cit.*, p. 12.

him, insisted upon the highest style of manners in the ministerial office, all the courtesy of the gentleman joined with the correctness of the scholar."[7]

The causes of bad manners are numerous. Defective early training is surely one. This usually applies, however, only to those conventions which are indispensable to social intercourse. Wherever there are contacts with our fellowmen, to proceed according to well-recognized customs is to reduce friction. To disregard them will only create confusion and misunderstanding as certainly as failure to heed the signal of a traffic officer. For example, if one is a guest in a private home during Annual Conference, he is expected to act as if he understood perfectly that a home is not a hotel. He will disturb the routine of the family as little as possible and make his convenience suit that of the family if within his power. And on returning to his own home, he will send a note of appreciation to his hosts for their gracious hospitality. To conduct oneself otherwise under circumstances such as these will open the way to censure. But defective conduct which grows out of ignorance of social conventions is not especially serious when one honestly intends to be thoughtful, modest, and courteous. He may inform himself concerning polite usages by studying a good volume on manners.

The situation is much more complicated when the cause is a wrong inner attitude of heart and mind. Vanity is one of these. This is responsible for the self-conscious assertion of oneself on small occasions—telling what others have said about one's sermons, parading one's hobbies and private affairs as if they must be of universal interest. "The vain man can scarcely be well-mannered; he is so absorbed in the contemplation of his own perfections that he cannot think of other people and study their feelings."[8] Irritability is another fruitful source of incivility, whether it is caused by weariness, illness, or constitutional churlishness. The irri-

[7] *Pastoral Theology*, p. 196.
[8] E. J. Hardy, *op. cit.*, p. 116.

tated person is always chiefly concerned with himself, full of fault-finding, and lacking in appreciation of others.

Probably every other source of bad manners, however, is gathered up under this—*disregard for other persons.* Bad pulpit manners are due to lack of respect for God and the congregation. All vulgar conduct—loudness, coarseness, silliness, boorishness, obtrusiveness of every sort—is due to lack of regard for the rights and feelings and presence of others. Reverence for others impels to love and sympathy, which prompts us to be courteous. Disregard for others impels us to throw away all self-restraint and let ourselves go according to the feeling of the moment.

The cure for bad manners is, of course, suggested by their several causes. If they are due to faulty education, then one should study some good guide to social conduct, watch the way in which others deport themselves, and eliminate that in one's own conduct which contrasts unpleasantly with their action. If vanity be the cause, then one must stop thinking of himself. If irritability, then one must learn to master his moods. If they are due to lack of respect for others, then one must learn to reverence personality wherever it is found, whether in God or a congregation, in adults or children. One who reverences all men because they are men will never quite abandon himself to say or do just what he likes. He will be concerned less with making himself comfortable and more with putting others at their ease. "To listen when we are bored, to talk when we are listless, to stand when we are tired, to praise when we are indifferent, to accept the companionship of a stupid acquaintance when we might, at the expense of politeness, escape to a clever friend, to endure with smiling composure the near presence of people who are distasteful to us—these things, and many like them, brace the sinews of our souls. They set a fine and delicate standard for common intercourse. They discipline us for the good of the community."[9]

[9]Agnes Repplier, *Americans and Others,* p. 26. Reprinted by permission of Houghton Mifflin Company.

3. UNREALITY. Among the influences which "unmake" a preacher, President (emeritus) Tucker, of Dartmouth, gives the primacy to *unreality*. This he defines as "the failure to get right correspondence between the expression and the comprehension of truth."[10] One less gifted with philosophic insight, and less skillful in saying harsh things sweetly, might define it simply as affectation, artificiality, insincerity, or plain "bluff."

a. This peril threatens *the intellectual life* of many ministers who pretend a knowledge which they do not possess, and affect an assurance which their attainments do not warrant. They are given to dogmatic utterance without offering solid reasons for their statements, and exalt their own unsupported opinions as the standards by which all in the community must stand or fall. At the best this intellectual unreality consists in affirming the ancient beliefs in ancient phraseology without verifying them in one's own personal experience; and at the worst it consists in grossly putting forth as one's own the thoughts and experiences of others. Conceivably it might consist in preaching less than one believes rather than more—in permitting the congregation to think that one accepts old statements of belief which, as a matter of fact, he secretly rejects.

b. Unreality breaks out too at the point of *the emotional life,* manifesting itself in the pulpit in a "ministerial tone," in "rhetorical courage," in gestures and voice artificially solemn or strenuous, in a religious fervor which one does not feel. In social contacts it expresses itself in gushing, and unctuous compliments on meeting people, in pretending to know or remember everyone, in excessive and flattering graciousness which does not represent one's true feeling. The necessity that is on the minister to make himself agreeable to all for the sake of their cooperation in his work strongly tempts him to become affected.

c. Moreover, unreality is reflected in the petty devices

---

[10] *The Making and Unmaking of the Preacher,* p. 62.

sometimes employed to give *an appearance of success in church work which would not otherwise be suspected.* For example, informing the church press each time the salary is increased, or an invitation is received to speak on some special occasion; special diligence in visiting just previous to the fourth Quarterly Conference in order to make a good report, even counting casual conversations on the street or at the post office as pastoral calls; Annual Conference reports of church and Sunday-school membership based on generous estimates rather than careful tabulations; reporting as "converted" all who bow at the altars of the church for any reason during special meetings; reporting large numbers received into church membership without explaining that a majority came by transfer, or that many were counted twice—once as probationers, and again when received into full membership. In these and countless other ways ministers may degrade themselves to make a "good showing." The preacher may be excused for lack of eloquence and brilliancy, but never for lack of candor and simple honesty.

4. Financial Matters. Delinquency in matters of finance hinders the effectiveness of some ministers.

a. This more commonly takes the form of *debt,* which trails them from charge to charge. It is easy to buy "on account," and the salary is generally meager. So the creditor may seem to be a real friend. But to pay is difficult, sometimes impossible, and good men have been impelled by sheer desperation to undertake disastrous ventures in speculation or "borrow" church funds in the hope of escaping from debt. Or it may be that they have become callously indifferent to their obligations, which is worse. The minister should borrow money sparingly; he should not run current bills in excess of his monthly salary; and when obligations fall due he should make no delay in meeting them. If he cannot pay when he promised, let him say so frankly and arrange for an extension of time, but never disregard the obligation.

b. Church Funds. The minister may become seriously involved through the careless handling of church funds. A few simple rules will save him trouble and possibly shame. (1) Never accept responsibility for administering funds which properly should be deposited with one of the church treasurers. (2) In case it seems imperatively necessary to become the custodian of church moneys, never deposit or in any way mix them with personal funds. Open separate accounts for them at the bank. And never borrow from them for private use. (3) Keep a careful and clear record of all receipts and expenditures of such moneys. (4) Insist that at regular and frequent intervals, all accounts shall be carefully audited by competent persons.

c. Supplementing the Salary. Frequently an insufficient salary, or sometimes plain commercial-mindedness, impels ministers to resort to various methods of increasing their income while continuing in the pastorate. Farming; investments in enterprises which promise large returns in interest or dividends; selling life insurance; breeding poultry, rabbits, or dogs for the market; buying and selling stocks, land, timber, or fruit orchards; taking agencies, or permitting their children to do so, to sell books, pictures, etc., to the community in which they live—these, together with writing and lecturing, are among the more common devices usually employed. Obviously, not all of these are equally objectionable. For example, to go on a Chautauqua circuit certainly comports more with the dignity of the ministry than to promote the sale of oil or mining stocks. There is great need for discrimination in these matters. The following observations would seem to be pertinent:

(1) The Methodist minister has taken a vow "to give himself *wholly* to the work of the ministry." Whatever more may be implied, this surely means that he shall have an undivided mind with reference to his work. Anything which seriously diverts his attention or makes large demands upon his time and strength must be pushed aside.

(2) While the church is obligated to provide a suitable

support for the minister and his family, it cannot be expected to do more than this. The ministry in whatever form must never become attractive by virtue of financial rewards. Its large compensations must ever be found in the peculiar aims and satisfactions of the work.

(3) There would seem to be no inherent impropriety in extra-ministerial labor along kindred lines, such as writing or lecturing, provided it is not allowed to interfere with one's main task.

(4) In the event that a minister cannot live on what the church will pay him he may honorably abandon the ministry for commercial pursuits, *but he may not follow them and continue in the ministry on salary.* Secular work is highly diverting and distracting. Moreover, the best conscience of the community insists that if the minister engages in it he should do so on terms of equality with others. He may not claim a subsidy in the form of a salary for religious work and then enter into competition with those who enjoy no such advantage, or, perhaps, have helped provide the subsidy for him.

(5) The minister should be thrifty so far as lies in his power. He is under obligation to save something out of his salary to provide comfort in old age or to protect his family in case of death. At the best his savings will be small. It is imperative then, that in investing them, he shall have regard, first, for the safety of his principal. Less than a rich man can he afford to risk his all in questionable ventures, and he may safely assume that any enterprise is questionable which seeks to finance itself on the small savings of salaried persons by the promise of large returns. *If it were a good investment, its promoters could get their capital from the banks.* And the minister cannot afford to invest his money in what the banks consider worthless. Life insurance is the wisest investment for the person of small salary. In case of early death, it returns many times the amount paid in premiums, while if one lives until the policy matures, at least a reasonable interest is returned for

the use of the principal. One will usually be very wise in refusing to invest in enterprises which promise more than five and a half or six per cent. It is the part of wisdom to consult a good banker before making an investment.

(6) A minister as agent should never seek to influence others in making investments. Much less should he appeal to the religious motive to risk their savings in highly speculative enterprises. This is beneath contempt. For similar exploitation of religious instincts and institutions in the interest of personal profit, Jesus became greatly angered and drove the money-changers from the Temple with a heavy corded whip. And honest men to-day are filled with a sense of outrage at such abuse of ministerial power.

5. MENDICANCY. The mendicant-priest and the begging-friar are familiar figures among non-Christians and Catholics. Theoretically, Protestantism makes no place for these professional "holy men" with their ostentatious poverty. But as a matter of fact the spirit of mendicancy obtrudes itself under all forms of religion. It has entered into the heart of every one who finds himself asking or expecting favors because he is a religious worker by profession, which he never would receive if he were not. Doubtless all are familiar with the reasons by which the clergy justify (to their own satisfaction) the custom of accepting presents, discounts, and special consideration of all kinds. But the fact remains that the finest spirits in the ministry have ever heard with whole-hearted approval Jesus' injunction to the twelve, "Take no wallet [begging bowl]."[11] Phillips Brooks exclaims bravely, "That which ought to be the manliest of all professions has a tendency, practically, to make men unmanly. Men make appeals for sympathy that no true man should make. They take to themselves Saint Paul's pathos without Saint Paul's strength. Against that tendency, my friends, set your whole force."[12] Perhaps a

---

[11]Luke 9. 3.

[12]By permission from *Lectures on Preaching*, p. 68f. Copyright by E. P. Dutton and Company.

better support for the ministry awaits the coming of a generation of preachers who will refuse to accept gratuities as a substitute for a fair salary.

6. LAZINESS. This may be physical, but it is more likely to be intellectual. In the interest of comfort there is a pronounced disinclination to wrestle manfully with the problems of thought which arise in religion. Some make themselves think they are too busy to study—as if one could ever be excused for neglecting the principal task because of any number of lesser ones. Intellectual apathy may go hand in hand with physical vigor. The man who likes to work in the garden may put in time there which properly belongs to his books. Moreover, his delight in human companionship may smother mental and spiritual culture. Under a pretext of social sympathy which takes him among the people he shirks the hard and lonely tasks of study and reflection.

7. IMPROPER SPEECH. *"Sin not with thy tongue!"* should be written in bold letters above the study table of every minister. It includes every sort of improper utterance: ungenerous and gossipy speech about one's brother ministers, inane story-telling and jesting, "smart" sayings which rankle and sting, as well as vulgarity and obscenity. Especially should the ecclesiastical buffoon be on his guard—the man who is full of Bible jokes. The hot wrath of Phillips Brooks blazes forth on all such. "There are passages in the Bible which are soiled forever by the touches which the hands of ministers who delight in cheap and easy jokes have left upon them. I think there is nothing that stirs one's indignation more than this, in all he sees of ministers. It is a purely wanton fault. What is simply stupid everywhere else becomes terrible here."[13]

8. COVETOUSNESS. The tenth commandment in the Decalogue (against covetousness) should have a conspicuous place in any rules laid down for the conduct of ministers,

---

[13]By permission from *Lectures on Preaching,* p. 54. Copyright by E. P. Dutton and Company.

amended, of course, to suit an ecclesiastical situation. Who has not met the minister who was envious of the esteem in which his predecessor is held? or who was jealous of his successor for captivating so readily the hearts of a former congregation? or who was so intent upon getting into a general office or a traveling secretaryship that he neglected his pastoral work? This is responsible for all that is offensive in "ecclesiastical politics"—unashamed and immodest self-seeking for ecclesiastical preferment. There is not so much of it as is supposed, but more than should be. A highly centralized form of church government, which requires a large number of general officers, may make it easy for men to sin in this way. But the best conscience of the church insists that anyone is disqualified for its high offices who self-assertively offers himself as a candidate or is active in promoting his own cause, whether he be a minister or a layman. The one serious criticism that may be made against our form of church government is that the administrative office is magnified above all others, and constantly operates to create dissatisfaction with the pastorate. If the pastorate could be restored in the consciousness of the church to the place of primacy among church offices, and the administrative office really be regarded as secondary, and so rewarded, covetousness might not disappear entirely but its forms certainly would be greatly modified.

9. Relations With Women. The most tragic experience that can come to a church is to have its pastor discredited because of immoral relations with women. Comparatively few ministers are unfaithful at this point—so few that the story of such a fall is told on the front page of every important newspaper on the continent, though he may have been previously the most obscure of men. Nevertheless, this type of delinquency is common enough to warrant particular mention in this chapter.

At two periods in his life a man may be in imminent peril from sexual appetite—once in youth before he has come to understand fully the significance of manhood, and again in middle age when, weary of life's prosaic responsibilities, the desire for romance flares up and tempts him to relieve the tedium of commonplace days by irresponsible adventure. It is in the second of these periods that the minister is most likely to fall, for the first will have passed as a rule before he has begun his professional career; and if it had not passed without serious mishap, he would not have been admitted to the ministry. In the later period his danger may be increased by a false sense of security growing out of his paternal relation to his own household. His fatherly consciousness may lead him to be more familiar with all women than he was as a younger man. And if, unfortunately, misunderstanding has arisen between himself and wife, leaving him to crave a sympathy which he thinks she does not give, the peril is still further magnified.

Two types of women may shake his self-control at this time; one is a young woman, attractive in personality and mystical in temperament, who may be very active in church work and thus thrown much in the pastor's company. Her interest in the things he counts most worth while may lead quite innocently on her part to an interest in herself which neither intended. If both are strong, they will remain masters of themselves. If either is weak, disaster may follow. The other is a middle-aged woman who shares with him the desire for romantic adventure which experience does not gratify in middle life. She too is likely to be physically attractive, religious by temperament, and will come into frequent contact with him in doing the work of the church. But life will have taught her so much that innocence can never be affirmed of her relation to the matter any more than of his. Of course a younger minister, especially if he is unmarried, is not free from danger, but the fact that most preachers who fall thus are between thirty-five and fifty years old suggests that the middle-aged man should be particularly on his guard.

In his relations with women, then, the minister should have strict regard for the following considerations:

a. Cultivate the habit of a clean imagination. No sin of this kind is ever committed without some degree of premeditation. Unclean thinking is always antecedent to unclean living. Behavior only reveals what has long been hidden in the "chambers of imagery."

b. Discipline the physical instincts by vigorous physical living. A young man is often in less danger than a middle-aged man because he is more active. Blood running fast and full of oxygen from exercise makes for pure thinking. David was betrayed into his sin with Bathsheba after he had given up the active life of camp and field for the passive life of court and palace. And many another man has gone wrong after he dropped into the sluggish physical habits of the forties and fifties.

c. In the matter of physical contacts, the minister should govern himself with the greatest restraint outside his own family circle. There is no conceivable emergency that can arise in pastoral or social relations which will give any warrant for sentimentally putting one's hand on a woman or otherwise coming into close bodily contact. And even to take her hand in both one's own in shaking hands is an exhibition of bad manners that is open to serious criticism.

d. Let him cherish constantly a sense of his responsibility for the spiritual and moral well-being of all in the community. So he will have a care that none are destroyed through his bad example.

e. Let him be sensible of his own everlasting need of divine grace. Let him, like Saint Paul, live in holy fear of failing to exemplify in his own life the gospel he preaches to others. "I buffet my body, and bring it into bondage: lest by any means, after that I have preached to others, I myself should be rejected" (1 Cor. 9. 27).